The Wrong War

CORNELL STUDIES IN
SECURITY AFFAIRS

Edited by Robert J. Art
and Robert Jervis

The Wrong War

AMERICAN POLICY AND THE DIMENSIONS OF THE KOREAN CONFLICT, 1950–1953

ROSEMARY FOOT

Cornell University Press

Ithaca and London

First published 1985 by Cornell University Press.

International Standard Book Number 978-1-5017-7206-1
Library of Congress Catalog Card Number 84-29305
Librarians: Library of Congress cataloging information
appears on the last page of the book.

*To my father
and in loving memory
of my mother*

Contents

[7]

Preface

During major wars, previously fluid conceptions often become stabilized, policies solidified. The Korean War was no exception. Though the lessons were often badly learned, over three years of war each of the major powers directly or indirectly involved underwent a particular kind of learning experience with respect to the other powers. For Washington, the conflict provided a tangible expression of expansionist Communist power that required previously considered responses to be implemented. For Moscow, witnessing the vast augmentation of American military resources in the war years, the conflict confirmed the wisdom of caution in international behavior and the need to acquire a technological and industrial base sufficient to rival that of the most powerful postwar nation. For Peking, the conflict established the reality of a hostile American presence in East Asia, displayed the limits of its alliance with Moscow, and demonstrated the value of an independent role in world politics.

A desire to explore those learning experiences was the stimulus for this study. The book is not a detailed history of the Korean War; many fine examples of that genre will shortly be published as a result of the opening of archival material. Rather, my focus is on American policy discussions during the Truman and Eisenhower administrations concerning the objectives and likely consequences of any expansion of the Korean conflict into China. Additionally, it traces the significance of the Sino-Soviet Treaty of Alliance in controlling the dimensions of that conflict.

There is a widely held belief that the Communist alliance was the chief restraint on expanded hostilities. The scholarly work of Sino-Soviet specialists, however, has illustrated the considerable strain in relations between China and the Soviet Union throughout the war, and it has recently become clear that U.S. administration officials were receptive to evidence of these tensions. This apparent contradiction between the conventional belief and specialist opinion provided my point of entry into the subject matter. But in working through the documentary material for the period, I soon found that the policy debate on the dimensions of the war not only gives crucial new insight into the American perception of Sino-Soviet relations but is also of more general significance in broadening our understanding of U.S. foreign policy in the Cold War years. The terms of the discussion had a major influence on America's later Asian strategy and policy toward China in particular. The debate also showed the nature of the constraints imposed on Washington's objectives. On the human level it revealed the tensions among policymakers created by their bureaucratic roles, individual experiences, and personalities. On the structural level it demonstrated the special strains imposed by America's hegemonic position. The discussions on the scope of the war set in train conflicts between a desire to act alone and a need to illustrate the universal quality of America's national interests; between a desire to demonstrate the overwhelming nature of U.S. power—militarily, economically, and politically—and a fear of failing in one or all of these areas.

In the end, the solution imposed on China and North Korea at the conclusion of the conflict confirmed, in the short term, America's dominant position in world politics. But it also engendered the conditions that would lead to a challenge of that dominance as America's values and priorities came to be questioned, and as Moscow and Peking diverged in regard to the appropriate response to the U.S. position. Such challenges contributed to the breakdown in bipolarity and to the establishment of a more complex international environment in which the criteria for leadership became more difficult to fulfill.

Research for this book could not have been undertaken without generous aid from a number of sources. An American Council of Learned Societies scholarship, combined with a Fulbright award, enabled me to spend six productive months in the United States, attached to the East Asian Institute, Columbia University. I am also grateful for the financial assistance of the British Academy, London; the U.S. Army Military History Institute, Carlisle Barracks, Pennsylvania; the International Communication Agency, U.S. Embassy, London; and the Harry S. Truman Library Institute, Independence, Missouri.

The assistance and advice of friends, colleagues, and archivists have been essential and highly valued throughout the project. I am particularly pleased to mention the patient efforts of Sally Marks and Kathryn Nicastro of the Diplomatic Branch of the National Archives, and Edward Reese and John Taylor of the Modern Military Branch. Many American and British colleagues have given generously of their time to discuss aspects of the text, and I was fortunate in having been able to test out some of my ideas on them at various venues, including the University of Sussex in England and Columbia University in New York.

I am especially indebted to Dorothy Borg, Tim Kennedy, Walter LaFeber, and Christopher Thorne, who each read and made constructive comments on an earlier draft of the manuscript. Robert Jervis, the coeditor of this series, has also offered many valuable suggestions. Marc Williams provided detailed written comments on some of my earliest thoughts about the issues I had undertaken to study. Lester Foltos kindly shared some of the documents in his possession pertaining to the period. Lord Oliver Franks responded to my questions with great candor and clarity. Anita O'Brien was generous with editorial advice; her genuine interest has sustained me at some difficult moments.

As a result of two periods of leave from the University of Sussex, my colleagues undertook increased teaching loads, and for this additional kindness I express my thanks. Tim Kennedy has remained enthusiastic, caring, and concerned throughout the long period of research and writing and has done everything possible to organize our life together in order that the work would indeed be finished. The members of my family, while somewhat in wonder at the length of time the project has required, has continued to be interested and supportive. Throughout my life, my parents have encouraged me in the various directions I have chosen to take; it is for this reason that I dedicate the book to them.

My thanks are due also to the Rare Book and Manuscript Library, Columbia University, for permission to quote from the Wellington Koo Papers; to Martin Wilbur of Columbia University's East Asian Institute, to quote from the Wellington Koo Oral History; to the Seeley G. Mudd Library at Princeton and George Kennan, to quote from Mr. Kennan's papers. Cambridge University Press has kindly granted permission to reproduce the map of Korea and surrounding areas, which opens Chapter 1 of this book, from Kalicki's *Pattern of Sino-American Crises.*

ROSEMARY FOOT

Sussex, England

A NOTE ON TRANSLITERATION

The Wade-Giles system of transliteration has generally been adopted for Chinese place and personal names, inasmuch as this is in keeping with the documents of the period.

Abbreviations

CCF	Chinese Communist Forces (People's Republic)
CCP	Chinese Communist Party (People's Republic)
CFM	Council of Foreign Ministers
CIA	Central Intelligence Agency (U.S.)
DPRK	Democratic People's Republic of Korea (North Korea)
FEAF	Far East Air Force (U.S.)
JCS	Joint Chiefs of Staff (U.S.)
JIC	Joint Intelligence Committee (U.S.)
JSPC	Joint Strategic Plans Committee (U.S.)
JSSC	Joint Strategic Survey Committee (U.S.)
KMT	Kuomintang (Taiwan)
NATO	North Atlantic Treaty Organization
NIE	National Intelligence Estimate (U.S.)
NSC	National Security Council (U.S.)
NSRB	National Security Resources Board (U.S.)
OIR	Office of Intelligence Research (U.S.)
PLA	People's Liberation Army (People's Republic of China)
POW	Prisoner of War
PPS	Policy Planning Staff (U.S.)
PRC	People's Republic of China
ROK	Republic of Korea (South Korea)
SE	Special Estimate (U.S.)

Chronology

1950

June 25   North Korean forces attack South Korean positions south of the 38th Parallel.

The U.N. Security Council adopts a resolution (with the U.S.S.R. absent and Yugoslavia abstaining) calling for "the immediate cessation of hostilities" and withdrawal of North Korean forces to the parallel.

U.N. members are requested "to render every assistance to the United Nations in the execution of this resolution and to refrain from giving assistance to North Korean authorities."

The U.S. administration decides to impose the Seventh Fleet in the Taiwan Strait and to increase aid to the French in Indochina.

June 27   President Truman orders U.S. air and sea units to give cover and support to South Korean troops.

The Security Council adopts a resolution recommending that "the Members of the United Nations furnish such assistance to the Republic of Korea as may be necessary to repel the armed attack and to restore international peace and security in the area."

June 30   President Truman announces that he has authorized the use of American ground troops in Korea and ordered the Air Force to conduct missions on specific targets in North Korea. General MacArthur has already ordered planes under his command to bomb targets north of the parallel.

July 7   The Security Council adopts by 7 votes (with Egypt, India, and Yugoslavia abstaining) a resolution requesting the United States to designate a commander for all forces being offered by U.N. members. General MacArthur is formally appointed.

Aug. 1   The Soviet delegate to the United Nations, Jacob Malik, ends Moscow's boycott of the organization and takes over the presidency of the Security Council.

Sept. 15   The American Tenth Corps, backed by naval and air power, launches a successful amphibious operation and lands at Inchon, 150 miles behind the enemy line. This enables U.S./U.N. forces to break out of the beachhead at Pusan and push rapidly northward toward the parallel.

Sept. 25   The acting chief of staff of the PLA warns that the Chinese will not "sit back with folded hands and let the Americans come up to the border."

Sept. 29   General MacArthur enters Seoul with President Syngman Rhee.

Sept. 30   South Korean forces cross the 38th Parallel into North Korea.

Oct. 3   Chinese Premier and Foreign Minister Chou En-lai issues his dramatic late-night warning to Ambassador Panikkar: PRC forces will enter the war if U.S. troops move across the parallel.

Oct. 7   The U.N. General Assembly adopts (47 to 5) a resolution recommending that "all appropriate steps be taken to ensure conditions of stability throughout Korea."

American troops cross the 38th Parallel.

Oct. 8   Mao Tse-tung issues orders to the Chinese "volunteer" forces to "resist the attacks of U.S. imperialism."

Oct. 15   President Truman and General MacArthur confer on Wake Island, discussing political arrangements for the unification of postwar Korea.

Oct. 25   Chinese units fight with ROK forces less than 40 miles south of the Yalu River.

Nov. 1   The first Chinese MIGs appear along the Yalu.

Nov. 6   General MacArthur reports men and materiel pouring across the Yalu, threatening the "ultimate destruction" of U.S./U.N. positions. He requests permission to destroy the Yalu bridges and pursue attacking MIGs into Manchuria.

Nov. 16   President Truman tries to reassure China and other nations that "we have never at any time entertained any intention to carry hostilities into China."

There is a general lull in the fighting and loss of contact between U.S./U.N. and Communist forces.

Nov. 24   China's special delegation to the Security Council, led by Wu Hsiu-chuan, arrives at the United Nations.

General MacArthur launches his "end-the-war offensive," and U.S./U.N. forces approach the Chinese border.

Nov. 26   The Chinese counterattack. General MacArthur announces on November 28 that his forces face an "entirely new war." In two days, November 30 and December 1, U.S./U.N. casualties exceed 11,000.

Dec. 5   U.S./U.N. troops withdraw from Pyongyang.

Dec. 11   The Tenth Corps begins its successful evacuation of Hungnam.

Dec. 16   President Truman declares a state of national emergency.

Dec. 22   Premier Chou En-lai rejects the 13-power draft ceasefire resolution because it makes no reference to China's calls for the removal of all foreign troops from Korea and withdrawal of the

Seventh Fleet from the Taiwan Strait, and offers no recognition of its claim to a seat in the United Nations.

1951

Jan. 1   The Communist offensive south of the 38th Parallel begins.

Jan. 4   U.S./U.N. forces evacuate Seoul.

Jan. 13   The U.S. delegation votes for a U.N. ceasefire resolution that promises a discussion of other Far Eastern questions.

Jan. 17   China rejects the ceasefire proposal, since "the purpose of arranging a ceasefire first [before negotiations] is merely to give the United States troops a breathing space."

Jan. 19   The U.S. House of Representatives passes a resolution calling on the United Nations to declare China an aggressor in Korea.

Jan. 23   The U.S. Senate adopts a similar resolution.

Feb. 1   The U.N. resolution declaring China to be engaged in aggression is adopted 44 to 7, with 9 abstentions.

Mar. 7   Seoul, changing hands once again, is recaptured by U.S./U.N. forces.

Mar. 24   General MacArthur issues his unauthorized statement to Communist commanders suggesting that the time is right "to confer in the field."

Apr. 5   General MacArthur's March 20 letter to the House Minority Leader, Joseph Martin, is made public; it criticizes the Truman administration's Far Eastern strategy and the concept of limited war.

Apr. 11   President Truman relieves General MacArthur as commander and appoints General Matthew B. Ridgway to succeed him.

Apr. 19   General MacArthur, speaking before a joint meeting of Congress, denounces the Truman administration for refusing to lift the restrictions on the scope of the war.

May 3   Hearings on the military situation in the Far East begin before the joint Senate Committee on Armed Services and Foreign Relations.

May 18   The U.N. General Assembly adopts a resolution recommending an embargo on the shipment of arms, ammunition, and other materials of strategic value to China and North Korea.

          The assistant secretary of state for Far Eastern Affairs describes the government in Peking as "a Slavic Manchukuo on a large scale" and "not the Government of China."

May 31   The Soviet expert George Kennan meets the Soviet ambassador to the U.N., Jacob Malik, for discussions on ways to end the conflict. The two meet again on June 5.

June 23   Malik's radio address calls for "a ceasefire and an armistice providing for the mutual withdrawal of forces from the 38th Parallel."

June 29   General Ridgway offers to meet the commander of the Communist forces in Korea to discuss a ceasefire and armistice.

July 1	General Kim Il-sung, commander of the North Korean forces, and General Peng Teh-huai, commander of the Chinese People's "volunteers," agree to truce discussions.
July 10	Armistice negotiations begin at Kaesong.
July 26	Agreement on the agenda for the armistice talks is reached.
Aug. 23	Communist delegates suspend armistice negotiations after alleged U.N. violations of the neutral zone at Kaesong.
Oct. 25	Ceasefire discussions resume at Panmunjom.
Nov. 13	The U.S. administration proposes acceptance of the current line of contact as the final demarcation line, provided other issues outstanding at the truce talks are settled within 30 days. U.S./U.N. ground action is permitted to continue.
Nov. 27	The demarcation line is established.
Dec. 27	No progress having been made on the other issues within the 30-day limit, the demarcation line is invalidated.

1952

Feb. 19	Delegates to the armistice talks agree that within 90 days after the signing of the armistice, a political conference will convene to discuss withdrawal of foreign forces and the peaceful settlement of the Korean problem.
Mar. 26	The U.S. secretary of state denies the use of bacteriological warfare by America and criticizes the Communists for refusing an impartial investigation of the charges.
Apr. 19	The U.S./U.N. delegation informs the Communists that an official poll shows only 70,000 of 132,000 prisoners of war willing to return home.
Apr. 28	General Mark Clark is appointed to succeed General Ridgway as of May 12.
	At an executive session at Panmunjom, U.S./U.N. delegates unveil a "package" proposal to be rejected or accepted in full: (1) no prohibition on the rebuilding of airfields during the armistice; (2) Poland and Czechoslovakia but not the Soviet Union to serve on a neutral nations supervisory commission; (3) prisoners of war to be repatriated only on a voluntary basis.
May 2	The Communists endorse part of the package but reject the principle of voluntary repatriation.
May 7	Both sides announce a stalemate over the prisoner-of-war issue.
June 23	Yalu River power installations are bombed for several days by U.S. airmen to induce a more cooperative attitude at the truce talks.
Aug. 29	The heaviest air raid of the war is launched against Pyongyang.
Sept. 28	The U.S./U.N. negotiating team delivers its final offer on the prisoner-of-war question.
Oct. 8	The proposal is rejected, and the U.S./U.N. announces an indefinite recess.
Oct. 15	U.S./U.N. troops launch a mock amphibious landing near Wonsan.

Oct. 24   General Eisenhower announces that if elected, he will go to Korea.

Nov. 4   In the presidential election, the Republican candidate, General Dwight D. Eisenhower, wins 55 percent of the popular vote.

Nov. 10   General James A. Van Fleet announces the mobilization of 2 new South Korean divisions and 6 regiments.

Dec. 3   The U.N. General Assembly endorses (54 to 5) the amended Indian resolution on the voluntary repatriation of prisoners of war. China and North Korea reject the resolution.

Dec. 5   President-elect Eisenhower ends a three-day visit to frontline units in Korea.

1953

Feb. 2   President Eisenhower announces in his State of the Union message that the Seventh Fleet will no longer be employed to shield Communist China.

Feb. 22   General Clark proposes an exchange of sick and wounded prisoners.

Mar. 30   Premier Chou En-lai agrees to the exchange and proposes that those prisoners unwilling to be repatriated be transferred to a neutral state.

Apr. 20   The exchange of sick and wounded prisoners begins at Panmunjom.

Apr. 22   President Eisenhower approves the activation of 2 further South Korean army divisions.

Apr. 26   Armistice negotiations resume.

May 13   General Clark is authorized to activate 4 more South Korean divisions, bringing total strength to 20 divisions.

May 20   The National Security Council decides that "if conditions arise requiring more positive action in Korea," air and ground operations will be extended to China and ground operations in Korea will be intensified.

May 22   The U.S. secretary of state, John Foster Dulles, meets with the Indian premier and hints at future expansion of the war.

May 25   The U.S./U.N. negotiating team presents its final terms and is given permission to break off the talks if these are rejected.

May 28   The U.S. ambassador to Moscow explains to the Soviet foreign minister the "seriousness and importance of this . . . step."

June 8   Truce negotiations resolve the prisoner-of-war question and the principle of voluntary repatriation is accepted.

June 17   A revised demarcation line is settled.

             President Rhee orders South Korean guards to release those North Korean prisoners resisting repatriation.

June 24   The Communists launch an offensive against ROK positions.

July 27   The armistice is signed at Panmunjom.

The Wrong War

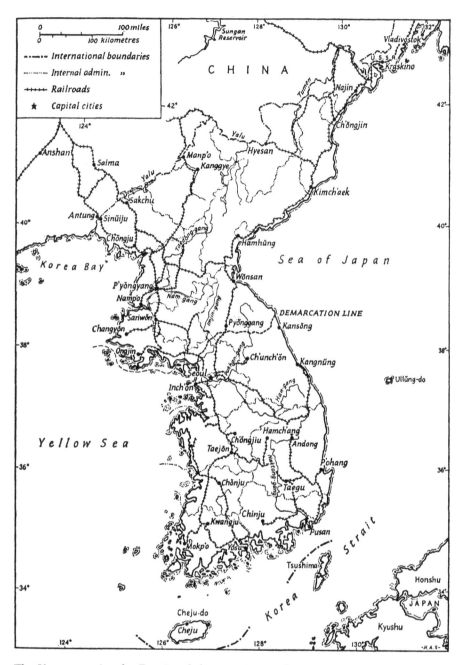

The Korean peninsula. Reprinted, by permission, from Jan Kalicki, *The Pattern of Sino-American Crises* (London: Cambridge University Press, 1975).

[1]

Introduction

In 1951, General Omar Bradley, chairman of the U.S. Joint Chiefs of Staff, succinctly stated the basis of the Truman administration's decision to confine hostilities during the Korean War to the Korean peninsula. America could not afford to expand the conflict into China, an area that was "not the critical strategic prize," he said. U.S. military capabilities were overstretched and overburdened; an expanded war that tied down its armed forces in Asia and caused damage to its collective defense effort in the North Atlantic area would provide the U.S.S.R. with an opportunity to take military advantage of the United States and the Western nations. For these reasons, he said, war with China would involve the United States "in the wrong war, at the wrong place, at the wrong time, and with the wrong enemy."[1]

To students of the Korean conflict, the logic of Bradley's memorable phrases has generally been viewed as unassailable. Thus the emphasis has always been on Korea as a limited war, and little attention has been given to policy discussions concerning the geographical expansion of the conflict. Yet despite the logic of Bradley's case and the presence of major constraints operating to inhibit the spread of hostilities, new documentary evidence shows the debate on expansion to have been much more extensive, rich, and complex than has hitherto been thought. Indeed, it was one of the most important and all-consuming questions of the period. Consequently, at many points of the war, the line between limited and expanded conflict was finely balanced.

Air and naval action against China was first contemplated in the early weeks of the Korean campaign as contingency plans were being drawn up. When the Chinese did finally intervene, therefore, those earlier discussions of retaliation served to bring the administration dangerously close to expanding the war, and closer still when the Chinese offensives in November and December 1950 brought U.S./U.N. forces to a point where it was thought likely that they would be compelled to withdraw from the peninsula. The expansion debate became more prominent still after about January 1952 because of the difficulty of concluding the armistice talks and the growing belief within the Truman and, later, the Eisenhower administration that the Chinese and North Koreans were deliber-ately delaying final agreement. It culminated in President Eisenhower's decision to take the war to China if the Communists rejected the U.N. Command's final terms on the issue of the voluntary repatriation of prisoners of war. Furthermore, the Eisenhower administration decided to expand the war not only geographically but also in terms of weapons: atomic warheads were to be used "on a sufficiently large scale" to bring the Korean conflict to a successful conclusion if the U.S. negotiating terms were not accepted.

The lack of knowledge about this debate on expansion and about the Eisenhower decision, and the previous lack of emphasis on the last 18 months of the Korean War have made our understanding of Korea as a limited conflict seriously deficient. The concentration has been on certain important phases of the fighting and the restraints operating to keep the war limited; elsewhere, the focus has been on the domestic setting within America: Senator McCarthy's and the Republican Party's criticisms of Truman and Acheson, especially as a consequence of the "Truman-MacArthur controversy." We have been deflected from closely examining the last 18 months of the conflict and the pressures for expansion by the administration's decision in the spring of 1951 to seek a negotiated settlement and, apparently, to renounce the goal of the reunification of Korea by force. The presumed clear-cut nature of that decision has been taken as establishing an appropriate stage at which to conclude comprehensive discussion of U.S. policy during the hostilities.

The availability since 1951 of virtually the whole transcript of the MacArthur hearings, held in May and June of that year to investigate the relief of General Douglas MacArthur from his command and his policy recommendations regarding the extension of the war into China, has reinforced still further the emphasis on this period as a termination point for the analysis of the war.[2] The congressional investigation provided an open, well-publicized debate of the merits and demerits of MacArthur's proposed retaliatory action in China, with the administration forcefully arguing the case for limiting hostilities. One aim of Truman and his advisers, however, was to undermine the general's position for domestic political reasons; thus it has always been unwise to treat the hearings as a totally accurate reflection of the administration's position regarding the extension of the war. Yet the investigation's conclusions have bolstered the belief that Truman's policies were cautious and circumspect, and prolonged the disregard of the views of those who between 1950 and 1953 favored solutions similar to MacArthur's: blockading the China coast and bombing China's air bases. The general was not alone in advocating such action, either before or after his dismissal.

This book, with its emphasis on the pressures to expand the Korean War, will therefore give a very different perspective on this "limited" conflict. Through the past neglect of these pressures to take the war to China, it has hitherto not been possible to show the depth of the strains inherent in maintaining a policy of restraint, nor how Korea pitted individuals and sections of the American bureaucracy against one another, nor how a nation possessing nuclear weapons but still relatively unsophisticated in its thinking about them envisaged their role in a conflict of this kind. Neither have previous analyses revealed the degree to which the conflict divided America from its North Atlantic allies, who had no doubts about the necessity of keeping the conflict contained.

Examination of the expansion debate also helps to explain the reasons for the enduring nature of American hostility toward China, at least until the late 1960s. Several members of the U.S. bureaucracy and the majority of the mass public regarded military action against China during the Korean conflict as a legitimate right that had been denied. Still others saw this denial as a lost opportunity to weaken a dangerous and expansionist foe.

Proponents and opponents of an expanded conflict expounded their arguments to both allied and domestic audiences. The primacy of European defense to the United States required that the Truman and Eisenhower administrations estimate the likely effect their Korean War policies would have on both the military buildup in Europe and America's political relations with its major allies within the North Atlantic Treaty Organization (NATO). And though domestic opinion had little direct influence on policy formation during the war years, neither president was immune to the suggestions and demands of domestic detractors and supporters, and both recognized the need to establish a sizable base of support for policy positions. But of central importance to the U.S. administrations was the need to develop reliable estimates of probable Soviet reactions to an expanded war, with reference to Russia's military support for China and to its potential military action elsewhere while America was preoccupied in the Far East. The focus here on the pressures to extend the conflict is thus additionally valuable in the light it sheds on U.S. perceptions of Sino-Soviet relations during the early years of their alliance.

Prior to the outbreak of the conflict in Korea, officials in Washington had been required to analyze the nature of the Sino-Soviet relationship in an effort to fix policy toward both the Chinese Communists and the defeated Nationalist regime. This activity probably influenced their later estimates. But the war in Korea served to sharpen the U.S. investigation of Sino-Soviet relations; indeed, the conflict made it imperative to seek a reliable assessment of the commitments involved in the military and ideological alliance between Moscow and Peking. Each phase of the conflict—the U.S. entry; the fighting between American and Chinese troops; the inconclusive truce negotiations—demanded that the United States make a serious attempt to calculate the likely responses of the two Communist powers. This "learning process" with regard to Sino-Soviet relations was significant not only in terms of the time spent on the analysis but also in terms of the situations in which it was undertaken: during a period of crisis and heightened tension in December 1950; at a time of apparent strategic stalemate in the spring of 1951; and through a period of protracted and acrimonious negotiations while fighting continued, from July 1951 to July 1953.

The conflict was significant also to the development of the Sino-Soviet dispute, since Peking found Soviet support to be less than steadfast during the war years. In 1950, just prior to the outbreak of hostilities on the peninsula, the U.S.S.R. and the People's Republic of China (PRC) had signed a Treaty of Friendship, Alliance, and Mutual Assistance in which defense clauses guaranteed mutual support in the event of an attack by Japan or any state allied with it. As U.S./U.N. forces crossed into North Korea, it appeared to the newly established government in Peking that American troops were taking the traditional Japanese invasion route into Manchuria, the industrial heartland of China. The PRC responded to this threat to its territorial integrity by entering the conflict in force, but it found aid from the Soviet Union both slow to arrive and somewhat less than generous.[3]

The war was, then, pivotal in undermining the relationship between Peking and Moscow. But additionally, and of major import to this book, America's leaders came to recognize the circumscribed nature of Soviet support for its major ally and the general cautiousness of Moscow's behavior during the period. One consequence was an increase in the vulnerability of China as it became clear that expanded hostilities would not necessarily provoke a third world war, or lead Moscow to initiate military action or heighten tension elsewhere. An examination of U.S. estimates of Soviet support for China has therefore made it possible to determine more precisely the degree of strategic benefit China actually derived from its alliance with the U.S.S.R. during the early 1950s. Such an approach represents a useful additional interpretation of the Sino-Soviet dispute, one not based on evidence derived from later Sino-Soviet polemics or from scholarly post-factum evaluations of Moscow's and Peking's behavior and statements (which may have been influenced by contemporary evidence of Sino-Soviet hostility).

In the light of the experience of such a key event as the Korean War,[4] conclusions that the United States drew then about the bilateral ties between Moscow and Peking appear to have held firm for some considerable time after the end of the fighting. Again, the popular belief is that China's entrance into Korea provided U.S. administrations with evidence that all Communist parties and leaders took their orders from Moscow, that Communist states should be treated as a monolithic bloc in which major interests coincided, and that it was fruitless to attempt to distinguish among such states. But the record shows that this depiction of U.S. beliefs is far too simplistic where China and the Soviet Union are concerned. America's long-term appraisal of the actions of Moscow and Peking in Korea established the basis for distinguishing between the U.S.S.R. as its "reasonable adversary" and China as its "irrational foe." The U.S. government concluded that although the Soviet Union was an opportunistic and aggressive power, it was also cautious. As its behavior between 1950 and 1953 demonstrated, Moscow had recognized that the two superpowers had certain interests in common; primary among these was the need to be wary of inadvertently provoking world war over issues that did not warrant so serious an outcome. China, on the other hand, came to be portrayed in America as a fundamentalist, violent, and revolutionary power that deserved to be punished for what was regarded as an unwarranted transgression of the norms of international behavior. Though détente with the Soviet Union was still some years away, the policy toward Peking, compared with that toward Moscow, remained stagnant for two decades, to the detriment of China's national security and its economic and diplomatic position.

Assessments made within the Truman and Eisenhower administrations of the risks associated with any expansion of hostilities into China depended on a variety of factors. In the early stages of the war, there was no unified perception of those risks. Greater agreement later on reflected the fact that more evidence was available on which to base an assessment of consequences and also resulted from the diminution of State Department influence as the war dragged on and policy became more militarized. The frequency and kind of contribution made to the policy debates varied according to the personal experiences and belief systems of the individuals involved, the bureaucratic roles they played, the inter-relationships among the decision makers, their responsiveness toward actors in the international and domestic settings, and their beliefs about America's military and diplomatic capabilities.

As was to be expected, power resources within the bureaucracy were not distributed equally, nor was the power structure entirely stable over the whole period of the war. Those with greatest access to the president tended to dominate the policy recommendation process. For most of Truman's period of office, Dean Acheson enjoyed a preeminent position; when policy recommendations tended to divide along departmental lines, therefore, the State Department often appeared to have predominated. For example, in the second half of 1949, Acheson broadly recommended a policy of limited accommodation toward the Chinese Communist regime and acquiescence in the fall of Taiwan. The Defense Department, however, was in favor of a far more punitive policy toward the Chinese Communists, advocating military assistance to the Nationalists in order to influence the outcome on the mainland and, later on, the disposition of Taiwan. Defense was much more concerned than State with the augmentation of Communist capabilities that would result from the capture of the Chinese mainland and then of Taiwan; State (with important exceptions) was more concerned with the impact that an interventionist policy on behalf of Chiang Kai-shek's discredited regime would have on the attitudes of the leaders of other Asian states and on America's European allies. Subsequently, during the Korean hostilities and during the consideration of extending the fighting to China, this bureaucratic split manifested itself again, with the military (particularly the commanders in Korea) advocating a harsher stance toward the Chinese than the diplomatic establishment, which was still more concerned with allied unity. Bureaucratic politics, therefore, were important in influencing policy decisions during the war, although on a number of key occasions this factor's impact on policy was an insufficient source of explanation.

Truman's decision-making style reinforced the distinctive departmental approach to problems. Truman liked to organize the policy-making process in terms of functional expertise, to allow each executive head to give his view from the departmental position. The president himself liked to play "the role of Chairman of the board, hearing sundry expert opinions on each aspect of the problem, then making a synthesis of them and announcing the decision."[5] President Eisenhower, on the other hand, preferred the "collegial" working relationship. He wanted to assist his executive heads in the process of "spontaneous mutual co-ordination," since he recognized that most significant policy issues would overlap departmental jurisdictions.[6]

Presidential style, then, affected the organization of the bureaucracy, but two structural changes that had occurred in 1947 were also of considerable significance in influencing the way decisions were arrived at. The National Security Act of 1947 created the National Security Council (NSC), which was designed to coordinate policy on national security issues within the executive branch, but the effect was to make the military more central in policy formulation. The act also created a unified Department of Defense in order to overcome the disunity among the services that had been prevalent in earlier years, but once again the effect was to increase the weight of the military perspective in policy deliberations.

Despite this emphasis on bureaucratic role, the "parochial" interests of the participants in decision making were generally diluted but occasionally reinforced by the personal relationships among executive heads. The well-known mutual antagonism between Secretary of State Dean Acheson and Secretary of Defense Louis Johnson tended to intensify the differences between their departments; indeed, Johnson worked to maintain a clear distinction between military and political factors. He has been described as "abrasive, cocksure, hyper-ambitious," and seemingly set on securing the Democratic Party's nomination in 1952. Acheson— "urbane, intellectual, lawyerly"—could not abide him, and the "time came when the two were hardly on speaking terms."[7]

By way of contrast, Acheson's relations with Johnson's successor, General George C. Marshall, were excellent if rather formal, and the Secretary of State became much less combative when the general took over at Defense for a year beginning in September 1950. Marshall had preceded Acheson at State and had himself been Army chief of staff when Omar Bradley (now chairman of the joint chiefs) was a subordinate commander. This previous governmental experience led Marshall to make a conscious effort to avoid meddling with the work of his successors.[8] Thus the opportunities for ensuring a harmonious Department of Defense and for building a policy consensus between State and Defense were much increased after Johnson's departure in September 1950, and they remained potentially greater throughout the Korean War period, when Marshall was succeeded by Robert Lovett. Lovett had once been undersecretary of state and, after a short break from government service, became Marshall's deputy in October 1950. His position within the bureaucracy was enhanced by his being Marshall's designated and then actual successor, and his previous close working relationship with Acheson ensured his playing a significant policy-making role. Despite improved relations between executive heads, however, there remained those within the lower reaches of both departments who had experienced the conflict and combat of earlier years.

Acheson's and Marshall's relations with their president were also reputed to be excellent. Truman and Marshall held each other in high esteem, the president venerating the general as "the greatest living American."[9] Truman, though not in awe of Acheson as he was of Marshall, worked very closely with him also. It has often been said that Truman's lack of foreign policy experience led him to appoint a strong and knowledgeable secretary of state, and their relations were such that apart from Marshall's time as defense secretary, Acheson had no peer at the White House. Nevertheless, though the secretary of state's views generally received priority in the president's deliberations, Truman was not "putty in Acheson's hands"[10] and would often overrule him at crucial moments. Truman was much more receptive than Acheson to domestic political pressures; he had come from ten years in the Senate and was still sensitive to congressional opinion. Republican criticism of his administration's China policy, for example, made its mark and led him to override some of Acheson's more accommodating moves toward the Chinese Communists in 1949 and early 1950. For these and other reasons, Acheson's influence with Truman may be termed considerable but not always decisive. In addition, Acheson was not well liked outside the bureaucracy, and McCarthyist attacks during the war decreased his ability to promote and build support for administration policies in the country at large. Hence, despite his favored position at the White House, in certain respects Acheson was vulnerable.

President Eisenhower's relationship with his secretaries of state and defense were notably different from Truman's. Not surprisingly, Eisenhower was virtually his own secretary of defense, treating Charles Wilson most of the time "neither as a deputy nor as a delegate, but rather as little more than an expediter of detailed presidential instructions."[11] Eisenhower was willing to delegate authority to John Foster Dulles, but they worked very closely together and were in touch daily. It was a "collegial working relationship. . . . They jointly perfected policies, but Eisenhower made the final decisions and Dulles executed them."[12] Eisenhower was less susceptible to congressional pressure than Truman had been, partly because of his enormous personal popularity, partly because he was adept at deflecting criticism away from himself and toward his executive heads through his use of the "hidden hand" strategy.[13] But he was still aware of his weakness of position with the Taft wing of the Republican Party and the need to cultivate the support of its members, especially after they came into positions of prominence in Congress in 1953.

Each of these and other significant policy makers entered the policy arena with the kind of simplified and structured beliefs about international relations that are essential in order to cope with a complex environment, that provide "the individual with a more or less coherent way of organizing and making sense out of what would otherwise be a confusing array of signals picked up from the environment by his senses."[14] The international events of the 1930s seem to have had great impact on those involved in framing foreign policy during the early 1950s. The defining experience of Dean Rusk's life, for example, had been America's failure to help the international community stop aggression in the 1930s.[15] Before becoming assistant secretary of state for Far Eastern Affairs in March 1950, Rusk had served briefly in the China-Burma-India theater during World War II, and as assistant secretary of state for United Nations Affairs. These experiences predisposed him to see others as aggressors, to be supportive of U.N. activities and collective security, to believe that the United States had "an obligation to stand" not just in one part of the world but everywhere it might be called upon to do so.[16]

Truman expressed similar feelings about the pre–World War II years; his own failure to support the League of Nations and his votes in favor of neutrality legislation haunted him after Pearl Harbor. This feeling of guilt, combined with a preference among U.S. policy makers for reasoning by analogy, meant that when North Korea attacked South Korea in June 1950, Truman's immediate point of reference was America's failure to act against Japan, Italy, and Germany in the 1930s. In his view, Communism was behaving in Korea just as Hitler, Mussolini, and the Japanese had behaved a decade or two earlier.[17]

Truman's guiding principles were that "world war was best avoided, that the Soviet Union was trying to take over the world, and that the United States should not be dishonored."[18] His beliefs about the Soviet leadership certainly were essentially simple: he viewed it with profound distrust, as a "wily adversary," unstable, unpredictable, and prone to take risks. Such an outlook made it difficult for Truman to take note of Soviet behavior that might have been regarded as moderate or cautious unless it was in response to countervailing force.[19] Moscow "respected nothing but force"; "only in the face of force [would] they talk and negotiate," he once said.[20] President Truman knew very little about China, especially before 1949, and had taken only an occasional, if significant, hand in administering China policy, but apparently he did not trust the Chinese Communist leadership, either.

Secretary of State Acheson had also first entered into the conduct of international relations when Hitler was at the peak of his power. The lesson that Acheson and others learned from Hitler was that it was pointless to try to understand the enemy's point of view; an opponent would come to terms only if your armed forces outstripped his.[21] He believed firmly in the deterrent power of military alliances and in negotiating only from a position of recognizable strength. These beliefs fundamentally influenced his approach to the Soviet Union and, in turn, reinforced the attitude of President Truman. In this respect, Acheson's views were very similar to those of John Foster Dulles, who was distrustful of the U.S.S.R. on all occasions and fearful of real negotiations, particularly when the adversary was in a position of strength. Dulles believed that when the adversary sought to negotiate, this was "a sign of weakness and/or failure"; he thought that under these circumstances it was necessary to push harder rather than to make concessions.[22]

It was in this area that Acheson and Dulles parted company with someone like George Kennan, the noted Soviet expert. Kennan was ready to recognize Moscow's concern for its own security and its basically cautious approach to foreign policy. But his influence in government circles had been on the wane since 1949, despite his renown, and in early 1950 he was replaced as head of the Policy Planning Staff (PPS) by Paul Nitze, whose analysis of Soviet intentions more closely reflected Acheson's own views.

The PPS's chief China expert was John Paton Davies, who was born of missionary parents in China and had had long experience in that country. But despite his extensive contact with the Chinese, Davies was somewhat less than sympathetic to their nationalist aspirations as they defined them, and he was keen to coerce the Chinese Communists, to "scold" them on a number of occasions in 1949 and 1950 for their failure to demonstrate their independence of Soviet leadership.[23] In the early part of the Korean War, he was one of those ready to contemplate retaliation against China, often evincing a more militant stance than some of his colleagues in the State Department.

Acheson, unlike his closest advisers, Dean Rusk and Philip C. Jessup, and unlike Dulles, was not a universalist. Whereas Dulles viewed "free world" interests as indivisible and was not willing to distinguish between areas of concern to United States security,[24] Acheson's major preoccupations centered firmly on Europe, particularly on relations with Britain. His major conditioning experiences in foreign affairs had involved the United Kingdom and Western Europe. He had been concerned with assistance to Greece and Turkey in 1947, the presentation of the Marshall Plan, and plans for postwar economic organization.[25] It is also a mark of his sympathy with the U.K.'s affairs that he spent more time with the British ambassador, Sir Oliver Franks, than with all other ambassadors combined. Franks enjoyed the privilege of full access to Acheson both during working hours and at home.[26] Concern for the Anglo-American relationship was central to Acheson's deliberations regarding policy toward China during the Korean War. His conception of Britain's crucial importance to the success of America's defense efforts in Europe and his determination to ensure allied unity on all possible occasions, as well as his personal rapport with Franks, led him to introduce the British government's perception of current and future events into many policy discussions. For these reasons, Acheson's individual preferences may be said to have reinforced his role as head of the diplomatic establishment in Washington.

Eisenhower as president was as concerned as Acheson and Truman had been to build a strong coalition of Western nations. His experience in the postwar years and as the first supreme commander of NATO reinforced his belief in the value of collective defense efforts in Europe. From this he hoped that with "time and Western steadfastness, 'world communism' might lose its monolithic expansionist qualities, and a strong, resourceful West could then take the lead in dissipating the cold war."[27] Acheson may not have had Eisenhower's optimism about the future, but in most other ways the two men were in agreement about the tasks that lay ahead for the United States. There was, therefore, a considerable degree of foreign policy continuity between the Truman and Eisenhower administrations.

Such, then, were the views of some of the central policy makers in Washington during the Korean War. The Cold War rhetoric; the attitude that Soviet power was harnessed to an expansionist doctrine; the essentially negative assessment of the value of diplomatic negotiations with Moscow; the perceived vulnerability of Western Europe to Soviet invasion or, more likely, to subversion from within; and projected changes in the balance of power within Asia— each of these aspects and perceptions of the international environment undermined the diplomatic approach to foreign policy in this era. The institutional changes that had brought the Defense Department into a position of greater influence in the policy-making process, and the partisan political pressures emanating from Congress (which demonstrated a dissatisfaction with the "passive" doctrine of containment), also had an effect in generating a perceived need to stand firm and to promote a more activist foreign policy. The crisis wrought by the Korean War and China's subsequent entry into the conflict crystallized these beliefs and brought forth the necessary support for a vastly increased defense budget to make this activism a reality.

During the early stages of China's intervention in Korea, decision making bore some of the hallmarks of crisis: that is, a perceived threat to important national goals, which surprised policy makers by its occurrence, and was seen to require an immediate response. Studies of crisis behavior have shown that during these periods, at both individual and group levels, there is a reduction in creative response, an inability to be receptive to information contrary to existing beliefs, and an increase in stereotypic thinking.[28] In the winter of 1950–51, U.S. decision makers appeared to rely on the personal belief systems described above and on the perceptions of primary policy makers such as Marshall and Acheson. Once the crisis atmosphere had abated in the spring of 1951, however, and it had become clear that U.S./U.N. forces would not be compelled to evacuate the peninsula entirely, a more decentralized method of decision making was established. In the later phases of the conflict, information could be gathered and evaluated over a longer period of time, and there was a consequent higher degree of bureaucratic involvement in the process of policy formulation. The increased opportunities for participation in policy making offered greater scope for the expression of departmental interests, thereby enhancing the effects of the institutional changes of 1947. Turning points in the war, therefore, also affected the way in which decisions were arrived at and determined the degree of influence of certain individuals' perceptions.

Though for many Americans the Korean War has probably paled into insignificance, the conflict should be seen as a major turning point in the Cold War. The fact that it was on the verge of becoming a wider and more dangerous Far Eastern conflict, in which the United States contemplated the use of atomic weapons against an Asian nation once again, has been obscured for too long.

Those readers wishing to focus primarily on this previously obscured aspect of policy making should turn to the later sections of Chapter 3 and to Chapters 4 through 7. These cover in a thematic way the arguments concerning the extension of the conflict from just prior to China's entry into Korea through the signing of the armistice agreement in July 1953. Each examines the bureaucratic debate within the U.S. administration, the domestic political and international settings for the discussion, the material resources available for an expanded war, and the intelligence estimates of likely Soviet response to attacks on China. Chapters 4 through 7 also contain material regarding the possible use of atomic weapons during the conflict.

More familiar ground is covered in Chapter 2 and the early part of Chapter 3. Chapter 2 surveys the external and internal settings for policy formulation in the months leading up to the Korean conflict, the Truman administration's attitude toward China, and its appraisal of Peking's relationship with Moscow prior to June 1950. Chapter 3 examines the U.S. decisions to enter the war, introduce the Seventh Fleet into the Taiwan Strait, and cross the 38th Parallel into North Korea. It also discusses the American perception of possible future Soviet and Chinese roles in the war. Despite the fact that these chapters deal with fairly well-known material, they are important in showing the wider context of American foreign policy and the context for America's early moves in Korea. They show, too, the early thinking about Sino-Soviet relations during the conflict, the roots of later policy divisions regarding military action against China; and they demonstrate that the idea of an expanded war was not solely connected with America's frustration at being unable to end the war on what it regarded as acceptable terms.

In military terms, although not in policy terms, the Korean War did, of course, remain limited. For most of the period, limited resources, allied pressure, and uncertainty about the military outcome operated to keep it so. But in the end these restraints were no longer sufficient, and the Eisenhower administration made a policy decision to present its ultimatum to the Communist negotiators at Panmunjom. The concentration on the pressures for expansion in the following chapters thus serves to demonstrate the thinness of the dividing line between a limited and an expanded conflict, and why that dividing line was crossed in policy terms in the spring of 1953. If the definition of Korea as a limited military conflict were to be relaxed, however, then in military terms as well the war did expand beyond Korea's borders. Leaving aside what befell Taiwan, between 1950 and 1953 the United States intensified its covert operations against the Chinese mainland; engaged in air reconnaisance over Chinese territory; bombed the Yalu River power installations and a chemical plant right on the Yalu in the knowledge that a few bombs might fall on the other side of the river; and supplied military advice to Nationalist Chinese troops, masquerading as "guerilla" forces, when they launched several large-scale raids against Chinese offshore islands.

Even in its strictly "limited" form, the war in Korea brought destruction and casualties of tragic proportions. The tragedy is all the more evident if one recognizes the war as essentially a civil dispute in its origins[29] and as wholly unnecessary in terms of its provocation of the Chinese. But supposedly intelligent and expert opinion in the United States dictated some of the moves in Korea, and many of the same decision makers were present in later years to influence policy formulation during conflicts involving the major Communist powers. If from this analysis we can learn something of the way in which U.S. administrations during the Cold War years established their attitudes and policies toward Peking and Moscow, then we may begin to comprehend matters that have been of consuming and enduring interest to U.S. foreign policy makers in the postwar era.

[2]

The International and Domestic Policy Settings

In the months preceding the outbreak of the Korean War on June 25, 1950, the appraisal of Soviet behavior and of the likely effect of the Communist victory in China on the strategic positions of the United States and the Soviet Union had become a major preoccupation of the Truman administration. The level of danger that Soviet activity posed to the United States and its allies was seen to depend on a variety of domestic and international factors, including the degree to which the Western nations—led by the United States—were able to demonstrate a unity and firmness of purpose, and the estimated relative strengths and capabilities of the two major power blocs. Bureaucratic and personal rivalries among decision makers also influenced the conclusions about the likely impact of Chinese and Soviet foreign policy. And though public and congressional opinion rarely had direct influence on policy toward Peking and Moscow, it could (depending on its intensity) indirectly affect the way policy was presented, and the method and timing of its implementation.

THE INTERNATIONAL SETTING

By the time of the conflict in Korea, the relationship between Moscow and Washington had become unproductive and hostile. International crises such as those involving Iran, Greece, and Berlin fed the hostility, as did events outside U.S. control, such as the U.S.S.R.'s explosion of an atomic bomb in August 1949 (two years earlier than Western intelligence had predicted) and the establishment of a Communist regime in China in October 1949. Amidst these developments, the U.S. government moved forward decisively with its policies toward Europe—providing aid to Greece and Turkey, introducing the Marshall Plan, and signing the North Atlantic Treaty. Toward Asia, however, its more tentative approach reflected strategic priorities centering on Europe, limited military capabilities that forced selectivity, and a more complex political environment in Asia. In addition, and of some consequence to America's China policy, officials in Washington had a better intuitive grasp of problems in Europe, given that the bulk of their experience had been in that region.[1]

In this tense political atmosphere, a joint State-Defense Department study group headed by Paul Nitze produced NSC 68, a comprehensive analysis of U.S. security objectives. Nitze, who had taken over from George Kennan in January 1950 as head of the Policy Planning Staff, thought such a study was urgently needed because, as he put it, "in the aggregate, recent Soviet moves reflect not only a mounting militancy but suggest a boldness that is essentially new—and borders on recklessness."[2]

The program advocated by NSC 68 required the allocation of vastly increased sums to the defense budget, and its language was startling and extreme—partly to persuade Congress that the dangers to U.S. security were immediate and great. The authors defined the "fundamental design" of the Soviet Union as "the complete subversion or forcible destruction of the machinery of government and structure of society in the countries of the non-Soviet world and their replacement by an apparatus and structure subservient to and controlled from the Kremlin." Since the United States was the "principal center of power in the non-Soviet world," Russia would try "by one means or another" to subvert or destroy its "integrity and vitality."[3] In view of the unexpected detonation of a Soviet atomic weapon in 1949, it seemed possible to the authors that within four to five years the U.S.S.R. would be able to launch a nuclear attack on the United States of such weight that Moscow would be capable of going on to win a world war.

NSC 68 had its detractors, notably George Kennan and Charles Bohlen, both leading Soviet experts in the Department of State. These analysts distrusted comprehensive policy documents of this kind and preferred to base prognoses of Soviet behavior on intentions rather than capabilities. But the document reflected the view of more powerful members of the Truman administration; Dean Acheson, for example, was strongly in support of the more militant stance that NSC 68 advocated, and the study group's position on the aggressive nature of Soviet power spurred the secretary of state into further activity. The North Atlantic Treaty had been signed in April 1949, but since NATO was in no sense a functioning organization at the time that NSC 68 was being prepared, Acheson expressed an urgent need to make America's commitment to Europe's security real rather than symbolic and pressed for rapid augmentation of conventional defense capabilities in the area. In Indochina, which the United States saw as the key to the stability of the whole of Southeast Asia,[4] the administration began actively to support French colonial rule in order to guarantee the survival of non-Communist regimes in Asia, and a stable government in Paris so that France might fulfill its mission as a vital part of the European security system. On May 8, 1950, the United States announced its first economic and military aid package to Indochina and France; after Korea, the aid was speeded up and increased. (By 1956, however, the last French forces had departed, and Indochina became a wholly American problem.)

Soviet-American hostility also reinforced the role of Japan as the central component of the U.S. security system in the Pacific. If Soviet access to the raw materials and natural resources of Southeast Asia were linked to the industrial war-making capacity of Japan, the security of the United States would be seriously jeopardized, it was argued.[5] In order to strengthen its relationship with Japan and stave off any Communist threat to that country, the Truman administration began to consider it essential to promote democracy and economic stability in Japan through a modification of U.S. occupation policies. If Japan were to resist Soviet pressure and emerge as a strong pro-Western ally, it would be necessary to support policies contributing to Japanese economic recovery and to work toward the completion of a nonpunitive peace treaty. With the outbreak of the Korean War, these goals were rapidly accomplished.

Prior to the conflict, the rapid U.S. demobilization policies following World War II accounted for a certain tentativeness in policy toward Asia, in comparison with the moves instituted in Europe. The U.S. decision to withdraw the 45,000 troops that were stationed in South Korea, for example, was taken primarily because of this manpower shortage, and because of other pressing obligations indicating that the troops could be used more profitably elsewhere. The Defense Department was acutely aware of its limited capabilities and perceptibly growing commitments. It never lost sight of the fact that between 1945 and 1947, U.S. military forces had shrunk from 12 million to 1.6 million men. Such shrinkage was reflected in the defense budget, which in fiscal year (FY) 1945 had stood at $81.6 billion but by FY 1947 had diminished to $13.1 billion. In June 1950, before the outbreak of the Korean hostilities, Congress had debated a budget for FY 1951 of $13.5 billion, about 5 percent of the gross national product (GNP) and 15 percent lower than the previous year's appropriations. Policies such as these were popular with Congress, with the electorate, and with Truman, who in 1949 had instructed the new secretary of defense, Louis Johnson, to hold defense spending below a ceiling of $15 billion.

Two major reasons have been suggested to explain a policy of reduced means at a time when the perceptions of Soviet intentions and capabilities were undergoing change. First, the belief had existed within the State Department during Marshall's day that vigorous rearmament might provoke the Soviet Union, too, into spending more on the military or, more dangerously, into taking rash action. The theory of deterrence was as yet an underdeveloped art, and "the question of 'how much is enough' rarely was squarely faced, let alone clearly answered."[6] Second, in the late 1940s large increases in military spending were generally thought to be a danger to the economy that would weaken the United States, thereby threatening national security. Economic publications such as *Business Week* and the *Wall Street Journal* predicted that a defense budget above $15 billion would produce inflationary pressures. These the business community wished to avoid, because inflation was likely to result in the imposition of governmental controls over wages and prices, restrictions on credit, and new taxation levels.[7]

Despite these fears, the confrontational stance outlined in NSC 68 and the pressure to maintain U.S. credibility with its allies in Europe and in Asia emerged as significant challenges to the low-budget philosophy. And with the outbreak of a war in Korea that was seen as having been instigated by the U.S.S.R., the fears of Truman and some of his advisers regarding an arms race or ram-

pant inflation were relegated to a position of secondary importance. The president thus formally approved NSC 68, and its ra-
tionale for increased defense expenditures, in September 1950. In
consequence, by 1953 defense spending was to rise to 14 percent of
GNP, representing an increase of $37.3 billion. In their study of
military preparedness before the Korean conflict, the joint chiefs
had set force objectives at 10 divisions, 281 major combatant naval
vessels, and 58 air wings. By September 1950 the objectives had
been revised upward to 18 divisions, 354 vessels, and 78 wings;
following China's entry into the war, the last two figures were
pushed still higher, to 397 naval vessels and 95 air wings.[8]

THE DOMESTIC SETTING

Although it was the Korean War that guaranteed the acceptance
of vastly increased defense budgets, the shock of the Soviet atomic
bomb and China's "loss" to Communism had already generated
fears of a dramatic shift in the balance of power in favor of Moscow. In this highly charged political atmosphere, evidence of espionage and intrigue accumulated, seeming to provide a partial
explanation for the U.S. "defeat" in China and successful Soviet
technological advances. In January 1950, Alger Hiss, a one-time
State Department official who had been present at the Yalta conference of 1945, was convicted of perjury for having stated under
oath that he had not passed classified documents to a Communist
agent. In February, the British scientist Klaus Fuchs, chief of the
Theoretical Physics Division of the British Atomic Energy Research
Establishment, who had once worked on the Manhattan Project,
confessed to having engaged in nuclear espionage on behalf of the
Soviet Union.

These and other alarming espionage revelations gave full rein to
the "paranoid" element in foreign affairs, providing valuable ammunition to Senator Joseph McCarthy and to conservative members of the Republican Party who were attacking the Truman administration for its foreign policy "failures." McCarthy made
public his first charges against the State Department in February
1950, charges that would destroy the careers of many Asian specialists and, more generally, damage the morale of the diplomatic
branch in Washington. Among the State Department's Asian ex-

perts lost to the administration were John Stewart Service, who was subjected to loyalty and security hearings virtually every year from 1946 to 1951 and was finally dismissed by Acheson in December 1951; O. Edmund Clubb, who was suspended in June 1951 and resigned in 1952; and John Paton Davies, who was transferred to an obscure post in Peru in April 1953 and was fired by Dulles on November 5, 1954.[9]

Congressional criticism, spurred on by McCarthy, was also responsible for certain significant personnel changes in 1949 and 1950. Walton Butterworth, who had finally been appointed assistant secretary of state for Far Eastern Affairs after Senate Republicans criticized his nomination, was replaced by Dean Rusk in March 1950, primarily because of criticisms and attacks during Butterworth's tenure. John Foster Dulles's appointment as State Department consultant in April 1950, though basically distasteful to both Acheson and Truman, was an urgent attempt to recreate the bipartisanship in foreign policy that was slowly being destroyed by criticism of the administration's Asian policy. Dulles promised he would be able to restrain Senators Robert A. Taft, Eugene Millikin, and Styles Bridges, but only "if Truman allowed [him] to plan some 'early affirmative action' against the 'Communist menace.'"[10]

McCarthy's damaging attacks on the State Department had dovetailed neatly with the charges that had been emanating primarily from the China bloc in Congress. Though the bloc was small, the infrequency of attempts to oppose its arguments led it to assume a position of influence far beyond its actual size. These "neo-isolationists," who were basically anti-European but in favor of an activist policy on behalf of Chiang Kai-shek, came to prominence with the defeat of the Republican candidate, Thomas E. Dewey, in the 1948 presidential election. Dewey's unexpected loss precipitated a movement within the Republican Party to reject the bipartisanship in foreign policy that had marked the approach of both presidential candidates to the 1948 campaign. The Democratic victory also resulted in a significant personnel change in Congress: Democratic Senator Tom Connally of Texas replaced the arch-exponent of bipartisanship, Senator Arthur Vandenberg, as head of the Senate Foreign Relations Committee.[11] Connally was less sure of himself than Vandenberg in this role, more unquestioningly supportive of Truman's foreign policy, and—because of his combative personality—less able to maintain unity within the committee.

This rejection of bipartisanship in policy toward Asia found support partly because of the general unease that accompanied evidence of irrevocable entanglement with the Old World, Europe, but it acquired its main impetus from the impending and then actual defeat of the Chinese Nationalists on the mainland of China. The heart of the China lobby's complaints was expounded expertly by one of its leading spokesmen in the House of Representatives: Walter H. Judd constantly urged the State Department to give Chiang its full support and so prevent "the communization of Asia." Judd, alive to the partisan benefits that could be derived from supporting McCarthyist tactics, also supplied the Wisconsin senator with material on the administration's China policy for his early speeches.[12] What Congressman Judd and others went out of their way to emphasize was that the administration had been "making every possible effort to help the . . . governments of Western Europe resist the further expansion of Communist control and no real effort . . . to help the Chinese government resist Communist expansion."[13] If the president had not presented his Truman Doctrine in 1947 as a containment policy of sweeping, global proportions but had made it clear to a wider public that containment demanded the setting of priorities and the distinguishing of major from minor interests, then Judd's point would not have been so difficult to answer. Neither would Chinese Nationalist emissaries in Washington and New York have been able to capitalize on the global rhetoric to promote their demands for military assistance.[14]

Acheson tried to respond to the charges by publishing the China White Paper in August 1949, which stressed that the outcome of the civil war in China was "the product of internal Chinese forces" that the U.S. could neither influence nor control. Short of a massive commitment of American ground troops in China, which no one wanted, the Nationalists seemed doomed to lose the fight for the mainland. But Acheson's attempt at explanation failed to convince the critics. On August 21, Senators Styles Bridges, William F. Knowland, Pat McCarran, and Kenneth S. Wherry issued a statement labeling the White Paper "a 1,054-page whitewash of a wishful, do-nothing policy which has succeeded only in placing Asia in danger of Soviet conquest with its ultimate threat to the peace of the world and our own national security."[15] This view of a "do-nothing" policy linked with the idea that a conspiracy to aid the

Chinese Communists existed among Communist sympathizers within the Roosevelt and Truman administrations cemented the alliance between McCarthy and the China bloc. This group and other Chiang supporters would make a range of demands in the next few years, including military aid to the Nationalist regime in Taiwan, assistance for a Nationalist return to the mainland, non-recognition of the Chinese Communist government, and denial of the PRC's place in the United Nations.

PERCEPTIONS OF SINO-SOVIET RELATIONS

Assessing the attitude of the Chinese Communists toward Washington and Moscow was problematical, to say the least, in such an international and domestic setting. The Soviet challenge to the U.S. nuclear lead and the general presumption of greater Soviet aggressiveness sharpened the American image of Moscow in 1949 and early 1950. Developments within China and Indochina appeared to provide further evidence of Soviet-led expansionism and the prospect of future augmentation of its economic and military capabilities, thereby enabling Moscow to overshadow the capacities of the West. To the administration's domestic critics, a policy of containment seemed too passive a response.

An attitude of uncertainty, coupled with ominous charges that "enemies within" were sapping U.S. strength as surely as the Communists without, made it difficult to develop a vocal and staunch domestic base of support for an enlightened policy toward the People's Republic of China. The general public was difficult to rally. It knew too little about Peking to be able to distinguish either between it and Moscow or between Mao Tse-tung and Chiang Kai-shek. Opinion polls showed, for example, that the majority opposed recognition of the PRC but had little enthusiasm for giving more aid to Chiang Kai-shek. Though the China White Paper of August 1949 was intended as a major effort to explain and publicize the administration's China policy, 64 percent of those questioned about the document in September 1949 had never heard or read anything about it.[16] The Truman administration therefore preferred to solve the China problem by awaiting the eventual downfall of the Nationalist regime—waiting for the dust to settle, as Acheson described it—before it made any definite policy moves.

The dramatic nature of the Nationalist collapse in China served to compound the problem of explaining the administration's China policy. The Communists were in control of Manchuria by November 1948 and of Shanghai by May 1949. By the second week of December 1949, the Nationalists had abandoned the mainland. Yet despite the press of these events and the legacy of policy explanations in previous years that projected Communism as an evil monolith, there were those within the State Department who thought the Truman administration could and should retain a flexible policy toward the Chinese Communists. Given time, they believed, America would eventually benefit from the independent and nationalist nature of the Chinese Communist movement and from Mao Tse-tung's "Titoist" tendencies, which would soon lead to an open split between his regime and Moscow. Acheson was inclined to favor this view because of his dislike of Chiang's regime, and because he realized there was no real alternative to recognition once the Chinese Communists had assumed control over the mainland. He tried to make such a policy more palatable by clinging to the belief that Mao was more nationalist than Communist and would not permit Soviet domination of his country.

The analysis of specialists within Acheson's department supported these arguments. The Policy Planning Staff made one of the earliest statements of the "Titoist" argument in 1948, a view that was incorporated into NSC 34 of October 13, 1948. NSC 34 suggested that Mao was not only another Tito but potentially even more of a heretic than Tito because he had been "entrenched in power for nearly ten times the length of time." The Kremlin would never be able to control such a large and populous country, it said, and if the Chinese Communists themselves acquired total control, they would be strongly tempted to assert their independence from Moscow.[17] The State Department's China expert, John Paton Davies, recommended early recognition of the Chinese Communist government in order to hasten the development of "Titoism."[18]

In early 1949 there were some indications that this analysis might be correct, that all was not right between Moscow and Peking. Cables from those capitals to Washington supported this assessment; and the consul general at Shanghai, John Cabot, whose views carried additional weight because of his previous duty in Yugoslavia, believed that if the Chinese were able to make independent decisions, "their eventual cooling off towards Soviets seems probable."[19] Some saw the supposed Chou En-lai demarche in May 1949 as signalling a Chinese desire for improved relations with the United States, and the June invitation to Ambassador John Leighton Stuart to visit Peking as evidence that there were still those within the Chinese leadership who desired something less than a close alliance with Moscow. An approach to American officials in January 1950, in which General Chen Yi was supposedly instrumental, also indicated that a moderate faction might eventually attempt to overthrow the supposed Stalinists inside the Chinese Communist Party.[20]

The negotiation of the Sino-Soviet Treaty of Alliance in February 1950 caused some consternation in Washington; however, its terms showed that there were tangible points of disagreement between Peking and Moscow. The negotiations took over two months to complete, and they did not contain the generous provisions of aid that the Chinese, it was presumed, had expected. In addition, continuing Soviet pressure in Sinkiang and Manchuria, as exemplified in the agreement, encouraged the United States to expect increased resentment in China. Rumors that Stalin demanded, and Mao resisted, the acquisition of five other ports in addition to Port Arthur and Dairen, and that Moscow sought to place large numbers of Russian "advisers" in police, army, and party positions, reached the State Department and gave it some reason to remain optimistic about a future Sino-Soviet split.[21] Speaking to the National Press Club in January 1950, Acheson again placed the blame for the "loss" of China on Chiang's incompetence, but he also suggested that his audience take heart from the fact that Stalin's ambitions would soon lead Moscow and Peking into conflict. Before the Senate Foreign Relations Committee in March, he asserted that the "very basic objectives of Moscow are hostile to the very basic objectives of China,"[22] despite the alliance.

Other factors, however, shifted the policy in a less constructive direction. Though the policy of encouraging "Titoism" in China received a boost from these signs of tension and from a realization of the magnitude of the task of bringing about any outcome other than Communist rule on the China mainland, the policy was never wholly secure or wholly acceptable, even within the administration. It was under attack from the China bloc in Congress, the Scripps-Howard and Hearst presses, the Pentagon, the president,

[47]

and certain influential officials in the State Department. It was undercut by events in China such as the arrest of the U.S. consul general, Angus Ward, at Mukden, by Mao's "lean to one side" speech in which he said that China must lean toward the Soviet Union and away from the imperialist West, and then by the Sino-Soviet treaty. Even Acheson revealed his basic hostility toward the Chinese when he ruled out a conciliatory policy and spoke in favor of letting the PRC learn "by bitter experience" what it was like to be Russia's ally.[23]

The president was hostile, too. The Chinese treatment of Ward upset him, and for a short time in 1949 he considered using force against Peking to get Ward and the U.S. consular staff at Mukden out of the country. He would blockade coal shipments from the northern ports of China en route to Shanghai to show the Chinese leaders that America "meant business" regarding the release of Ward, he said, and if China attempted to break the blockade, the United States "should be prepared to sink any vessels which refused to heed our warning."[24]

Acheson was able to deflect Truman from such a course of action, but the president's ideas suggested that he might have felt more in tune with a policy that unreservedly projected China's Communist leadership as a tool of the Soviets, allowing his administration to adopt a more punitive policy toward the new regime in China. Truman was suspicious, as were other U.S. officials, about the Peking leadership's motives in approaching American personnel such as Stuart and Clubb. The American intelligence establishment did not place much credence in the Chou demarche, suspecting that "notions of a schism within the Chinese Communist Party were fraudulent ideas peddled by its Stalinist leaders in an effort to obtain Western aid and trade."[25] Consul General Clubb's telegram from Peking on June 2, 1949, reinforced this view: "Communist desire continue diet Soviet political bread but eke out diet with American economic cake."[26] Huang Hua's overture to Ambassador Stuart was rejected in part because of the expected domestic fallout in Washington that would result from Stuart's trip to Peking. But Truman was also wary of demonstrating any softening of attitude toward the Chinese Communists;[27] he felt it might encourage them in their aggressive behavior toward U.S. officials in China. Suspicions, inflexibility, and an unbending domestic political setting thus made the U.S. government slow to implement any moves designed to advance the relationship with the Chinese Communists.

There was also great uncertainty as to when Sino-Soviet hostility was going to manifest itself. In June 1949, Clubb said that "it would be premature to accept development of Titoism at this juncture."[28] In December, Acheson had suggested taking the long view and being prepared to wait six to twelve years.[29] In February 1950 a State Department working group examining Indochina policy assumed that "an effective split" between the two Communist states was at least three years away.[30] The joint chiefs were inclined to the view that it would never manifest itself. As they had written in June 1947, "Communists in China are frequently described as differing basically from communists found in other parts of the world. . . . It is believed . . . that the Chinese Communists, as all others, are Moscow inspired and thus motivated by the same basic totalitarian and anti-democratic policies as are the communist parties in other countries of the world. Accordingly, they should be regarded as tools of Soviet policy."[31] There is little evidence that they ever deviated from this view. From 1948 onward they argued that a CCP victory on the mainland would significantly alter the world balance of forces to Moscow's advantage, and therefore that large-scale, supervised military aid should be given to the Nationalists.

This assessment inevitably affected the joint chiefs' evaluation of the strategic implications of a Communist takeover of Taiwan. Requested in November 1948 and again in February 1949 to comment on such a possibility and its probable effects on U.S. security, they described it as "seriously unfavorable," since it would be a major contribution to enemy capabilities allowing possible domination of "the sea routes between Japan and the Malay area, together with a greatly improved enemy capability of extending his control to the Ryukyus and the Philippines."[32] Given the disparity between America's military strength and its global commitments, however, they reluctantly recommended using only diplomatic and economic means to deny the island to the Communists. In the meantime, the United States could seek to deter the Chinese Communists from invading the island by "the stationing of minor numbers of fleet units at a suitable Formosan port or ports, with such shore activity associated therewith as may be necessary for maintenance and air communication."[33]

At this stage, Acheson managed to block such an attempt to tie the United States more firmly to the island on the grounds that doing so would undercut his policy of promoting Soviet and Chinese enmity. It was essential, he said, to avoid "an American-created irredentist issue just at the time we shall be seeking to exploit the genuinely Soviet-created irredentist issue in Manchuria and Sinkiang."[34] But later, with the Nationalist retreat to Taiwan, the political pressures building in Congress in support of Chiang, and the availability of $75 million in funds granted under the Military Assistance Act for the "general area of China," the military seized an opportunity to present renewed suggestions for aid to Taiwan. On December 23, 1949, the joint chiefs advocated "a modest, well-directed, and closely supervised program of military aid," combined with increased psychological, diplomatic, and economic support. They also suggested that General Douglas MacArthur, Commander in Chief, Far East, be permitted to send a mission to the island to survey requirements.

Again, Acheson counterattacked by explaining State Department policy. Meeting on December 29 to clarify the JCS thinking of the 23rd, Acheson reiterated the central components of the "Titoist" view: "In the Soviet effort to detach the northern tier of provinces in China exists the seed of inevitable conflict between China and the Soviet Union. Mao is not a true satellite in that he came to power by his own efforts and was not installed in office by the Soviet Army. This situation is our one important asset in China and it would have to be for a very important strategic purpose that we would take an action which would substitute ourselves for the Soviets as the imperialist menace to China." The joint chiefs, Acheson said, had not demonstrated their claim that the loss of Taiwan would really breach U.S. defenses; thus it was not worth paying the international political price that would follow from the course recommended by them.

The joint chiefs were bowed by this but not yet beaten. Pointing straight to the domestic political weaknesses of the State Department's policy, Bradley said in reply that the JCS were "presenting a purely military point of view which reflected the fact that Congress had appropriated money to support these people who were resisting Communism and that he recognized that political considerations might override their views."[35] It was obvious that he and the joint chiefs remained unconvinced of the merits of Acheson's argument.

The president and the National Security Council formally approved Acheson's policy position later that day, but the military were still able to influence Truman in the direction of their desired policy. Bradley, for example, was instrumental in having certain phrases inserted and others removed from Truman's January 5 press statement on the Chinese civil war and the future of Taiwan. Although intended to clarify the U.S. government's position with regard to the Nationalist regime, Bradley's suggestions served to muddy the statement's meaning. With the addition of the words "at this time" to the assertion that the United States had "no desire to obtain special rights or privileges, or to establish military bases on Formosa," Bradley was able to indicate that options regarding Taiwan were to be kept open. He also managed to delete a denial of any U.S. desire to detach the island from the Chinese mainland.[36]

Although the State Department had more or less won the latest battle with Defense over China policy, the Pentagon derived strength for its position from the fact that its high-level officials were united in their views, whereas the State Department's were not. Secretary of Defense Johnson sympathized entirely with the opinions of his joint chiefs. Indeed, Johnson's contacts with Chinese Nationalist officials, particularly with their ambassador to Washington, Wellington Koo, were frequent. On a number of occasions, Johnson and the assistant secretary of defense, Paul Griffith, discussed the possibility that Nationalist government strategy might effect a change in the U.S. administration's China policy. Griffith, for example, suggested ways in which the Nationalists could exert pressure on Acheson, and he even encouraged them in the belief that public opinion might soon force Acheson to leave office.[37] General MacArthur, also a staunch supporter of Chiang Kai-shek, added his support to the joint chiefs' views on the significance of Taiwan. The general provided ammunition as well for Truman's domestic political critics, on one occasion making public a secret State Department guidance memorandum requesting its foreign service officers to minimize the strategic significance of the loss of Taiwan.[38]

Within the State Department, however, there was no such unity as the Pentagon displayed; those who clearly sympathized with the Defense Department's view of the administration's China policy were unhappy about the prospective loss of Taiwan to the Communists. One of these was Dean Rusk, who became assistant secretary of state for Far Eastern Affairs on March 28, 1950. Rusk, sensitive to arguments about the strategic importance of Taiwan, immediately set about reversing the drift away from support for the island. He forwarded to Acheson optimistic reports of Taiwan's potential for survival, followed by the assertion of the U.S. military attachés in Taipei and Hong Kong, that extensive Soviet aid to China would culminate in the fall of Taiwan and eventual Chinese Communist pressure on Southeast Asia—an area that both State and Defense had agreed was of vital strategic importance to the West. Rusk was giving Acheson this information, he said, "for background, as the President's statement of January 5 regarding Formosa does not contemplate the supplying of military aid," and increased Soviet support for a possible invasion of Taiwan might "prompt further strong recommendations, official and otherwise, for countervailing aid to the Nationalist Government."[39]

In May, Rusk and Defense Department officials agreed that within the bounds of existing U.S. policy, they should provide assistance to the Nationalists. This would include a State Department request to Truman to release some of the $75 million for "covert actions in support of resistance on Formosa," and a policy of facilitating the granting of export licenses to the Nationalists for the purchase of military equipment in the United States.[40]

John Foster Dulles agreed with this activist policy in support of Chiang; both he and Rusk considered that Taiwan was a plausible place to draw the line against Communism. On May 30, Rusk prepared to send a draft memorandum to Secretary of State Acheson, identical to one Dulles had prepared on May 18, which repeated his and Dulles's view that Taiwan was the place where a "stand might be taken" because it possessed certain geographic and political advantages: "It is not subject to the immediate influence of Soviet land power. It is close to our naval and air power. It is occupied by the remnants of the non-Communists who have traditionally been our friends and allies. Its status internationally is undetermined by any international act and we have at least some moral responsibility for the native inhabitants. It is gravely menaced by a joint Chinese-Russian expedition in formation. The eyes of the world are focused upon it."[41] He further reflected the views of the Defense Department when he wrote that "the loss of China to Communists" who were "junior partners of Soviet Communism . . . marked a shift in the balance of power in favor of Soviet Russia and to the disfavor of the United States."[42]

Although it is not known whether Acheson saw this memorandum, or what his response was if he did, the appointment of someone like Rusk with such firm views regarding China policy at this time was undoubtedly crucial to the development of that policy. Rusk was certainly able to influence others apart from Acheson, such as Ambassador-at-Large Philip C. Jessup, Paul Nitze of Policy Planning, and Livingston Merchant, Rusk's deputy. At a meeting with these three and others to discuss Taiwan policy, the participants were generally agreed that a U.N. trusteeship for the island should be proposed to Acheson, and that naval units should be stationed there, "under circumstances sponsored by the United Nations,"[43] to prevent the fall of Taiwan.

Prior to the outbreak of the Korean War, then, the China policy that Acheson and others in the State Department had promoted was being undermined. The policy, which had projected the Chinese Communists as nationalists as much as communists, and which had expected them to be fiercely resentful of any encroachment on their national sovereignty or territorial integrity, was threatened at its heart by those within the Truman administration who desired to detach Taiwan from the mainland. On June 25, 1950, the developing policy toward Taiwan would enter a crucial new phase when Acheson recommended the interposition of the Seventh Fleet in the Taiwan Strait. This recommendation indicated that the secretary of state saw some merit in the view that domination by the PRC would open up the island to Soviet power, and illustrated the ambivalence of his thinking with regard to China. Following the advancement of this kind of assessment of Sino-Soviet relations, the Korean War seriously eroded a policy whose foundations had already been subject to attack, although the "Titoist" strategy was not regarded as completely inoperable in its original form until China's intervention in the conflict.

But even before the outbreak of hostilities, the administration was divided and uncertain about the nature of the Sino-Soviet relationship, and unclear about the role China would play in the world as a newly established Communist state. The signals from China were confusing: it was difficult to assess the Chinese leadership's motives and to weigh evidence, obtained indirectly, that suggested disunity on foreign policy issues in Peking. Acheson's approach increased the somewhat superficial nature of the evaluations of PRC behavior and of the Sino-Soviet relationship. He was not really interested in the Chinese or in their country; what was important to him about dividing Peking from Moscow was the continuance of a policy of containment by new means, through the Chinese Communists. As always, Moscow was at the heart of his thinking and at the core of the "Titoist" strategy.[44] This made his policy vulnerable to the arguments of opponents and to events outside U.S. control, such as the outbreak of the Korean War, which could be interpreted as undermining its operational basis— although not its basic premise.

The Cold War atmosphere had sharpened in Asia by 1949; if the Chinese Communists were to demonstrate their independence, it had to be soon. Unfortunately, a necessary ingredient for the administration's China policy was time: time to demonstrate that Chiang's regime was doomed to extinction, that Americans could coexist with a Communist cum nationalist government in China without its undermining U.S. security, and that a wedge could be driven between Moscow and Peking. A gradual approach of this kind was difficult to maintain in the late 1940s as the Truman administration struggled to build "situations of strength," allied unity, and a domestic consensus. Energies were directed primarily toward the European theater and only secondarily toward the promotion of other vital interests in Japan and Southeast Asia. The predominance of these areas, combined with differences between State and Defense over the strategic value of Taiwan, divisions within State itself over this question, the countervailing activities of the China bloc, and the PRC's own policies toward Washington and Moscow made the progress of the China policy inordinately slow and prevented a sustained effort to promote it.

Policy deliberations during the Korean War demonstrated the durability of the influence of these external and internal factors. Concern with European policy, disagreements over China, vocal congressional criticism all had their effect, as did the two conflicting strains behind China policy—one that advocated a harsher, more punitive stance towards Peking, and the other that favored a more passive role based on the perception of potential and actual conflicts of interest between Peking and Moscow. During the Korean hostilities, and particularly when U.S. and Chinese troops were engaged in battle on the peninsula, these opposing positions came together in unexpected ways to influence the appraisal of the Sino-Soviet relationship and the question of extending the war into China.

[3]

The U.S. Appraisal of
Chinese and Soviet Policy:
June 25–October 15, 1950

The U.S. decision to intervene in the Korean conflict with air, naval, and ground forces occurred at a time when America was seeking to enhance the strength and stability of the Western alliance and to build a greater degree of domestic support for its foreign policy goals. Many policies of consequence flowed from the initial decision to enter the war, none of greater importance for America's relations with China and the Soviet Union than the agreements to "neutralize" the status of Taiwan and, in particular, to cross the 38th Parallel into North Korea.

The emphasis here is on the influence that Moscow and Peking had on the U.S. decision-making process. How was their relationship to the conflict interpreted? What were the expectations regarding their potential participation in the war, individually or jointly? And what kind of contingency plans did the administration draw up to deal with the potential military and political moves of the two Communist states?

THE MAJOR POWERS AND THE TWO KOREAS

Within a few months, China was to be heavily involved in securing the survival of the North Korean government as a separate entity. Yet, ironically, prior to June 1950 the United States considered China to be the least concerned of the major powers with events in either North or South Korea. Peking's influence in Pyongyang was probably as great as Moscow's, but its ties were categorized in Washington as being "weak and superficial."[1]

In the months preceding the outbreak of the war, China's preoccupations were basically domestic. Its leaders' priorities were to complete the revolution by taking over control of the territories of Tibet and Taiwan, and to grapple with the formidable tasks involved in unifying the country and feeding the population. As Mao said on June 23, the "test of war is basically over." It was now time to "enter the new era of socialism unhurriedly and with proper arrangements when conditions are ripe and when transition has been fully considered and endorsed by the whole nation."[2] To help with the urgent task of rebuilding the devastated rural areas, some People's Liberation Army (PLA) troops were to be transferred to productive tasks, and defense spending was to be severely curtailed. Although certain combat units were still needed for the takeover of Tibet and Taiwan, basic demobilization was to be carried out in 1950. Liu Shao-ch'i, in his May Day address, explained the new government's thinking: "After Taiwan is liberated the enemy's blockade and bombing will naturally end, the country's military expenditures can be greatly reduced, a great increase in investment in economic construction can then be made; and our country can move ahead on the road to transitional economic construction."[3]

The Soviet Union, on the other hand, was regarded in Washington as being strongly committed to the maintenance of Kim Il-sung's regime in North Korea, which it had helped to establish in 1948. Although Kim was much more of a nationalist than Washington would allow and was at least as close to Peking as he was to Moscow,[4] and despite the fact that the Red Army's presence had diminished in North Korea by 1949, U.S. officials in Washington and Seoul stated that the Democratic People's Republic of Korea (DPRK) was completely under Soviet control. It had about the same degree of independence as the Mongolian People's Republic, in their view. As the CIA put it on June 19, 1950, North Korea was "a firmly controlled Soviet Satellite that exercises no independent initiative and depends entirely on the support of the USSR." The Soviet embassy at Pyongyang was "headquarters for the four- to five-thousand-man Soviet mission in northern Korea," which was "infiltrated as advisers throughout the government, economy, and political organizations" of the country. The military forces were "entirely the product of Soviet planning and depend heavily on the large Soviet military missions for training at higher command levels and for tactical advice down to the battalion level."[5] Officials in Washington believed that any idea of independence for North Korea was a "complete fiction."

In many respects, America was firmly committed to its client state in South Korea, its "creation" in postwar Asia,[6] yet the greater public awareness of the various strands of that relationship made it appear more ambiguous than the Soviet relationship with the North. The initial American decision to station troops in Korea, which was not made until late in World War II, represented a deliberate denial of Far Eastern territory to the Soviet Union, whose troops originally were intended to occupy the whole of Korea. By 1947, however, the strategic value of the peninsula south of the 38th Parallel was being closely examined in the light of America's demobilization policies and increasing commitments in Europe. In general, the U.S. Defense Department accorded little strategic significance to Korea in the event of another world war— the major planning preoccupation.[7] Thus, by the autumn of 1947, a decision had been made to withdraw the 45,000 U.S. troops stationed in the country. As noted earlier, at a time of severe manpower shortage, the troops were needed elsewhere. American strategy had to take advantage of its "high technology/low-manpower orientation";[8] it would rely on naval and air power to defend its interests from island bases—a plan known as the "defensive perimeter" concept.

But there was a considerable period between the decision to withdraw the troops from South Korea and their actual departure. Not until June 1949 did the last of these forces leave, and as they did so, the Korean Military Advisory Group established by the United States expanded, thereby demonstrating the ambivalence of America's position. Even though the military and strategic commitment to the Republic of Korea (ROK) appeared to have been downgraded, the United States recognized that it could not entirely "'scuttle' and run from Korea without considerable loss of prestige and political standing in the Far East and in the world at large."[9] In addition, with the United Nations involved in the maintenance of a separate South Korean regime, NSC discussions increasingly linked the issue of U.S. credibility to the prestige of that international body. The overthrow of a U.N.-supported South Korea by a Soviet-dominated regime would "constitute a severe blow" to U.N. "prestige and influence . . . in this respect the interests of the U.S. must be regarded as parallel to, if not identical with, those of the UN."[10]

There was no doubt that the U.N. was to be strongly associated with South Korea's political future. In Dean Acheson's speech to the National Press Club in January 1950, he excluded the country from America's defensive perimeter in the Pacific area, but he declared that any move against the ROK would be grounds for invoking "the commitments of the entire civilized world under the Charter of the United Nations." U.N. involvement was further secured through the establishment of a new commission to "observe and report on any developments which might lead to or otherwise involve military conflict in Korea." The commission was also urged to use its influence to remove "other barriers caused by the division of Korea" and to help secure the unification of the country.[11] Despite the emphasis on international support for the maintenance of Syngman Rhee's regime, however, this was not the end of the bilateral relationship with the ROK, since the military advisory group continued its work, and the U.S. political commitment was maintained through the provision of arms and economic assistance.

In view of the ambiguity of U.S. policy in South Korea, it is possible, though not certain, that neither Moscow, Peking, or Pyongyang bargained on such a prompt American military response to the North Korean attack. According to Khrushchev's memoirs, Kim Il-sung came to Moscow to gain Stalin's support for a plan to take over the South. Despite Stalin's doubts about the sagacity of this action, Kim convinced him that the war would be won quickly, before the United States had time to become involved. Mao Tse-tung, who was also in Moscow during the winter of 1949–50, apparently approved Kim's plans, saying that "the USA would not intervene since the war would be an internal matter which the Korean people would decide for themselves."[12]

THE U.S. INTERVENES IN KOREA

International Aspects

There was little doubt in the minds of officials in Washington that the Soviet Union was directly involved in planning the North

Korean attack across the border on June 25, 1950, thus vindicating many of the assumptions contained in NSC 68. According to the State Department's Office of Intelligence Research (OIR), there had been "indications since early June that the USSR had been reviewing its Far Eastern policy"; these deliberations had involved the Soviet ambassador to the United States and the Soviet representative on the Allied Council for Japan, perhaps in an effort to estimate the likely U.S. reaction to a North Korean invasion. Since the North Korean government was completely under Soviet control, there was "no possibility that the North Koreans acted without prior instruction from Moscow."[13] The first considered CIA reaction to the attack stated quite categorically that it was Soviet inspired: "The invasion of the Republic of Korea by the North Korean Army was undoubtedly undertaken at Soviet direction and Soviet material support is unquestionably being provided. The Soviet objective was the elimination of the last remaining anti-Communist bridgehead on the mainland of northern Asia; thereby undermining the position of the U.S. and the Western Powers throughout the Far East." The intelligence memorandum went on to highlight the nub of the issue for the Truman administration: "By choosing Korea as the area of attack, the USSR was able to challenge the US specifically and test the firmness of US resistance to Communist expansion."[14]

It was this interpretation of the attack that most appealed to Truman and Acheson. Stalin, like Hitler, was testing their resolve; failure to oppose him would embolden the Soviet leader to proceed with further aggressive acts in the future.[15] In addition, U.S. credibility and prestige were considered to be at stake. A concern with "formulism" led policy makers to ask not what was the price of what it was about to do in Korea, but what was the price of not doing it. The answer was "a dreadful picture of defeats and miseries."[16] Unwillingness to intervene in support of a recognized ally in Asia would mean that U.S. determination to resist Soviet pressure would be questioned elsewhere, particularly among governments in both Europe and Asia that were concerned about the level of American support they would receive in the event of a Soviet-inspired attack. More generally, the American conception of harmony in the international system would be seen to have been violated and aggression rewarded—while the United States stood by. As Charles Bohlen put it, "All Europeans to say nothing of the

Asiatics are watching to see what the United States will do."[17] George Kennan agreed and told the British ambassador on June 27 that although South Korea was not strategically important to the United States, "the symbolic significance of its preservation was tremendous, especially in Japan."[18]

U.S. entry into the conflict would even benefit the policy of driving a wedge between Moscow and Peking, the OIR noted. A stiffening of the U.S. position in the Far East that included "effective measures to forestall Chinese Communist capture of Formosa" might lead Peking "to view the Korean adventure as a move by the USSR in disregard of Chinese Communist interests." Moreover, if the "adventure" should fail, the Chinese Communists might begin to question what advantage they derived from the Soviet alliance. They "would be impressed not only by the relative weakness or ineptness of the USSR in its Korean adventure but also by the threat of the newly militant posture of the US in the Far East, a threat that had all but been created by Soviet blundering. As a consequence, the strength of the Chinese Communists' ties to the USSR would be significantly weakened."[19]

In many ways, the allied response to the U.S. decision to intervene in Korea was all that had been anticipated. General MacArthur reported from Tokyo that the Japanese were immensely relieved; they interpreted it to mean, he said, that the United States would "vigorously defend them against [a] Russian invasion."[20] Averell Harriman, President Truman's special assistant, reported that prior to the U.S. decision to intervene, the Europeans were "gravely concerned" that the Americans "would not meet the challenge." Afterward, they too were greatly relieved.[21]

All of America's major allies voiced their support and perceived the decision as a turning point in the Western alliance. Lester Pearson, Canada's foreign minister, said later—in response to the U.S. military action and the subsequent U.N. involvement—that he felt "very excited about this historical precedent."[22] British ministers feared that the overrunning of South Korea would result in a disastrous loss of prestige for the Western allies, whereas an allied success in South Korea would "undoubtedly have a salutary effect on all non-Communists in Malaya."[23] The United Kingdom and the majority of other countries in the U.N. thus voted in support of the resolution that committed the organization to involvement in the conflict. Even India, despite certain misgivings, accepted the

U.N. resolution calling for military support for South Korea, a decision that delighted the Truman administration.

Despite Moscow's and Peking's loud protestations about what they described as the South Korean invasion of the North, their overall responses might best be termed circumspect. *Pravda's* coverage of the outbreak of the war was described by Ambassador Alan G. Kirk in Moscow as "deadpan."[24] The Soviet reply to the U.S. *aide-mémoire* calling on Moscow to disavow responsibility for the North Korean invasion indicated to Acheson that the Soviet Union was not going to be directly involved in the fighting;[25] it was going to treat the conflict as a civil confrontation. Admiral Roscoe H. Hillenkoetter reported to the NSC's consultants, meeting on June 29, that there was little evidence of Soviet support for the North Koreans and little Soviet military activity anywhere in the Far East.[26] Neither did Truman seem to think that the Soviets posed much of a direct threat in Korea. On July 8 he told the cabinet that he had "talked to the Lutheran Bishop of Berlin yesterday. He said 70 percent of the Russian attitude is bluff."[27] At about the same time, the Soviet Union showed some interest in encouraging peace moves in Korea, which the hard-line American ambassador to Moscow described as "genuine."[28] It appeared to Washington in early July that the U.S. response to the Soviet "test" had forced Moscow into a retreat.

There was still the possibility, however, that the Russians intended to embroil the Americans in a conflict with "Asian satellite forces" in order to wear down U.S. military capabilities. Although subsequent analyses of China's role in the early months of the war have shown that Peking was extremely cautious,[29] the Truman administration described Peking's reaction to the Taiwan Strait decision (discussed below) as "hostile and provocative". The next step in the "Communist strategy" might be a Chinese attack on Taiwan, or the introduction of Chinese forces into North Korea in order to tie the United States down in a wasteful and debilitating Asian war.[30] On July 9, MacArthur reported "a combination of Soviet leadership and technical guidance with Chinese Communist ground elements" within the forces he was confronting, but that same day the State Department described his telegram as "ambiguous," adding that no other source had confirmed the actual presence of Chinese troops.[31] Later in the month, there were reports that Premier Chou En-lai had made it "quite clear . . . that China had every intention of avoiding implication in the present hostilities."[32]

Given the response to MacArthur's allegation, Chou's statement, and Washington's failure to take seriously Peking's subsequent threats to intervene, it seems unlikely that China's involvement in hostilities was regarded as a strong eventuality or a grave problem at this stage of the war. On the whole, therefore, allied and Communist reactions to the U.S. decision to intervene in Korea were, respectively, supportive of the action and unrestraining; both probably encouraged further bold steps.

The Domestic Setting

For domestic reasons, too, it seemed that now was the time to "draw the line" with respect to Communist "aggression." The policy discussions reflected in NSC 68 had gained a number of prominent adherents within the Truman administration to the view that the Soviet Union might begin undertaking "piecemeal aggression" or "wars by proxy." The North Korean attack served to confirm these predictions and promoted the type of analysis contained in the document. The fact that the administration's Asian policy had been under sustained attack in the preceding months may also have encouraged a forceful response to the North Korean move.

It took very little time, therefore, after official word of the attack was received, to make the decision to intervene. Acheson thereafter played the leading role in all stages of the decision-making process, advocating in the first days that naval and air forces be committed to the Korean theater, urging increased military aid to Indochina and the Philippines, and proposing that the Seventh Fleet be installed in the Strait of Taiwan. Although the military were hesitant to commit overstretched U.S. combat forces to Korea, on June 30 they were forced by the continuing retreat of South Korean units to respond to MacArthur's call for a regimental combat team and a buildup of two divisions in Korea. Admiral Forrest P. Sherman, the chief of naval operations, also proposed a naval blockade of North Korea, which was agreed upon.[33]

Within the United States, the administration received widespread support for its decision: in early July, 77 percent of those polled approved of America's intervention in South Korea. Clark Clifford, a member of the White House staff, told Truman that "approval of your action is surprisingly universal."[34] Members of the Republican Party, including such staunch critics of Truman's Asian policy as Senators William F. Knowland, Styles Bridges, and Alexander Smith, unanimously supported the administration's action. Even Senator Joseph McCarthy gave his grudging approval, as did Truman's erstwhile Republican opponent in the 1948 election, Governor Thomas E. Dewey of New York.[35] Senator Robert Taft doubted the constitutionality of Truman's action but made it clear that he would support a joint resolution affirming congressional approval of the president's decision, if one were introduced. In the first days of the conflict, he repeatedly reiterated his support. The House voted to extend the Selective Service Act for one year; and when Truman asked Congress on July 19 for an additional $10 billion for defense, removal of limitations on the size of the armed forces, and authority to establish controls over the economy, his requests were generally—although not enthusiastically—supported.[36]

Anti-Communist liberals also rallied behind the president's decision to fight in Korea. The Americans for Democratic Action heaped praise on the president and commended him for following in the traditions of Franklin Roosevelt's "quarantine" speech.[37] None of the major daily newspapers opposed involvement, either. A *New York Times* editorial of June 28 called the decision a "momentous and courageous act"; the *Washington Post* credited Truman with having given the free world the leadership it desperately needed, and called his eventual decision to send ground troops to Korea "as wise as it was inevitable."[38] The *National Guardian* was almost the only journal to oppose the decision from the outset.[39] There was, then, a widespread domestic and international consensus that the North Korean attack was Soviet inspired and represented a challenge that the United States had to meet at once, or face the consequences in the future.

TAIWAN AND THE SEVENTH FLEET

The International Setting

If the decision to intervene in Korea received international and domestic support of gratifying proportions, the Taiwan decision met a more mixed reception. It was a two-part decision that involved, first, imposing the Seventh Fleet between the Chinese mainland and Taiwan to prevent attacks by either party on the other, and second, neutralizing the status of Taiwan, with the recommendation that its future be decided at the same time as a final settlement in Japan or by the United Nations.

The plan to patrol the Strait of Taiwan was not referred to the U.N., and the president, for one, recognized the need to "lay a base" for the action.[40] Presumably, he expected criticism from other governments, since there was already considerable internal support for such a move. Contingency plans for general war with the U.S.S.R. also provided for the neutralization of Taiwan in order to prevent Moscow from establishing air and naval bases there.[41] Since on June 26 no one could be definite about Soviet intentions, it was thought prudent to prevent the island from falling into Communist hands. Finally, it was recognized that should a Chinese attack on Taiwan occur simultaneously with the Korean invasion, the level of international tension would be such that general war by miscalculation would become a real possibility. Hence the decision to interpose the fleet was also designed to circumscribe the area of the hostilities.

Acheson made clear the extent to which he was prepared to exaggerate his view of Peking's role in the conflict in order to gain allied support for the Taiwan move. In a message sent to Britain's Foreign Minister, Ernest Bevin, on July 10, Acheson predicted an all-out Communist assault on Asia, with "Chi[na] as one spearhead" and "immediate objectives in Korea, Indo-China, Burma, the Philippines and Malaya and with medium-range objectives in Hong Kong, Indonesia, Siam, India and Japan." It was therefore impossible to hand Taiwan over to either Moscow or Peking, the latter of which "at the least is encouraging aggression against its neighbors in open cooperation with Moscow," and could militarily exploit this "strategically located island."[42]

The British government remained unconvinced. In its view, the U.S. attitude was driving Peking into the arms of Moscow and creating disunity within the United Nations. Certainly the government of India, the U.N.'s leading Asian member, found that the linking of the Taiwanese and Korean questions had made it difficult to give wholehearted support to the U.N. actions to repel North Korean aggression.[43]

The decision to neutralize the Strait was also partly responsible for complicating America's attitude to Soviet peace moves made in July. According to Bohlen, Soviet press handling of Moscow's attempts to find a peaceful solution to the conflict in Korea continued to confirm that the leadership seriously wanted to find a way to end a situation that threatened to get out of hand.[44] Nevertheless, Washington thought it likely that they would exact some "unacceptable price" for a return to the *status quo ante bellum*—such as the expulsion of Nationalist China from the U.N. and the return of Taiwan to the mainland—and so discouraged Moscow's attempts to formulate a negotiating position. Acheson argued in predictable terms that concessions would whet the Soviet appetite and encourage its leaders to be more aggressive elsewhere.[45]

Chinese Communist reaction to the Taiwan Strait decision was, not surprisingly, "immediate and authoritative"[46] in contrast to its cautious response to the outbreak of fighting between North and South Korea. On July 6, Chou En-lai sent a strongly worded message to the secretary-general of the U.N. denouncing the "armed aggression against the territory of China in total violation of the United Nations Charter."[47] To the Chinese, the decision was confirmation that the United States intended to maintain its support for Chiang Kai-shek—indeed, to reinforce the relationship, as shown by the decisions to increase aid to his regime, and to send a military mission to Taiwan at the end of July. Unbeknown to the State Department (again reflecting the poor relations between State and Defense in this policy area), MacArthur seized an opportunity to lead the military mission. Although the joint chiefs advised that he send a senior officer to survey the needs of the island, they added, "However, if you feel it necessary to proceed personally on the 31st, please feel free to go since the responsibility is yours."[48] MacArthur, needing no more than this tacit support, arrived in Taipei for two days of talks.

At the conclusion of the trip, both Chiang and MacArthur released statements that stressed a high degree of military coordination between Nationalist and U.S. forces in the event of an offensive launched from the mainland. Such comments caused great uneasiness among allied governments, who feared that MacArthur might be instrumental in widening the conflict in Asia. But for China, of course, such activity was of direct and immediate significance. In Peking's perception, Korea was being used as a pretext for strengthening U.S. forces in the immediate vicinity of the mainland, forcing postponement of the invasion of Taiwan, and giving heart to the remnants of Chiang Kai-shek's supporters and other rebel groups in the southern provinces. China's security and territorial integrity thus came to be tied closely to the fortunes of the North Koreans.

The Domestic Setting

The largely unfavorable international response to the Taiwan decision was not paralleled in the domestic arena. Support for the action, which was portrayed as necessary in order to circumscribe the conflict, was expressed in several major newspapers, with the notable exception of the *St. Louis Post-Dispatch.*[49]

For the China bloc in Congress, the Taiwan decision and Mac-Arthur's visit to Taipei represented a real breakthrough for their policy of enhancing U.S. support for Chiang's regime. It temporarily slowed their attack on the administration by removing their central target—the failure to support the arch-anti-Communist, Chiang Kai-shek. Some critics did interpret the decision more as a means of preventing Chiang from attacking the mainland—Chiang "leashed," as it were—and providing the opportunity for the Chinese Communists to transfer their troops to the Korean region. At this stage of the war, however, their criticisms were muted by the overall encouragement that the Taiwan decision had given those who wanted to tie America more closely to the Nationalist regime: the China bloc in Congress, certain officials in the Washington bureaucracy, and MacArthur in Tokyo.

The secretary of defense and his subordinates had been determined to state the case for the protection of Taiwan at the first meetings held in response to the outbreak of the war, and General Bradley, on June 25, made the first order of business the reading of MacArthur's latest memorandum, which detailed the strategic value of Taiwan. Perhaps to secure administration unity on the issue and to appease Truman's political critics,[50] it was soon thereafter that Acheson proposed stationing the Seventh Fleet in the Strait of Taiwan. He may have been attempting to draw the teeth of others who were ready to suggest a policy likely to receive presidential support, thus securing his preeminent position with the chief executive and within the bureaucracy. Alternatively, he may have been genuinely influenced by Rusk's previous efforts to alter his position on support for Chiang's regime, or simply responding to the requirements of the strategic plan for the island in time of war.

Whatever his reasons, the secretary's recommendations regarding Taiwan undermined his previous policy of disengagement from Chiang, if not from the island. Acheson had not meant the decision to reactivate those ties, as he made clear following the outbreak of the war; he said he thought it most undesirable that the United States "should get mixed up in the question of the Chinese administration of the Island," and the president agreed.[51] But over the next weeks, Acheson had to resist fierce efforts by Johnson, Mac-Arthur, and Chiang himself to ally America even more closely with the Nationalists. Chiang's offer of 33,000 troops for use in Korea was a shrewd move that appealed to Truman, whose first inclination was to accept the offer on the grounds of its contribution to the multilateral composition of the U.N. forces.[52] Though the proposal was rejected, it remained in place to plague Acheson and the State Department during subsequent stages of the conflict. Johnson also advocated during this period that the Chinese Nationalists be permitted to launch preemptive attacks on any Communist amphibious concentrations that threatened Taiwan or the Pescadores. Acheson was quick to scotch this idea, reminding Johnson that America "was not at war with Communist China"; neither did it wish to become involved with Chinese Communist forces or to extend the U.S. commitment in the Far East.[53]

But despite Acheson's and Truman's desire to avoid greater entanglement with the Chinese Nationalist regime, the administration, having conceded the strategic importance of the island, found it impossible to keep its distance from Chiang. It was difficult not to follow through on the strategic assessment of the value of Taiwan with, at a minimum, a policy of military aid and advice to the island's occupants. This was granted in August; by October, Acheson and Dulles had agreed on the need to work through the United Nations for the permanent neutralization of Taiwan.[54]

CROSSING THE 38TH PARALLEL

International Reactions

Against this background of increased U.S. commitment to Taiwan, China's hostility and its suspicion of American motives reached a new intensity in August 1950. The concrete expression of that hostility became centered on the 38th Parallel and the question of whether U.S. forces would cross that line. China made the crossing a *casus belli*, whereas the United States saw the movement north as a unique opportunity to diminish the size of the Communist bloc and as a way of probing Soviet and Chinese intentions.

Syngman Rhee was responsible for bringing the question to the forefront of international attention on July 13. The North Korean attack had, he said, "obliterated the 38th parallel and . . . no peace and order could be maintained in Korea as long as the division at the 38th parallel remained." This prompted a denial from an "American army spokesman," who declared that the United States intervened solely to push the North Koreans back across the line and would "use force if necessary" to prevent Rhee's troops from advancing beyond the parallel.[55] On that same day, however, Truman made it clear to the press that the question of crossing the parallel was an open one, which he would decide when it became necessary to do so. On July 17 the president asked the National Security Council to prepare substantive recommendations on the matter.[56]

The U.S. administration correctly anticipated that allied and neutral states in the U.N. would be uneasy about discussion of the future status of the parallel. But in many ways the position of these states was anomalous in that they were members of an organization that had been working for the unification of Korea and was now being presented with a slim opportunity to carry through such a policy. Some, like the British and Indian governments, opposed any movement into North Korea, but though they sought ways of negotiating a peaceful settlement, they found that the military momentum of operations in Korea outstripped their political activity. In addition, the British were reluctant to put their case too forcefully in Washington. As Bevin told the British chiefs of staff in October, though he agreed with their fears that a move across the parallel would lead to the widening of the war, should they voice these views and a military opportunity be lost, the British "might be blamed for subsequent military difficulties."[57]

The Indian government fared little better in its efforts to prevent the crossing. In August, India proposed that invitations be issued to both North and South Korea to negotiate an end to the conflict, with the help of neutral nations, at the U.N. This useful and potentially productive approach was damaged, however, by the observations of the American ambassador to the U.N., Warren Austin. On August 10 he suggested that the United Nations had a moral obligation to reunite Korea: "Korea's prospects would be dark if any action of the United Nations were to condemn it to exist as 'half slave and half free' or even one-third slave and two-thirds free. The United Nations has consistently worked for a unified country, an independent Korea. The United Nations will not want to turn from that objective now."[58]

Domestic Reactions

Congressional critics of Truman's policy in Asia agreed that a great opportunity to reunite Korea was at hand, and they were ready to sneer at any action that demonstrated caution with respect to such a move. Not long after the outbreak of the fighting, they had developed the new theme that "Korea was but one link in a chain of events that stretched backward at least to Yalta,"[59] an argument that marked the revival of McCarthy's conspiracy theory and prompted the Wisconsin senator, among others, to renew the attack on the State Department. "American boys" were "dying in Korea," he said, because "a group of untouchables in the State Department" had undermined congressional attempts to aid South Korea. Acheson soon came under renewed personal attack. He had given Russia "a green light to grab whatever it could in China, Korea, and Formosa,"[60] and Truman had rendered the country ill-prepared to fight a war. Now, the president was compounding his failure by not acting resolutely in the Asian conflict. General MacArthur's frequent statements alleging the appeasement of Communism in Asia increased the vulnerability of the Truman administration on this score.

As early as July 6, Senator Taft agreed that U.S./U.N. troops would have to "march right on over the 38th parallel and at least occupy the southern part of North Korea,"[61] and with the success of the Inchon landing on September 15, many congressmen stepped up their demands for more resolute action. Typical of the more unrestrained attacks upon the executive branch was Congressman Hugh D. Scott's suggestion that the Truman administration would not sanction the crossing of the parallel but would wait until Congress had adjourned before saying so. "The Hiss Survivors Association," he said, "down at the State Department who wear upon their breasts the cross of Yalta, are waiting for Congress to go home before they lift the curtain in the next act in the tragedy of Red appeasement."[62] With the impending midterm elections in mind, the GOP was attempting to deny the administration's willingness to cross the parallel and trying to identify itself with MacArthur and his program for the military conquest of North Korea.

The Democrats, too, were alive to the political benefits that might be derived from an aggressive policy in Korea, and they badly needed a ready weapon to use against the Republicans, who were going to link the theme of "Communists in government" to the outbreak of the Korean War and make it the main plank in the November election campaign.[63] Aware of these tactics, the Truman cabinet, meeting on September 29, outlined its electioneering plan: to stress the successful Democratic record in the fight against Communism in Greece, Iran, Turkey, and Western Europe. Acheson's remarks suggested that Korea shortly could be added to this list of successes. He reported that the 38th Parallel was to be ignored, and plans were being developed to set up a commission to go into the country. Korea, he said, would be "used as a stage to prove what Western Democracy can do to help the underprivileged countries of the world."[64]

Major newspapers also increased the pressure for a movement north of the parallel. According to State Department surveys, a growing number of newsmen viewed a divided Korea as untenable, and as early as July, columnists such as Walter Lippmann regarded a return to the status quo as impossible. Most editorials in October described the parallel as a "purely fictitious line"; it should be ignored, and U.N. policy should be pushed to its "logical conclusion." Joseph Alsop demanded to know why the United Nations and Washington were "shilly-shallying" about the issue.[65] Only Arthur Krock among leading newspaper correspondents warned of the disastrous political consequences that would follow if the movement north resulted in a Pyrrhic victory, but his note of caution had little impact; after the parallel had been crossed, the *Christian Science Monitor*, *New York Herald Tribune*, *Philadelphia Inquirer*, *New York Times*, *Baltimore-Sun*, *New Republic*, *San Francisco Chronicle*, and many others acclaimed the decision.[66]

The Bureaucratic Debate

In a number of respects, the general assumption of the press that the Washington bureaucracy was vacillating over the decision to cross the parallel was incorrect. The debate within each department was heavily weighted toward taking such action. Perhaps to build support for the decision to move north, those who favored doing so expressed views that were often more consistent with their personal beliefs than with their bureaucratic positions. There was not a straight State versus Defense division on the question; on occasion, members of the Defense Department would stress the international benefits of moving north, while some in State argued more narrowly for the solid military advantages.

MacArthur entered the deliberations early. He had no doubts about his mission, as he made clear to Generals J. Lawton Collins and Hoyt S. Vandenberg during their visit to his headquarters on July 13. MacArthur told them that he intended to destroy North Korean forces; afterward, the problem would be to "compose and unite Korea." He added that "it might be necessary to occupy all of Korea, although this was speculative at the time."[67] With a strong belief in total victory and a tendency to equate negotiation with appeasement, MacArthur advocated military means to reunify Korea, even at a time when U.S./U.N. military action held out just a hint of a promise of a successful conclusion to the campaign.

The U.N. commander's optimism about the military situation in mid-July may also have had a significant impact on Truman's thinking about crossing the parallel. In receipt of a message from MacArthur that stressed the increasing strength of U.S./U.N. positions in South Korea and the diminishing strength of enemy forces, the president stated in a special message to Congress on July 19: "We are determined to support the United Nations in its effort to restore peace and security to Korea, *and its effort to ensure the people of Korea an opportunity to choose their own form of government free from coercion*" (emphasis added).[68]

The joint chiefs thought it made no military sense to halt at the 38th Parallel, a line that "from the point of view of military operations . . . has no more significance than any other meridian." Failure to move forward would mean a renewal of military instability. Of greater international significance, crossing the parallel would provide "the United States and the free world with the first opportunity to displace part of the Soviet orbit," thus disturbing "the strategic complex which the USSR is organizing between its own Far Eastern territories and the contiguous areas." They also advanced an argument similar to that of the OIR memorandum of June 25 (quoted above) on the effect of a success in Korea on the

Sino-Soviet relationship: "A free and strong Korea could provide an outlet for Manchuria's resources and could also provide non-communist contact with the people there and in North China." As a result, "elements in the Chinese Communist regime, and particularly important segments of the Chinese population, might be inclined to question their exclusive dependence on the Kremlin. Skillfully manipulated, the Chinese Communists might prefer different arrangements and a new orientation." Moreover, "throughout Asia, those who foresee only inevitable Soviet conquest would take hope."[69] Once again, the benefits were seen to be as much psychological as strategic.

John K. Emmerson, of the State Department's Northeast Asian Affairs division, was as excited as members of the Defense Department with regard to the possible ramifications of success in Korea: "If the Soviet Union, having mistakenly judged the odds in Korea and having failed to involve Chinese satellite forces, should write off Korea for the time being, as it did Iran in 1946 and Berlin in 1949, we should be presented with the greatest opportunity in Asia since the war. Such a Soviet decision would presumably indicate that the Kremlin would not risk general war at this time, that it had no present intention of committing Soviet resources on any large scale in the Far East, that Peiping and Moscow policies were not identical, and that Manchuria—not Korea—would serve as a Soviet strategic base. . . . Facing this happy situation in which Moscow has suffered a defeat we should do everything in our power to widen the rift between Moscow and Peiping and to win the support of Asiatic populations whose Communist allegiance has run no deeper than a negative acceptance of what sounded the better of two alternatives."[70]

Not everyone in favor of crossing the parallel drew out the wider benefits of this policy. Dulles, for example, advanced straightforward military arguments for ignoring a boundary which, "if perpetuated as a political line," would provide "asylum to the aggressor." A failure to destroy North Korean forces would imply "either the exposure of the Republic of Korea to greater peril than preceded the June 25 attack or the maintenance by the United States of a large military establishment to contain the North Korean army at the 38th Parallel."[71] As early as July 1, John M. Allison, director of the Office of Northeast Asian Affairs, had advocated going as far north as the Manchurian and Siberian borders, if militarily feasible, and following this with U.N.-supervised elections.[72] On July 22, his views acquired greater prominence when he was placed in overall charge of studies on future Korean policy.[73] Two days after this appointment, he attempted to broaden the appeal of his position by becoming the exponent of the American moral conscience. The United States should serve notice, he declared, that aggressors will not go unpunished. He conceded that crossing the parallel might entail risks, "but I fail to see what advantage we gain by a compromise with clear moral principles and a shirking of our duty to make clear once and for all that aggression does not pay—that he who violates the decent opinions of mankind must take the consequences and that he who takes the sword will perish by the sword." Even the prospect of a new world war did not seem overly to perturb Allison: "That this may mean war on a global scale is true—the American people should be told and told why and what it will mean to them. When all legal and moral right is on our side why should we hesitate?"[74]

Some members of the Policy Planning Staff, however, wanted to hesitate. Soviet specialists Kennan and Bohlen were against movement north of the parallel because of the U.S.S.R.'s sensitivity to its borders. In a long memorandum to Acheson, Kennan stressed the unease and the humiliation Moscow would feel if U.S. forces moved north and if the American navy patrolled waters that the Russians saw "almost as theirs."[75] The PPS also argued that a movement into North Korea might bring Moscow and/or Peking into the war, and that crossing the parallel would lose America valuable support in the United Nations. But in response to pressure from Dulles and Allison, among others, and in response to the improved military situation, the PPS shifted its position to the point of advocating a postponement rather than a rejection of the move, waiting on "political and military developments in the future."[76] Ambassador Kirk in Moscow agreed: the United States should be prepared to take advantage of any temporary military vacuum in Korea but not move north until it could evaluate the Soviet willingness to risk a showdown in the favorable terrain of Korea.[77]

Kennan alone consistently urged restraint.[78] He pressed Acheson to abandon any idea of crossing the parallel, to ignore those who were "indulging themselves in emotional moralistic attitudes" and carrying the country toward "real conflict with the

[73]

Russians."[79] But whether Acheson listened very closely to his advice at this time, on the eve of Kennan's departure from the State Department, is difficult to gauge. The secretary of state saw little point, in August, in arguing the matter "until the actual military situation developed further," but he was clear that the idea of moving north should not be abandoned.[80]

The decision to cross the parallel if doing so should prove militarily feasible finally seems to have been made at the end of August, in time for the meeting between the U.S. secretary of state and the U.K. foreign minister. On September 11, Truman approved NSC 81/1, which authorized ground operations north of the parallel, provided there was no entry into South Korea of major Soviet or Chinese forces, no announcement of intended entry, and no threat to counter U.S./U.N. military operations.[81] A final decision was to be made in the light of "the action of the Soviet Union and the Chinese Communists, consultation and agreement with friendly members of the United Nations, and appraisal of the risk of general war."[82]

Following the success of the Inchon landing in mid-September (with its indication of MacArthur's apparent invincibility), evidence of support from the U.N., combined with the U.S. appraisal of likely Chinese and Soviet roles in the war, Secretary of Defense George C. Marshall informed MacArthur on September 29: "We want you to feel unhampered tactically and strategically to proceed north of 38th parallel."[83] The next day, South Korean troops crossed into North Korea, followed by U.S. forces on October 7.

THE APPRAISAL OF SOVIET AND CHINESE ROLES

The discussion concerning possible Soviet and Chinese moves in Korea and U.S. response to these projected actions was one of the most interesting of those that took place in Washington, given its impact on policy toward China during later stages of the war. Initially, it was thought that direct Soviet entry into the hostilities was unlikely, because it would entail the risk of general war. The United States considered it possible, at first, that the Korean operation was a feint to lure U.S. forces away from some more vital area where a Soviet attack was planned, but with the passing weeks there were no indications of Soviet preparations for such an attack.

Alternatively, it had earlier been suggested that the Soviet Union intended to use "satellite forces" (most likely Chinese) to tie down American troops in a theater of secondary importance, thereby sapping U.S. strength. Whatever the Soviet purpose, however, its major reaction was expected to come before the actual crossing of the parallel by U.S./U.N. forces. The Truman administration was quite certain that the "rolling back" of a presumed Soviet satellite in an area so strategically important to the U.S.S.R. would inevitably evoke a response. NSC 81/1 recorded that the reaction might be military or might involve attempts to secure a negotiated settlement before U.N. forces reached the parallel. In the unlikely event that Moscow took no action of any kind, "there would be some reason to believe that the Soviet Union had decided to follow a hands-off policy."[84] U.S. policy would depend upon that response.

Moscow's failure to make any of the expected threats concerning the action the Soviets would take if U.S. forces crossed into North Korea was to prove fatal for the Chinese and North Koreans. Such passivity gave encouragement to those within the U.S. administration who wished to see a military settlement to the Korean unification problem, and to those who wanted to impress on the Communist bloc the resilience and effectiveness of American military power.

Several events in August and September contributed to the view that the Soviet Union did not intend to play any significant role in the war. Moscow's attempt to negotiate an end to the war in August was poorly timed, since it increased the boldness of those in the United States who sought to achieve wider goals in Korea. The Soviet return to the Security Council that month, after its boycott to protest Taiwan's retention of China's U.N. seat, had also made Moscow appear weak and ridiculous to some within the Truman administration. Rusk, for example, had been prepared for Malik to make his first statement on August 1 an objection to the continued presence of the Chinese Nationalists; he then expected to hear a call for the admission of the PRC and, after the ritual negative vote, to see the Soviet delegate walk out.[85] Malik did not do this, but later in the month he expanded on the earlier Indian proposals for an end to the "civil war" in Korea and called for the withdrawal of all foreign troops after a conference involving both Korean governments.

The Defense Department also took Moscow's response to U.S. military activity in August as further evidence of the U.S.S.R.'s cautious approach to the Korean hostilities. The bombing of the oil supply depot at Rashin (or Najin) in North Korea, only 17 miles from the Soviet border, did not lead to any harsh protest, and the Russian failure to respond in the expected manner seemed to indicate that the State Department had exaggerated Soviet sensitivity to its borders. State had disapproved of the kind of attack that was made on Rashin—by three sweeps of B-29 bombers in poor visibility—because, as Kennan pointed out, Rashin was "less than 100 miles from the entrance to the road-stead of Vladivostock and . . . the Soviet authorities are pathologically sensitive even to any reconnaissance activities, let alone actual bombings, in that vicinity."[86] The Defense Department (still under Johnson) argued, however, that 17 miles was "well clear of the frontier," was within the terms of the president's directives, and anyway was not more likely to evoke a response from the Soviets than any other aspect of the Korean campaign. In a letter to Acheson, Johnson suggested that State keep out of the matter; the 17-mile restriction was, in his opinion, "intended only to guard against the possibility of frontier violation and not to provide for political determination as to which military objectives within the area of North Korea may or may not be bombed."[87]

When the president was first brought into the disagreement he seemed to side with the military, instructing General Omar Bradley that "he was to go after any targets which were being used to furnish supplies to the North Korean troops."[88] Not until September 11, when Acheson made a direct appeal to the president, did the Defense Department halt a proposed renewal of the bombing program. The secretary of state pointed out that these air attacks could well force Moscow to enter North Korea in order to provide better protection for its border. As evidence of the dangers of such activity in poor weather conditions, Acheson referred to the episode on September 4 when a Soviet plane had been shot down over the Yellow Sea.[89]

The problem, though, with both Acheson's and Kennan's analyses was that despite the Soviet Union's concern about these incidents, it did nothing to indicate a stepped-up involvement in Korea as a result. Instead, its propaganda increasingly emphasized that U.S. activity in North Korea threatened China most. In the

U.N., and at a reception for Acheson at the Waldorf-Astoria in New York, Soviet diplomats appeared relaxed and friendly as they talked about the necessity of ending the Korean War.[90]

In October, with U.S. forces poised to enter North Korea, American planes strafed a Soviet aerodrome. The U.S. embassy in Moscow was disconcerted by this mistake and pointed out that the incident occurred within perhaps the "most important and sensitive Soviet military area in [the] Far East and one of similar concern [to] China lying only 10 miles to [the] west."[91] The Soviet protest, however, again seemed mild, perhaps because Moscow did not want to heighten tension at a time when U.S. forces were ready to cross the parallel. Whatever the reason, the Moscow embassy telegrams of the time show that the U.S.S.R. continued its conciliatory moves throughout September and October.[92] In early October at the U.N., Vassili Kasaniev of the Secretariat sought to use Hans Engen of the Norwegian delegation as an intermediary between the Soviet and American governments. During a lunch on October 4, Kasaniev told Engen that "MacArthur should agree to stop at the 38th Parallel. The North Koreans would then lay down their arms, and, third, a United Nations Commission would be allowed to go into North Korea to hold elections, et cetera."[93] Further conversations ensued, but the process was too slow and, by October 7, too late: U.S. troops had crossed into North Korea, and the Soviets discontinued their peace efforts.

The smugness with which the U.S. counselor to Moscow, Walworth Barbour, described these Soviet efforts probably reflects rather accurately the attitudes of others within the U.S. administration who were buoyed up by the stunningly successful Inchon landing: "The amiable side of Soviet countenance beginning to emerge into sharper focus with increasing rapidity wears not cheerful grin of a good comrade but rather forced smile of an exposed scoundrel. Failure of Soviets to intervene openly in Korea, mild tone of their recent notes on POWs and strafing of Soviet airfield, recent overtures apparently seeking a CFM [Council of Foreign Ministers' meeting] on Germany, their attempts, halfhearted as they may appear, to seem co-operative in UN are not indications of basic Soviet change of heart but may be early ephemeral fruits of policy of containment and building of areas of strength."[94] As Emmerson had already noted, if (as appeared increasingly likely) the Soviet Union had misjudged the odds in

Korea and was now writing the "adventure" off for the time being, the United States might be facing the greatest opportunity in Asia since the Second World War.[95] The U.S. government found much to be optimistic about in late September and early October.

Naturally, the administration had made contingency plans in the event that major Soviet units should enter Korea while U.N. forces were operating in the North or "satellite" forces undertake simultaneous or successive acts of armed aggression. Under such conditions, the United States was to assume that global war was probably imminent and, while still making every effort to localize hostilities, prepare to execute emergency war plans. But the analyses overwhelmingly predicted action of some kind before the parallel was crossed, and when no such action occurred, it appeared increasingly likely that the Soviet Union had adopted a hands-off policy toward Korea, as NSC 81/1 had suggested it might.

The Soviet failure to act prior to October 7 explains the change in emphasis in the CIA report of October 12. Whereas previously the agency had been fearful that U.S. entry into North Korea would run a grave risk of precipitating general war,[96] by mid-October it had drawn back and concluded: "Since the beginning of hostilities the Soviet Union has sought in its official statements and in its propaganda to give the impression that it is not involved in the Korean situation." Overall, the agency suggested, Moscow would not consider that its prospective losses in Korea warranted direct military intervention and the risk of war unless it had decided that global war would be in Soviet interests. The CIA covered its options by stating that the U.S.S.R. was in a position to conduct "general war of limited duration now," if its leaders desired to do so, but conceded that there was insufficient intelligence for reliable prediction.[97]

Besides these few cautionary remarks, there was not much being said to dent Truman's optimism. At the Wake Island conference with MacArthur on October 15, no one present—neither Bradley, Rusk, Philip Jessup, nor the president—contradicted the U.N. commander's conclusion that the chances of Soviet (or Chinese) interference were "very little. Had they interfered in the first or second months it would have been decisive. We are no longer fearful of their intervention."[98]

Unlike the Soviet Union, however, China had issued explicit threats about the actions it would take if U.S. forces crossed the

38th Parallel. August marked the start of its more aggressive stance, but the most forceful warnings were made in late September and early October as U.S. forces were poised to enter North Korea. Unfortunately, many of the Chinese messages were passed through the Indian ambassador to Peking, K. M. Panikkar, who was regarded in Washington as emotional, unstable, and strongly biased in favor of Mao's regime. On September 25, Nieh Jung-chen, acting chief of staff of the PLA, told Panikkar that the Chinese would not "sit back with folded hands and let the Americans come up to the border."[99] Even more dramatic was Chou En-lai's late-night meeting with Panikkar on October 3 in which the Chinese premier made it unmistakably clear that if U.S. troops crossed into North Korea, Chinese contingents would enter the war. "The South Koreans did not matter," Chou explained, "but American intervention into North Korea would encounter Chinese resistance."[100]

Although some people in the State Department were inclined to take Chou's warning seriously, the majority appeared to go along with Acheson in regarding it as "a bluff, pending more information." The secretary of state described the Chinese as taking part in a "poker game," and although he agreed that there was a risk involved in pushing north, "nevertheless there had been risk from the beginning and at present," he believed, "a greater risk would be incurred by showing hesitation and timidity." He also implied that since U.S./U.N. forces were already advancing, "it was too late now to stop this process."[101]

In early July, when there was concern that Chinese forces might be used in Korea to tie U.S. troops down in an area of secondary importance, Secretary of the Army Frank Pace, ever concerned to weigh U.S. troop levels against those of the enemy, had pointed to the presence of some 200,000 Chinese Communist troops on Korea's northern border, about ten days' march from the fighting.[102] With U.S./U.N. forces already outnumbered more than two to one, those troops could easily force an evacuation from Korea. John Paton Davies, during the same period, had suggested several other reasons why the Chinese might take action in the Far East, including "irredentism, expansionism, Soviet pressure and inducements, strategic anxieties, ideological zeal, the enormous demands of internal problems, emotional anti-Americanism—and miscalculations of [U.S.] intentions."[103]

But by October such thoughts had been put aside; the threat of Chinese intervention was seen to have receded because the most favorable time for Chinese troops to have entered, as Kirk said, "was logically when UN forces were desperately defending the small area of Taegu-Pusan, when the influx of overwhelming numbers of Chinese ground forces would have proved the decisive factor." The background material prepared by Dean Rusk for use at the Wake Island conference confirmed this view: hence the general reluctance to contradict MacArthur's statement that there was little chance of a Chinese entry in Korea.[104]

O. Edmund Clubb, director of the Office of Chinese Affairs, was the only high-ranking officer who consistently, from early October until the time of Chinese entry, cautioned that it was not safe to regard Chou's statement to Panikkar as a bluff. Clubb interpreted the message to mean that Peking and Moscow were "prepared to risk the danger of World War III, and [felt] ready to meet that danger."[105] But Clubb's analyses throughout the war had generally been more alarmist than the majority view. In July, for example, he had argued, against the opinion of all other major figures in Truman's administration, that the Soviet Union might want to precipitate global war before the year was out.[106] Clubb was in a decided minority again in October, supported only by Livingston Merchant (Rusk's deputy) and U. Alexis Johnson of Northeast Asian Affairs, who suggested that China's threats should be treated with "extreme seriousness" rather than too readily discounted.[107]

The comments of James R. Wilkinson, the American consul-general in Hong Kong, were also cautionary but too inconclusive to force a reassessment of China's interests in Korea. Chinese troop movements to Manchuria might be, he said, "a cold war maneuver, a massing for defensive purposes or preparations for active support of the North Korean army." There was little doubt in his mind that the presence of U.S./U.N. forces on the Manchurian border would be seen as a "serious danger" in Peking; on the other hand, Wilkinson acknowledged, China had enormous internal problems that had to be given priority.[108]

These few voices of warning were therefore largely ignored, as were the manifold expressions of China's intent. The CIA summarized the majority view on October 12: "Despite statements by Chou En-lai, troop movements to Manchuria, and propaganda charges of atrocities and border violations, there are no convincing indications of an actual Chinese Communist intention to resort to full-scale intervention in Korea."[109] The failure of China's deterrent efforts are shown only too well by that statement.

China's intentions were misperceived for a variety of reasons. A report produced by the Joint Intelligence Committee (JIC) on July 6 explained that because of restiveness in North China and other unspecified areas, and the PLA's role in maintaining internal security, a large-scale redeployment of troops to North Korea could not be undertaken.[110] The CIA memorandum quoted above laid even greater emphasis on China's domestic preoccupations. War with the United States would mean, it concluded, that the PRC's entire domestic program and economy would be jeopardized by the strains involved and the material damage that would be sustained; this in turn would encourage anti-Communist forces to such an extent that "the regime's very existence would be endangered."[111]

The JIC also considered that the past combat experience of the PLA soldiers was inappropriate to the operations in Korea. Their previous fighting had involved "hit and run" guerilla tactics; they had never met "a well-trained force with high morale equipped with modern weapons and possessing the will and the skill to use those weapons." In addition, China had "practically no capability" of reinforcing or supporting the North Korean navy and not much in the way of an air force either.[112]

Acheson pointed to the lack of Chinese interest in Korea. In the secretary's view, "it would be sheer madness" for the Chinese to enter the Korean War when their great problem was with Soviet domination along their northern borders.[113] The CIA supported this argument in October when it suggested that Peking's acceptance of the major Soviet aid necessary to prosecute a war against the United States would increase Soviet control in Manchuria to a most unwelcome extent. What was more, the agency argued, if Chinese intervention should prove unsuccessful, resentment in China would cause the leadership to be accused of "acting as a Soviet's catspaw."[114]

It was also believed that since China wanted to take its seat in the U.N. (as shown by Chou's telegram to that organization and *People's Daily* editorials demanding the admission of the Communist representative and the unseating of the Nationalist delegation),[115] the PRC was unlikely to prejudice this presumably primary goal by intervening in Korea or invading Taiwan. In addition, the U.S, administration assumed North Korea to be a Soviet satellite rather than a particularly close ally of China; therefore, why should China fight on its behalf, or Moscow permit Chinese encroachment on a Russian sphere of influence? Furthermore, in order to protect China from extremely costly human and material losses, Moscow would have to provide Peking with powerful air cover and naval support.[116] Such protection would constitute Soviet intervention, as far as the United States was concerned at the time, and thus invite global war. In this way, the question of possible Chinese intervention in Korea became closely tied to an assessment of Moscow's willingness to risk general war. By October, few in Washington or Tokyo seemed to believe that the Soviet Union was willing to take those risks.

Policy toward China during this period was based on the twin assumptions that legitimate Chinese interests were in no way threatened by U.S. action in Korea, and that the Chinese had given primacy to their domestic policies. The inability to perceive the situation from the Chinese perspective was compounded by the startling military momentum generated after the Inchon landing, by Moscow's failure to make any of the expected military moves before U.S./U.N. forces crossed the 38th Parallel, by congressional and press pressure to accomplish the unification of Korea, by the perceived unreliability of the source transmitting the messages from Peking, and by the inability of such nay-sayers as Clubb, Merchant, and Johnson to make any real impact on the decision-making process.

One other factor may also have encouraged a disregard of China's October signals: that is, the optimistic assessments of America's ability to deal militarily with any Chinese intervention. It is surprising to find, given the outcome of a limited war in Korea and the prevailing view that the United States constantly desired to limit the hostilities to Korea, that retaliation against China was regularly included in the contingency plans drawn up in the first months of the war to deal with a possible Chinese entry. From the outbreak of hostilities, the general assumption seems to have been that if Chinese troops entered Korea, the United States would have legitimate reasons for attacking China itself. George Kennan was probably the first to suggest this; on June 30 he said that if regular

PLA units became involved in Korea, "we would have adequate grounds for air and sea attacks on targets in Communist China directly related to the enemy effort in Korea." He added, though, that whether or not America "would wish to make use of this pretext would be a matter for consideration in the light of circumstances prevailing at the time."[117]

Kennan's phrasing was subsequently incorporated verbatim into NSC 73 of July 1, which added that while it was a matter for operational decision, "it is our assumption that we would not hesitate to oppose any Chinese Communist forces which might engage themselves against us in the Korean theater, or any movement of such forces to the Korean theater."[118] On July 12, John Paton Davies suggested that the message be passed to China via India that if the Chinese joined the North Koreans in force, "they will have imposed upon us the necessity of retaliating." This did not mean that the United States was going to become embroiled in an attempt to occupy China, but it could take "naval and air action against military objectives contributing to the Chinese aggression in Korea." He went on to suggest that if China were to engage in widespread aggression "from Korea to Indochina (and even Burma)," the United States could take bombing action that would result "ultimately . . . in the destruction of the rail, water and road carriers of the Chinese transportation system and the thin industrial base of Chinese economy."[119]

Even if Davies's remarks were intended only as a threat to be conveyed to the leaders in Peking (in fact, the threat was never passed on, as far as is known), it was an alarmingly aggressive scenario for so early a stage of the war. Perhaps for this reason, Acheson raised an objection the same day in a memorandum to Davies's superior, Paul Nitze: "As to widening the theater of operations by attacks on Chinese territory generally, as against attacks on forces coming in—I should think this unwise as constituting an invitation to the Russians to join the Chinese under their treaty."[120] As the memorandum shows, however, even Acheson contemplated attacks on Chinese territory to the extent required to prevent their forces from entering Korea.

Acheson's cautionary remarks did not immediately enter into the NSC's deliberations. NSC 73/1 (July 29) and NSC 73/4 (August 25) repeated that in the event of the overt use of organized Chinese forces in Korea, the United States would not become engaged in a general war with China, but "as long as action by UN military forces now committed or planned for commitment in Korea offers a reasonable chance of successful resistance, such action should be continued and extended to include authority to take appropriate air and naval action outside Korea against Communist China."[121]

It was not until late August, when the debate concerning the crossing of the parallel began to crystallize, that thinking was refined on the response to a possible Chinese entry. On August 31 a draft State Department memorandum distinguished between Chinese operations south and north of the parallel. In the event of Chinese (or Soviet) occupation of North Korea, it recommended that U.N. forces reoccupy Korea up to the 38th Parallel. If, however, major Chinese units were openly employed south of the parallel, U.N. action was to be continued as long as successful resistance proved possible, and retaliatory action against China was to be authorized, to include air and naval action outside Korea. In addition, it was suggested that if Chinese units moved into South Korea, the matter should be put before the U.N. Security Council with the object of condemning the Chinese as aggressors.[122]

These recommendations were incorporated into NSC 81/1, signed by President Truman on September 11. The document's conclusions were subsequently transmitted as a directive to General MacArthur on September 27, but the details of retaliatory action were not specified.[123] Indeed, in an amplification of the directive to cover the contingency of Chinese entry anywhere in Korea, and without prior announcement, MacArthur was warned that he must "obtain authorization from Washington prior to taking any military action against objectives in Chinese territory."[124] Washington had decided not to give MacArthur the freedom to pursue the action against China outlined in NSC 81/1, perhaps because of frequent examples of the general's penchant for broadly interpreting his directives, particularly where China was concerned. Perhaps Acheson had taken notice of George Kennan's blunt remarks in August that the latitude enjoyed by MacArthur had led to a "state of affairs in which we do not really have full control over the statements that are being made—and the actions taken—in our name."[125] There may, too, have been an unacknowledged and underlying sense of unease building in early October as a result of China's threats and MacArthur's zeal. The British may have contributed to this unease by conveying to Acheson their very real concern about the Chinese statements of early October, and their awareness of MacArthur's desire to hit back at the Chinese if the PLA should enter the fighting. On October 3, for example, the U.K.'s political representative in Japan, Alvary Gascoigne, reported a conversation in which the general had said that if Chinese units entered Korea, he would "immediately unleash his air force against towns in Manchuria and North China including Peking." Chou En-lai, MacArthur believed, must realize that he would do this and that the U.N. Command had at its disposal a "vastly greater potential in the air, on the ground and on the sea." Therefore, the general deduced, Chou's statement to Panikkar was "just blackmail."[126]

Washington must have been as aware as the British were of MacArthur's cavalier attitude toward bombing China, since he made no secret of his desire to take such action. At a meeting with General Matthew B. Ridgway in August 1950, he had again discounted the view that the Chinese might engage their forces in the war, but he had added, "I pray nightly that they will—would get down on my knees" in order to have an opportunity to fight the Chinese Communists.[127] But in case Washington was not fully aware of MacArthur's outlook and of the strength of British feeling on the subject, Bevin sent a message to President Truman (on the eve of the Wake Island conference) strong enough to embarrass the British ambassador in Washington. Emphasizing the British view of the serious consequences that would flow from an attack on China, Bevin bluntly suggested that the president should make certain that the U.N. commander had "categorical instructions . . . not to take action outside Korea without the express orders of the President." And preferably, the president's sanction would not be given to the general without prior consultation between the U.S. and U.K. governments.[128]

Bevin's first suggestion had already been taken care of, but the policy conclusions of NSC 81/1 and their "promise" of retaliatory air and naval action against China still stood in October. From this document and from earlier discussions that contemplated bombing attacks on the Chinese mainland should its forces enter the conflict, MacArthur almost certainly assumed he would have the authority to undertake such action, and would relish it.

Mao issued the order to the Chinese People's "Volunteers" to "resist the attacks of US imperialism" on October 8, one day after U.S. troops had crossed the parallel. But U.S./U.N. forces met little resistance in North Korea for the next two weeks, and so optimistic was Washington that there was talk of withdrawing the Eighth Army by Christmas and of sending one division to Europe by January.[129] The war seemed to be almost over; the prospects for Korean unification appeared good and the U.N. northward movement irresistible.

In mid-October, the dominant view was that the Soviet Union did not want to risk general war by becoming embroiled in Korea: The probe to test the resolve of the United States was turning out badly, and there were signs that Moscow was trying to extricate itself from the war altogether. In recent months, the Soviet Union had tolerated the bombing of Rashin close to its borders, only mildly protested the strafing of one of its aerodromes and the shooting-down of one of its planes, initiated peace moves at key points of the war, placed primary emphasis on the Peace Movement as a method of mitigating tensions, and abstained from raising the pressure in any of the other so-called trouble spots around the world. Finally, Russia—like China—had convinced U.S. officials of its intended noninvolvement in Korea by missing what was regarded as its most opportune moment to intervene—before U.N. troops had crossed the 38th Parallel. Unfortunately, the Truman administration did not regard Soviet caution as an opportunity to initiate negotiations to end the war; rather, Truman's and Acheson's distrust of Russian motives led them to push home their advantage by attempting to "roll back" Communism.

As for China, Washington concluded that it was unlikely to enter the war because of the PRC's inappropriate and low military capability, its domestic problems, its desire to take its seat in the U.N., and its reluctance to become further dependent on Moscow, militarily and diplomatically. Only Clubb, Merchant, and Johnson had suggested that Chou's warnings of China's impending entry into Korea might be more than a bluff. But they seemed unable to make any impression on their immediate superiors, Rusk and Allison, who argued strongly from early July onward for the military unification of Korea.

And if the Chinese should enter the war and move south of the parallel, it seemed surprisingly noncontroversial—between July and October—to consider retaliation against the Chinese mainland. Significantly, no one was arguing at this stage that such action would run a grave risk of precipitating world war. Acheson had issued a note of warning that bombing on a general level in China might lead to the invoking of the Sino-Soviet Treaty, but this thought does not seem to have been taken up elsewhere within the administration (except by Clubb) at this stage.

Acheson was in a somewhat anomalous position. He had argued forcefully against bombing Rashin, so close to a sensitive border area, but no Soviet protest was forthcoming as a result of this action; and he also undermined the argument designed to prevent activity near the Soviet border by not contesting the dominant view that Moscow did not intend to become overtly involved in Korea. With regard to China, he continued to assert, as he had before the Korean War, that its major foreign policy preoccupation was to fend off Soviet encroachments on its territory, and that its interests diverged from Moscow's in Korea. Yet this analysis weakened his warning that the Sino-Soviet alliance might be invoked if Chinese territory were bombed.

Finally, the secretary of state supported the view that the Chinese, if left to themselves, would not enter Korea; if they did, it would have to be conceded that they were, after all, subject to Moscow's will. Acheson's change of policy toward Taiwan had already led him to make a concession to the argument that Peking and Moscow would act in concert in time of war, partially revealing the strategic weakness in his earlier position on Taiwan.

It would be an exaggeration to conclude that these slight inconsistencies particularly affected the secretary's relations with other policy makers in Washington in the early autumn of 1950. In the next few months, however, the anomalies would be further exposed, possibly contributing to a diminution of Acheson's influence on Korean War policy.

[4]

China's Intervention and the U.S. Response: October 1950–February 1951

The Wake Island conference of mid-October 1950 vividly illustrated that the Truman administration considered U.S./U.N. forces to be on the verge of victory in Korea. Major themes discussed at the conference were the political arrangements for the unification of postwar Korea and the speed with which U.S. troops could be redeployed to more strategically vital areas. As late as October 31, the joint chiefs still thought the campaign was going well enough that they could refuse further Latin American military contingents.[1] One month later, however, the spectacular military gamble undertaken in Korea was shown to have been tragically ill-considered. George Kennan described the United States then as the victim of "an absolutely unbelievable and stupendous military blunder."[2] Indeed, it would involve the United States and the United Nations in a costly and destructive conflict for another two and a half years.

A rigid adherence to previous decisions and an inability to receive and interpret new and countervailing evidence contributed to the debacle, and policy makers in Washington were as guilty of such rigidity as was the UN commander in Korea. On October 25, Chinese "volunteers," as they were described in Peking, fought with ROK forces at Onjong, less than 40 miles south of the Yalu. In the next few days, Chinese forces engaged South Korean and American troops at several points, and on November 1 the first MIGs appeared along the Yalu. To General Omar Bradley, the Chinese actions were puzzling: they were "half-way between" the either large-scale or marginal involvement in Korea that had been anticipated.[3] Believing that the most appropriate time for a decisive Chinese entry had passed, the U.S. administration dismissed the first signs of Chinese troop activity as a limited move designed to save face after Chou En-lai's threats or to protect the hydroelectric installations along the Yalu. MacArthur's directives, in the event of open or covert employment of major Chinese units without prior announcement, were to continue the action as long as he believed his forces had a reasonable chance of success. In the early stages, there was nothing to indicate that his mission might not be successfully completed.

Intelligence and reconnaissance estimates also tended to support the view that this was a limited incursion by the Chinese. Although MacArthur's headquarters believed that 34,000 Chinese troops had entered Korea by November 3 and that there were 415,000 troops in Manchuria ready to cross if called upon,[4] Lt. General George E. Stratemeyer, commander of the Far East Air Force referred on November 4 to 15,000–30,000 troops then in Korea, and implied that only Russia was in a position to import additional forces of any magnitude. Moscow could move an estimated 300,000–450,000 troops into North Korea in less than three days if it chose to, he said, accompanied by 600 to 1,000 airplanes. In his view, however, such a move would mean the major powers were on the verge of World War III, "so the likelihood of such action at this time appears not to be on the cards."[5] It was a familiar restatement of previous assessments regarding the probable Soviet role in the war, which took very little account of Chinese interests in a conflict on its Manchurian border.

Not until November 6 were the first alarms sounded about extensive Chinese involvement in Korea, and an intense debate begun about the possibility of a change in MacArthur's orders. The general's telegram of that date, in which he reported men and materiel pouring across the Yalu and threatening "the ultimate destruction" of U.N. positions, succeeded in shocking his superiors,[6] and the sense of urgency that it conveyed forced immediate consideration in Washington of two issues: how to slow down or prevent the augmentation of Chinese strength in Korea, and how best to deal with the MIG fighter planes that had begun to operate along the Yalu in support of the Chinese "volunteers." MacArthur's reaction to both these situations had been predictable: on November 5, he had instructed Stratemeyer to fly his combat crews "to exhaustion" in order to destroy the bridges the troops were using to cross the river border; additionally, he wanted to pursue the MIGs into Manchuria.

In Washington and key allied capitals, the response to China's entry into North Korea was more circumspect. MacArthur was eventually granted permission to bomb the Korean end of the Yalu bridges, but not before he had been asked to detail the imperative nature of his request, or before he had used the ploy of a direct appeal to his commander in chief to lift restrictions that might well, he said, "result in a calamity of major proportions for which I cannot accept the responsibility without [the president's] personal and direct understanding of the situation."[7]

Washington was concerned that should inadvertent bombing of Manchuria occur, it might intensify the Chinese efforts in Korea or lead to the outcome that administration officials had all but dismissed as a possibility: Soviet entry into the conflict. The deputy-secretary of defense, Robert Lovett, who had first held up MacArthur's order to bomb the Yalu bridges, voiced these fears to Acheson and Rusk. Rusk also pointed to the diplomatic repercussions that would follow, noting that the United States had made a commitment not to take action involving possible attacks on Manchuria without consulting the British. In addition, and probably of more crucial importance to Rusk, the British cabinet was meeting that very morning "to reconsider their whole attitude towards the Chinese Communist Government and . . . ill-considered action on our part might have grave consequences."[8]

The outcome of these deliberations was that the U.N. commander's request to disable the bridges was granted in such a way that it satisfied no one. He was permitted to bomb only the Korean end of the structures, forbidden to bomb any dams or power plants along the Yalu, and enjoined to exercise extreme care to avoid any transgression of Chinese territory. That the avoidance of Chinese territory could not be guaranteed concerned the State Department and America's allies; for the Air Force, restricting bombs to one end of the bridges was a stipulation virtually impossible to carry out.[9] The bombing, in fact, turned out to be very inaccurate; for example, one napalm raid resulted in the destruction of 60 percent of the city of Sinuiju but missed the adjacent bridge.[10]

"Hot pursuit" of Chinese aircraft was not permitted under any conditions, despite the basic concurrence of Truman, Acheson, Marshall, and the joint chiefs that this request should be granted.

In this case, the allies seem to have been decisive in preventing the territorial extension of the hostilities. On November 13 the State Department had sought governmental reactions in London, Canberra, Ottawa, and Paris; and had informed its ambassadorial staffs in Ankara, New Delhi, Wellington, The Hague, Moscow, and the United Nations that "it may be necessary at an early date to permit U.N. aircraft to defend themselves in the air space over the Yalu River to the extent of permitting hot pursuit of attacking enemy aircraft up to two to three minutes flying time into Manchurian air space." Governmental agreement was not required, only their reactions were sought. When they came, they were wholly and unanimously adverse. Some governments stressed that it might lead to the very thing they were supposed to be attempting to avoid: the extension of hostilities. Others pointed out that such action would be regarded as a unilateral U.S. move and, as the Dutch remarked, "would afford the basis for a Soviet charge that the UN was only a front for the U.S."[11] This forceful and unanimous rejection had its effect, and "hot pursuit" was denied.

There is little doubt that the Defense Department and MacArthur resented the maintenance of the Chinese "sanctuary" in Manchuria. Earlier in November, the secretary of the Air Force, Thomas K. Finletter, and the chief of the Air Force, Hoyt S. Vandenberg, had told Rusk they felt "very strongly that the whole world should understand the great problem created by forces which are in position to attack UN forces from within a safe haven." MacArthur informed his superiors that the sanctuary was making life intolerable for the men under his command and having a major impact on "the morale and combat efficiency of both air and ground troops."[12] Nevertheless, "hot pursuit" was prohibited in deference to the wishes of allied governments, who, at a time of great international uncertainty, were able to exert maximum influence on U.S. war policy.

BRITISH AND FRENCH CONTRIBUTIONS
TO THE POLICY DEBATES

Fears of an extended war that would divert the United States from the task of rebuilding Europe dictated European reaction to the events of the first two weeks of November. The fillip that the onset of Korean hostilities had provided to European defense preparations had begun to flag by October, discussions having stalled over the question of West German rearmament and its future role in European defense. A possible large-scale war between the U.S. and Chinese forces was thought likely to delay the resolution of these differences, since it would draw American resources and interests away from Europe and toward the Far East. In addition, both Britain and France had since 1948 been operating under the assumption that a harsh policy toward the People's Republic would serve only to cement a Chinese alliance with the U.S.S.R.

These assessments had contradictory effects on the policy of America's major allies: Britain and France did not want to jeopardize their relationship with the United States by refusing to follow its foreign policy lead, yet they were to go further than America was prepared to do in providing reassurances to the Chinese in order to avoid a costly war of attrition between the United States and China and to prevent Peking from being pushed into Moscow's embrace.

The British, in particular, were active in advancing plans intended to bring U.N. forces to a halt well south of the Yalu River, and they put forward for U.S. consideration the idea of a demilitarized buffer zone in Korea, to be administered jointly by the U.N. and the PRC. Both right and left, government and the opposition in Britain were in favor of preventing any further advance into North Korea. The Americans, however, were not in favor of establishing any buffer zone that did not call for a comparable demilitarized area on the Chinese side of the border. In predictable language, Acheson described as unwelcome Foreign Minister Ernest Bevin's proposal for a U.N. resolution advocating a buffer zone, since "giving up the part of Korea we do not yet occupy would at this time undoubtedly be interpreted as a sign of weakness."[13] By November 24 the British, reluctant to risk open disagreement with the Americans on any aspect of Korean War policy, concluded that it was not "expedient to address further representations to the US Government or Chiefs of Staff."[14]

The U.S. debate over the British proposals for a demilitarized zone illustrated the split within the administration on how best to respond to the situation created by China's entry into Korea. The State Department were willing to consider the establishment of a buffer area on both sides of the Yalu, but within the Pentagon and at MacArthur's headquarters, any talk of buffer zones was distasteful. It reminded MacArthur of the approach to policy in the 1930s; for him, "the widely reported British desire to appease the Chinese Communists by giving them a strip of Northern Korea finds its historic precedent in the action taken at Munich on 29 Sept 1938." He went on: "To give up any portion of North Korea to the aggression of the Chinese Communists would be the greatest defeat of the free world in recent times. Indeed, to yield to so immoral a proposition would bankrupt our leadership and influence in Asia and render untenable our position both politically and militarily." MacArthur warned his government against following "in the footsteps of the British," who were already morally bankrupt in his view, and "who by the appeasement of recognition [of the People's Republic of China] lost the respect of all the rest of Asia without gaining that of the Chinese segment."[15]

Major General Charles L. Bolté, the Department of the Army's assistant chief of operations, fresh from a visit to MacArthur, supported the general's views on military requirements and marshaled familiar arguments against stopping the U.S./U.N. military action short of the border. "Certain elements of the Department of State," Bolté wrote, "are of the opinion that action should be taken to halt the military conflict in Korea on the grounds that further offensive action by UN forces will prevent the continued localization of the conflict." But in Bolté's view, there would be grounds for halting the moves to unify Korea only if further offensive action ran "too great a risk of general war." The Chinese on their own could not succeed in driving U.N. forces from Korea "unless materially assisted by Soviet ground and air power," in which case the U.S. plan was to withdraw from Korea and prepare for global war. In the absence of Soviet assistance of this kind, he could see no reason for holding back the planned UN mission to unify Korea.[16]

The demilitarized zone concept was not spiritedly defended by Acheson at the State-Defense meeting on November 21, probably because of the known opposition of Secretary Marshall and others within the military, and because a lull in the fighting had permitted MacArthur's forces to push their approach to the designated zone. And no one seemed to understand in the latter part of November what the Chinese were up to. Bradley confirmed that despite aerial reconnaissance, MacArthur still did not know the reason for the absence of contact with the enemy during this period.[17] As Acheson explained to the British on November 21 and again on November 24, the results of MacArthur's planned offensive would "make much more clear many matters which are now obscure."[18] Or, as a State Department spokesman much more bluntly stated to U.S. diplomatic correspondents, it was very hard to figure out the Chinese intentions because they had intervened so late; therefore, "we are going to go ahead and force the issue now."[19]

The Chinese added to Washington's confusion on November 21 by releasing 27 wounded U.S. prisoners of war, captured 18 days earlier; with a friendly pat and wave, their Chinese captors directed them to return to their units.[20] Rather than seeing this action and the lull in the fighting as an opportunity to negotiate a settlement, U.S. officials were nonplussed; they still found little to indicate that MacArthur's mission might not be terminated successfully.

If the State and Defense departments were able to reconcile their differences over the issue of a demilitarized zone, in the Defense Department's favor, they achieved only an unsatisfactory compromise with respect to the French government's attempt to provide reassurances to the Chinese via a U.N. resolution. The French hoped to diminish the tensions in Korea and prevent large-scale Chinese intervention by reassuring Peking that U.N. forces would not attack its territory. They proposed a General Assembly statement making clear the U.N. Command's intention to refrain from bombing the Yalu River power installations, and a U.N. resolution specifying that the Chinese border was to remain "inviolate." On November 8, Marshall and Truman had approved a resolution stating that the U.N. would not violate the Manchurian border "unless the Chinese Communists continued their action in Korea."[21] But the French felt that the final condition was an implied threat, which it was, and the State Department proposed to modify it. The Army's Plans and Operations Division, however, found such a guarantee to the Chinese unacceptable, since it "would permit continued harassment by Chinese planes executing tactical strikes from nearby Manchurian bases." In a memorandum to the Army Chief of Staff, the division went on to express a desire to leave open the possibility of operations across the Chinese border. There was "no guarantee," the memorandum stated, "that US air and ground forces may not, in the near future, be required to operate across the Chinese frontier even before the General Assembly has had the opportunity to adopt such a resolution."[22] General Marshall appeared to agree; on November 10 the secretary of defense said to Acheson that while it was the view of both State and Defense that some form of reassurance to the Chinese was called for, "I believe it should be made clear that a sanctuary for attacking Chinese aircraft is not explicitly or implicitly affirmed by any United Nations action."[23]

The compromise wording the State Department worked out retained the word "inviolate" with regard to the border but weakened the implied resolve by calling "attention to the grave danger which continued intervention by Chinese forces in Korea would entail for the maintenance of such a policy."[24] The resolution as finally drafted presumably went some of the way to satisfy the Defense Department's request to leave military options against China open, but it undercut the French government's attempt to diminish China's fears for its security.

The Defense Department's rejection of the buffer zone and dislike of the French-sponsored U.N. resolution should not be seen as evidence that the military would not have preferred a political solution to the conflict in Korea at that time, or were not concerned about a possible war with China; they were. On November 9 the joint chiefs clearly stated their fear that a war of attrition with the Chinese would inevitably wear down U.S. strength to the benefit of Russian interests. But they did not believe the Chinese capable of driving U.S./U.N. forces out of Korea without material Soviet assistance in the form of naval and air power. Such Soviet support would imply the imminence of a third world war and in that event the United States would withdraw from the peninsula[25]—the same reasoning Bolté used to quash the notion of establishing a demilitarized zone in Korea. Although the joint chiefs conceded in early November that the risk of global war had increased, there were no firm indications that the U.S.S.R. intended to engage in general hostilities; thus there was no reason to change the orders to the U.N. Command.[26]

THE INTERNAL DEBATE ON THE "END-THE-WAR OFFENSIVE"

Calling a halt to MacArthur's offensive in Korea was difficult to suggest when there appeared no really convincing reasons for doing so. Besides, MacArthur had regained his optimism in mid-November and was confident of the success of his impending "end-the-war offensive." His stature with the joint chiefs was still at an all-time high, as it was with Truman's domestic political critics. The Truman administration, for domestic reasons, needed a success against Communism of the kind MacArthur's offensive promised. In the period before the congressional elections of November 7, the GOP had discovered that criticism of Truman's Korean War policy was a vote winner. Harold Stassen's November 5 address in support of Republican candidates described the Korean War as "the direct and terrible result of five years of building up Chinese Communist strength through the blinded, blundering American-Asiatic policy under the present national Administration. . . . five years of coddling Chinese Communists, five years of undermining General MacArthur, five years of snubbing friendly freedom-loving Asiatics, and five years of appeasing the arch-Communist, Mao Tse-tung."

The war created a climate in which McCarthyism could dominate the election campaign. Even the most distinguished Republicans embraced McCarthy's tactics, including Senator Robert Taft, who accused the administration of "strong Communist sympathies," and Senator Alexander Wiley, who like Stassen thought there had been a deal of "Communist coddling."[27] The conflict also kept Truman from the hustings, a considerable loss for the Democratic Party. The results of the elections, which gave the Republicans 28 additional seats in the House, and five in the Senate, were a clear signal to Truman that the Republicans were continuing to make gains from their harsh criticism of his Asian policy, and the Republicans evidently intended to pounce upon any new evidence of "appeasement" toward the Chinese Communists.

A matter of timing also worked against U.S. attempts to gain a better understanding of China's intentions in Korea. On November 10, Chou En-lai cabled that the Chinese delegation would arrive at U.N. headquarters about November 18 to discuss the Taiwan issue. It was also made known that the group would have authority to discuss the conflict in Korea. Unfortunately, the party did not reach Lake Success until November 24, the day MacArthur launched his "final" offensive. An earlier Chinese arrival might just have provided the opportunity for both sides to probe intentions through diplomatic contacts, a ploy that Acheson had tried unsuccessfully through Swedish officials in mid-November.

It was also the case, perhaps, that the voices of those who were seriously concerned about a full-scale Chinese involvement in Korea were not powerful enough. The assistant secretary of state for public affairs, Edward W. Barrett, totally disagreed with the suggestion that only 18,000 Chinese "volunteers" were in Korea; he said that they were building up to at least 100,000 and perhaps hundreds of thousands of troops.[28] O. Edmund Clubb, who had been perturbed about China's intentions in Korea since late September, on November 1 reminded Rusk of the reported presence of 15 Soviet divisions in Manchuria and 40,000 Soviet artillery troops—attired in Chinese uniform—in the Yangshi mountain area near Fengcheng. But though he called for a slowing of military operations, discussions with America's allies, and new political estimates "to the end that, in our haste to win a battle, we shall not lose the war," Clubb weakened the force of his warning on November 7 by saying that the battle for Korea should be continued "pending definitive developments."[29] Later in the month, the questions that had arisen with regard to bombing air bases north of the border in Manchuria and "hot pursuit" across the Yalu consumed his thoughts. As a result, he devoted his energies to developing arguments not in support of calling a halt to the military operations in Korea but only against the extension of hostilities into Manchuria.[30] Since Clubb previously had been out of step with the thinking on Soviet and Chinese intentions, his views carried less weight at this time. His contention that the Soviets, with China as one spearhead, were following a timetable en route to the initiation of World War III, was dismissed by John Paton Davies, for example, as being "out of character" for Stalin, whom Davies regarded as a supreme opportunist and realist.[31]

Other officials who could have influenced the policy deliberations regarding China's intentions were also changing their positions at a rather slow rate. Davies did caution on November 7 that the Chinese might be "on the rampage," but he still did not want U.S./U.N. forces to call a halt. Any withdrawal of forces from Korea would be humiliating, he said, and would shake confidence in the United States, whereas falling back to a purely defensive position "would be interpreted by the Kremlin and Peiping as a precipitate retreat inviting bold exploitation."[32] He recommended seeking a localized solution to the conflict while preparing for the possible outbreak of World War III, proposals that neither reined in MacArthur nor substantially changed policy. On November 14 he was awaiting clarification of China's military objectives but hinted that it had become a military decision as to whether the U.S. should attempt to advance the "military position on the ground or fall back to a defensive position."[33] He was more forthright on November 17 when, at last, he recommended a "retirement of all UN forces to a defensive position at the neck of the Korean peninsula."[34] But the bracketing of this suggestion with a call for the establishment of a buffer zone in the northern regions of Korea undermined the impact of his apparently lone voice. And it was shortly thereafter that Acheson deferred consideration of the zone concept, since it was not attractive to the military and was tainted by its equation with appeasement.

CIA reports were also somewhat contradictory and unhelpful in November. The warning the agency gave the administration on November 8 was grave indeed: it reported 30,000 to 40,000 Chinese troops in Korea itself but 700,000 over the border in Manchuria, a capability that could, if fully applied, force the U.N. forces to withdraw to defensive positions farther south. In the CIA view, China had full freedom of action and was dictating the tactical moves in Korea. Overall, the risk of general war had substantially increased, indicating "either that the Kremlin [was] ready to force a showdown with the West at an early date or that circumstances [had] forced them to accept that risk."[35]

One day later, however, the head of the CIA sent a memorandum to the NSC that confused these earlier conclusions about Moscow's intentions. General Bedell Smith wrote on November 9: "The probability is that the Soviet Government has not yet made a decision directly to launch a general war over the Korean-Chinese situation. There is a good chance that they will not in the immediate future take such a decision." At what point Moscow would decide to launch a general war, intelligence was unable to predict. The CIA director went on to support military arguments for removing restrictions on the geographical area of military operations by arguing that "action by U.N. forces to attack troop concentrations or airfields north of the Yalu River, or to pursue enemy aircraft into Chinese territory would not increase the already substantial risk that the situation may degenerate into a general war involving Russia. In other words," he wrote, "the Kremlin's basic decision for or against war would hardly be influenced by this local provocation in this area."[36]

As will be shown later, the introduction of these ideas concerning Soviet intentions brought an unfortunate twist to the argument that proved difficult for Acheson to overcome, since it appealed to the hard-liners in his own department and the Pentagon. John Paton Davies, for example, basically agreed with the CIA director; on November 7 and 14 he had argued that localized and limited activity in Manchuria (meaning air and naval action of a "purely punitive and attritive character" in south Manchuria and China proper) would "not necessarily mean that the U.S.S.R. would honor its alliance with Communist China. The likelihood of that occurring would increase as we departed from retaliatory air and naval action and expanded the conflict in two respects—toward the Soviet frontiers and onto the ground."[37]

Allied reactions to the idea of "hot pursuit" and the desire not to provoke full Chinese intervention in Korea, if it could be avoided, prevented wider acceptance of these arguments. In a statement to the press on November 16, President Truman tried to make clear that the United States had no intention of carrying the hostilities into China. But as of the start of the last week of November, the U.S. was still not certain whether it had "provoked" China or not, whether the Chinese were engaged in a full-scale or a limited offensive in Korea. As the CIA put it, the available evidence was "not conclusive."[38] All major branches of the U.S. administration, therefore, expressed the need to probe Chinese intentions further; thus the military orders to MacArthur still remained unchanged. At a State-Defense meeting on November 21, Lovett reported that he had received nothing from General MacArthur to indicate that he could not accomplish his mission. At the same meeting, Marshall emphasized the apparent State-Defense consensus on the next moves in Korea. He expressed "satisfaction that Mr. Acheson had stated his belief that General MacArthur should push forward with the planned offensive," and Acheson acknowledged the difficulties inherent in establishing a demilitarized zone.

But one potentially significant change did emerge at the meeting which, had it been carried through, might have averted part of the military disaster that was soon to follow: agreement was reached on a proposal to be put to MacArthur that instead of pushing to and then holding the line at the Yalu River, he should—for military reasons—hold the high ground to the south of it.[39]

After Acheson, Marshall, and Averell Harriman left this meeting, there was inconclusive discussion with regard to policy to be followed if MacArthur's offensive failed. Admiral Forrest P. Sherman and General Vandenberg, the chiefs of the Navy and Air Force respectively, believed that the Chinese should in that event be told to "quit or we would have to hit them in Manchuria"— further evidence perhaps that military men regarded retaliation against China as the next logical step in the military operations. With no one apparently dissenting from this opinion, the discussion moved on to another of the joint chiefs' major concerns: how to augment troop strength in Korea and still send the promised divisions to Europe.[40]

Little was proposed at that meeting with any great conviction. Over it all hung either the promise of a successful military offensive led by MacArthur or the threat of a full-scale Chinese military intervention in the war, and no one seemed to know which was most likely. As a reflection of these contrary indications, the joint chiefs relayed the new suggestion to MacArthur that after the offensive he hold his forces on the terrain dominating the approaches to the Yalu, but it was only too apparent that they expected a negative reply to a proposal designed to reduce Chinese fear of U.N. military action against Manchuria. The joint chiefs weakened the force of their recommendation by stating: "While it is recognized that from the point of view of the Commander in the field this course of action may leave much to be desired, it is felt that there may be other considerations which must be accepted"; holding the high ground south of the Yalu was "suggested as a course of action upon which we would appreciate your comments."[41]

Predictably, the result was another blast from General MacArthur. A failure to follow through with the total destruction of all enemy forces in North Korea would be regarded by the Koreans as a betrayal, he said, and "by the Chinese and all the other peoples of Asia as weakness reflected from the appeasement of Communist aggression." U.N. forces now held the initiative in Korea, MacArthur argued; the time had passed when the joint chiefs should be studying the risks of Chinese entry.[42]

The "end-the-war offensive" therefore went ahead on November 24 as planned, soon to be blunted and thrown back by a heavily augmented Chinese army. Peking had used the mid-November period to assess U.S./U.N. reactions to their initial attacks, to prepare against counterblows in Korea and in Manchuria, and to step up mobilization.[43] Nearly 300,000 Chinese troops had entered Korea, ready to engage the Tenth Corps and Eighth Army. U.S./U.N. troops were immediately forced into a long retreat that eventually took them south of the 38th Parallel. All talk of Peking's sensitivity to its border areas or desire to protect its hydroelectric installations on the Yalu now seemed foolish; Chinese divisions appeared ready to push enemy forces off the peninsula entirely.

THE CHINESE COUNTERATTACK AND THE U.S. RESPONSE

The days immediately following the Chinese counteroffensive were probably the worst the Truman administration had experienced. In two days, November 30 and December 1, U.N. casualties exceeded 11,000. The Eighth Army and the Tenth Corps together could put slightly more than 110,000 men in the field against an estimated 256,000 Chinese and 10,000 North Koreans.[44] Recriminations were rife. America's allies tended to blame the United States for provoking the Chinese; Washington officials publicly blamed themselves for not realizing the depths of Chinese "deviousness" and privately blamed MacArthur's intelligence facilities. The general took "credit" for exposing Chinese perfidiousness through his "reconnaissance in force"; he blamed Washington for not allowing him to use America's full military arsenal against the Chinese. Truman's Republican critics agreed with the general on this last point. They attacked the U.N. allies for their appeasement of the Chinese and lack of support for the American way of war, and they renewed their demands for the removal of Acheson.

The Truman administration's explanation of China's actions emphasized Peking's alliance with Moscow. As a result of the clashes between U.S. and Chinese troops on November 26 and the casualties at the end of the month, there was much less hesitation in Washington about portraying China as a full-fledged member of the so-called International Communist Camp. T. J. Cory sent a memorandum to his fellow members of the U.S. delegation to the General Assembly, explaining the deductions that were being made concerning China's motives. North Korea was, he said, definitely within the Soviet orbit: "It follows from this that the new intervention in Korea stems not so much from the national interests of China as it does from the Chinese Communist role as a member of the Moscow-directed International Communist front. From this it follows in turn that the Chinese Communist intervention should be viewed as part of a global Communist program rather than in the more limited context of Manchuria or even of the Far East."[45] The State Department's Office of Chinese Affairs was now certain that Peking "was definitely on the Moscow line" and that the possibility of reorienting Peking away from Moscow was "negligible."[46]

Clubb's earlier analyses seemed to have been vindicated, and he continued to emphasize that Chinese actions should be seen as part of a Soviet strategic design: China's intervention in Korea was "largely meaningless" unless it was "regarded as a component part of a global Communist plan." The "international character of Chinese moves" was demonstrated for him by the "energetic repair and construction of airfields" taking place in China, indicating that "preparations are being made for use of Chinese fields by the Soviet air force." Enlargement of the conflict would be difficult to avoid, he felt, particularly if U.N. action were carried over the border into Manchuria or into China generally. In these circumstances, the Communists would be provided with an opportunity to invoke the Sino-Soviet treaty; with U.S. forces thus tied down in Korea and Europe, "Communist blows" would be struck elsewhere, possibly against Japan, Hong Kong, and Indochina.[47]

This time the CIA was much more in tune with Clubb's analysis. The agency believed that the U.S.S.R. and its "satellites" viewed their "current military and political position as one of great strength in comparison with that of the West" which they would exploit as far as possible. The estimate also stated quite unequivocally that the Soviet Union would "come openly to the military support of China, under the terms of the Sino-Soviet Treaty, in the event of major US(UN) operations against Chinese territory."[48]

Both Rusk and Acheson began to make much of the fact that China had been involved in the planning of the North Korean invasion for a long time and that the two offensives had collided: it was "obviously fantastic [to] suppose that [an] offensive involving [a] half million men c[ou]ld have been prepared impromptu."[49] As Acheson said at the NSC meeting on November 28, what had taken place was "a progressive uncloaking of the extent of this involvement until now there was a fullscale attack."[50] From this explanation, Rusk felt able to argue that the Chinese response "should not be on our conscience since these events are merely the result of well-laid plans and were not provoked by our actions."[51] It was a fantastic piece of rationalization designed, presumably, to bring some comfort to the administration in a time of despair.

Throughout this period, Acheson never deviated from his real concern regarding the war: at the NSC meeting on November 28 he concentrated the discussion, when possible, on the effects the setbacks in Korea were having on European opinion and on security policy in Europe. He tried to direct attention away from the immediate problems in Korea and toward the global picture, including an emphasis on the intentions of the Soviet Union. In this regard, he was as remiss as everyone else in failing to make a real attempt to examine China's motives and in neglecting to examine the situation in Korea from Peking's perspective. As he was to remark to the British Prime Minister, Clement Attlee, a few days later, he had "probably been more bloodied . . . than anyone else" in attempting to distinguish in public between Chinese and Soviet interests, and he thought it was no longer possible to act on the basis of a future split between the two Communist allies.[52] In formulating policy at this time of crisis, the administration saw or was forced to portray China's entry into Korea not as a Chinese decision based on Chinese interests but as an indication of a new phase in a Soviet-directed campaign. Thus an analysis of Soviet intentions and purposes was deemed of paramount importance, including an assessment of the type and extent of support the Soviet Union would give its most valuable ally.

One CIA assumption was that the presumed Soviet backing for China's entry into Korea indicated a greater readiness on Moscow's part to initiate a third world war. At a conference at the Pentagon on December 1, the CIA chief referred to a new estimate the agency was working on that outlined "a much better case than they previously thought for Russians plans for war soon." He concluded, "They probably do not plan on war now but are willing to have it if they can bog us down in Asia."[53]

Many advantages were considered to accrue to Moscow should U.S. military forces become embroiled in Asia, benefits of enormous strategic importance to the U.S.S.R. A long war in Asia would likely create dissension between the United States and its allies over the conduct of that conflict, and plans for the defense of Western Europe under the North Atlantic Treaty would probably be obstructed and delayed.

Germany was of foremost Soviet concern; on November 3, closely coordinated with military events on the peninsula, Moscow had proposed a four-power foreign ministers' conference on the German problem. On December 15, the U.S.S.R. sent notes to the British and French protesting the proposal for West German rearmament, and accepted the Western powers' suggestion that the conference first consider the broader causes of East-West tension. Washington viewed these tactics as deliberately divisive, and Acheson saw real signs in early December that these Soviet moves were beginning to bear fruit. There was a "virtual state of panic" among allies in the United Nations, he said, and accusations that U.S. leadership had failed. A general lack of confidence was halting European defense plans and creating a resurgence of neutralism in Germany.[54]

This preoccupation with the effects of China's entrance into Korea on Soviet capabilities and intentions made Washington receptive to intelligence indicating that Moscow was enhancing Peking's ability to engage in a war of attrition. Far East Air Force (FEAF) estimates passed on in December showed that Moscow had made good its promise to deliver combat aircraft to China. China was believed then to possess 650 aircraft, and 400–500 Soviet air force planes were thought to be ready for use at bases around Dairen.[55] Although FEAF estimates were above those of the Joint Intelligence Committee, it was agreed that there had been a steady augmentation of Chinese air strength in November and December, sufficient for the Chinese to launch an air attack on U.S./U.N. forces and to give tactical air support to ground troops.[56]

It was a bleak and dangerous time for all parties in Korea. For the Truman administration, the atmosphere of crisis was generated not just by the shock of the military defeats but by its unpreparedness to deal with the new and unforeseen circumstances. During periods of crisis, decision makers often assume the adversary's options to be wide-ranging and unconstrained while their own choices appear circumscribed and narrow; this kind of response to the new crisis in Korea was reflected in the debate within the administration in late November and early December. But the difference in position was perceived not only in terms of the number of policy options available but also in terms of the level of sophistication of those options. In late November the Soviet Union was thought to be operating on the basis of a master plan at the global level; the U.S. policy makers saw themselves as reactive and parochial. Moscow, it was assumed, could decide on global war at a time of its own choosing, or on instigating a debilitating conflict between China and the United States in order to benefit Soviet policy in Europe and Japan. On the other hand, if it preferred to, the U.S.S.R. could sit on the sidelines directing military operations, at the same time launching a peace offensive designed to "strengthen its pretensions as the champion of 'peaceful settlement,' and for the purpose of creating confusion in the United States and Western Europe."[57] U.S. policy makers, meanwhile, faced the necessity of responding negatively to an urgent request to augment its already overstretched military forces; of dealing with a domestic and an international front in disarray; and—within the administration itself—of building a policy consensus to determine the most appropriate response to the Chinese onslaught.

U.S. DOMESTIC AND INTERNATIONAL ACTIVITY

Since U.S. ground force capabilities in the Far East on the eve of the Korean War were minimal, it had been a tremendous gamble in the first place to enter the war, and subsequently to cross the 38th Parallel with the troops then available. In October 1950 the gamble seemed to have paid off, but by early December, MacArthur was warning that unless he received immediate reinforcements and replacements, he would have to set about evacuating his forces. The U.N. command had been fighting with under-strength units even prior to China's entrance into Korea; after the heavy losses suffered in late November, the weakness in military strength became intolerable.[58]

The impossibility of meeting MacArthur's requests for more troops was made abundantly clear at the NSC meeting on November 28, where the secretary of the Army, Frank Pace, stated that the only unit available to send was the Eighty-second Airborne Division. New National Guard units would not be ready until March 15, he said, and no individual replacements would be available until January 1.[59] Not surprisingly, under these circumstances, MacArthur again raised the question of utilizing Chiang Kai-shek's ground troops, who were, he said, the only source of trained reinforcements available for early commitment to the U.N. side in Korea. Again, the joint chiefs denied the general's request, making it clear that serious international consequences could flow from a decision to employ these troops: doing so might disrupt the unity of the U.N., and the Commonwealth countries might find it wholly unacceptable to have their forces fighting alongside Nationalist troops.[60] The joint chiefs also suggested that such a move might lead to the extension of hostilities to Taiwan and other areas. Their emphasis on the likely disruptive international consequences of a decision to use Chinese Nationalist troops, however, surely reinforced MacArthur's belief that America's allies—particularly the British—were the single most important factor in determining Korean War policy.

The joint chiefs sympathized with MacArthur's position, but little could be done immediately to alleviate the problem of resources. In the longer term, however, the United States could augment its capabilities in the Far East. On December 1, Truman asked Congress for supplemental defense appropriations of $16.8 billion, and on December 16 he declared a state of national emergency, accompanied by an increase in defense production, an expansion of the armed forces, and wage and price controls.

Two other proposals implemented in December were intended to deflate the power of the Chinese in the longer term. On the 3rd the United States imposed an all-out economic embargo on trade with China, and on the 16th the Department of Commerce issued orders prohibiting U.S. ships and aircraft from visiting Chinese Communist ports.[61] Of course, American trade with China had become effectively nonexistent by December 1950 anyway, but this symbolic move was designed to show that the administration was taking action and to encourage U.S. allies similarly to deny their exporters access to China. In the main, it was directed at the British, whose Far Eastern economic interests made it more painful for them to tighten up on the delivery of items that found their way into China.

In the short term, faced with the prospect of a possible withdrawal from Korea and a further series of military defeats, attempts were made to shore up Truman's domestic and international support. Such moves were deemed to be imperative in the domestic arena, since polls on December 8 had shown the State Department that public opinion was in a "desperate condition" and was "waiting for leadership" from the government. Gallup survey data also indicated that after China's entry into Korea, Truman's popularity had reached a new low: 49 percent of those sampled disapproved of his leadership, and only 36 percent approved of his administration as a whole. Acheson fared little better than the president: of those who could identify the secretary of state, only 20 percent viewed him favorably, while 30 percent thought he should be replaced. Once Chinese intervention had increased the prospects for a long battle, rather than a speedy and decisive victory, support for the war effort dropped precipitously. By early January, 66 percent of those surveyed thought the United States should pull out of Korea, and 49 percent believed it had been a mistake to go in in the first place.[62]

Administration critics in Congress reflected and reinforced these expressions of public disapproval and discontent. Though congressional demands were often contradictory, their tone contributed to the atmosphere of crisis in Washington during the winter. The majority of the Republican Party, with Robert Taft at its head, "alternately called for both militancy on a scale advocated by MacArthur and withdrawal; decided that the Korean intervention was a monumental blunder; attacked the United Nations and our allies; and demanded at least a limited disengagement from our involvement in the defense of Europe." Senator Taft's inconsistency stemmed from his being "caught amid his anticommunist militancy about Asia, his lifelong hostility toward extensive overseas involvement, and his partisan opposition to Truman." In the winter of 1950–51, despite his previous support for the move, he focused on the possible unconstitutionality of Truman's original action in sending troops to Korea, and he called for the withdrawal of U.S./U.N. forces to a defensible line in Japan and Taiwan.[63] Senators William F. Knowland, Alexander Smith, Harry P. Cain, and Homer E. Capehart enthusiastically endorsed MacArthur's request (described below) to strike at the Chinese bases and supply lines, and to impose a blockade of the Chinese coast. McCarthy went further in his direct attacks on the administration: on December 2 he sent a telegram to the president, demanding to know why Truman was letting Acheson and the rest of the "crimson clique in the State Department" run amuck with the lives of American soldiers; moreover, he threatened to start impeachment proceedings against Truman, and he urged that Acheson and Marshall be dismissed. Democrats Pat McCarran and James Eastland also called for Acheson's resignation,[64] and in late November, columnists

Joseph and Stewart Alsop began a campaign in the *Washington Post* designed to effect Acheson's removal from office.[65]

It was to improve domestic support for the administration that Truman decided on the psychological ploy of declaring a state of national emergency on December 16, a move not considered vitally necessary for material reasons. Acheson and the Policy Planning Staff had suggested it as a method of regaining something of a national consensus. To obtain the widest support, they thought, it was probably "advisable to declare that the Kremlin threat to the security of the United States has created an unlimited national emergency."[66] They hoped that the impression of a resolute executive branch would calm the populace and produce a favorable international effect as well, since the degree to which other nations would be induced to work with the United States depended, it was thought, not only upon material assistance from America "but also upon the steadiness, the calmness and the self-possession that is now shown by the Government and the people of the United States."[67]

One way of demonstrating government steadiness, some officials argued, was to "hold the line" in Korea, sticking by the ROK even though conditions were beginning to dictate otherwise, and to continue with plans to build up the military and economic resources of Europe. Dulles and MacArthur seem to have been the only ones who dissented from aspects of this view, and both let congressional leaders know of their feelings. In a meeting with Republican Senators Eugene Milliken and Taft, Dulles argued that in Asia the United States should more closely limit itself to "areas subject to sea and air power, which fits our natural role." Although he did agree that a beachhead should be held in Korea for political reasons, he would clearly have preferred that America extricate itself as soon as possible from the "major military disaster" that had befallen it. With regard to the Truman administration's European policy, he revealed that his views were somewhat distant from those of his State Department colleagues. He doubted, for example, that an effective European army could be created in time to deter a Soviet attack, and if not, "the question of the best use of our economic, military and manpower resources would need to be reconsidered."[68] In this respect, Dulles gave some support to the neoisolationist arguments being voiced in Congress and to MacArthur, who for years had been arguing that the Roosevelt and

Truman administrations contained those who were "so infatuated with the safeguard of Europe that they would sacrifice Asia rather than see any support diverted from Europe."[69] And MacArthur, like Dulles, favored reliance on America's air and naval power, arguing in December that greater emphasis be put on these branches of the armed forces operating in Korea.[70]

Kennan and Rusk, however, argued forcefully against any thought of ground-force evacuation, and they were successful in convincing Acheson, Lovett, and Marshall of the need to put this thought aside. On December 4 both Rusk and Kennan brought up the example of the British decision to hold during World War II even when "the odds were overwhelmingly against them."[71] As Rusk said on a later occasion, "upright behavior [was] worth many divisions." To abandon South Korea to its fate would set a poor "example of what it means to be a friend of the US."[72] Rusk even drew some comfort from the enhanced U.S. military capability that the Korean War had brought about: though military losses were considerable, at least the country was more powerful now than it had been on June 25.[73]

Acheson's well-known aversion to America's appearing as a weak or defeated nation reasserted itself, and he agreed that a surrender in Korea would be conceding that Russia and China were the most powerful forces in the Far East. In line with his view that power implies domination, he concluded that if the United States gave up the fight in Korea, "all Asians would hurry to make the best deals they could" with Moscow and Peking,[74] an outcome he could not allow.

It was also thought necessary for U.S. troops to remain on the peninsula and win back some ground in order to achieve an acceptable position for negotiation. Though many allies and nonaligned states desired an immediate ceasefire, the United States at that time did not embrace the idea enthusiastically. In early December a ceasefire at the 38th Parallel was considered to be the best the military could hope for, but negotiating from a position of weakness was considered difficult and unwise, if not downright distasteful: the Communists were bound to exact a price that the United States was unwilling to pay.

The British presented an additional complication. With their strong fear of an expanded conflict in Asia, they announced themselves willing to make concessions to the Chinese to secure a cessation of hostilities. In a terse summary of the Truman-Attlee discussions of December 4 (the first of several meetings in Washington), Acheson characterized the situation as follows: "At this time we [the U.S./U.N.] had no choice but to negotiate with the Chinese. These negotiations would, of course, extend beyond Korea and it was certain the price the Chinese demanded would be Formosa, a seat in the UN, and recognition."[75] The British delegation might have found this acceptable, but without a doubt neither the secretary of state nor the president would allow such concessions to be wrung from the United States while there was still a slight hope that defeat in Korea could be avoided.

There was also a growing danger that other U.N. members would introduce a ceasefire resolution whose terms the United States would find politically unacceptable. The U.S. administration thus made it quite clear to the United Kingdom and other governments that it would not accept a ceasefire to which any political strings were attached. The resolution the Asian states had drafted by December 11 turned out to be objectionable to America primarily from the military point of view: it did not contain provisions that could prevent a further increase in Chinese forces and supplies at the front, which would prove serious if the Chinese decided to violate any truce agreement. The secretary of defense emphasized that it was essential for the U.N. commission to have access to all of Korea in order to provide protection against such violations. He added that imposing this condition "might in fact result in the Communists refusing the ceasefire"—an outcome that he would find acceptable.[76]

The United States obviously disliked U.N. involvement in ceasefire arrangements, but it had to be endured in order to maintain some semblance of U.S./U.N. unity. Fortunately, as far as the Truman administration was concerned, the Chinese rejected the 13-power draft resolution because it failed to include any reference to China's call for the removal of all foreign troops from Korea, withdrawal of the Seventh Fleet from Taiwan, and recognition of its claim to the U.N. seat. The U.N. ceasefire commission refused to accept China's rejection as final, however, and on January 11 it submitted a new formula that promised a discussion of the questions the Chinese delegation had raised earlier. The United States voted for this revision on the 13th, despite the domestic uproar it would cause, in order to maintain unity with the other U.N. members, who supported the resolution in overwhelming numbers.

This decision indicated that at this stage of the war, U.N. and allied support was marginally of greater significance to leading U.S. decision makers than was domestic political criticism, but as Acheson later described it, the choice of whether to support or oppose the resolution "was a murderous one, threatening on one side the loss of the Koreans and the fury of Congress and the press and, on the other, the loss of our majority and support in the United Nations." U.S. support of the resolution was decided upon "in the fervent hope and belief that the Chinese would reject it"[77]—which they did, because it called for the truce to come before the discussion of political questions. As Chou En-lai charged in a telegram to the U.N., "The purpose of arranging a ceasefire first is merely to give the United States troops a breathing space."[78]

China's rejection was the signal for the United States to play its major political card (albeit one with serious military overtones): that of branding the Chinese Communists as aggressors in Korea. On August 31, a draft State Department memorandum had said that if Chinese units moved south of the 38th Parallel, the matter should be put before the U.N. Security Council with the object of securing the condemnation of the Chinese as aggressors; again, at the NSC meeting on November 28, Acheson had repeated that America must "go forward in the UN to uncloak the Chinese Communist aggression."[79] The move was also discussed extensively during the Truman-Attlee meetings of early December and with the French premier, Rene Pleven, at the end of January.

Britain, France, Canada, and India were particularly anxious about America's intention to force through a resolution condemning the Chinese, believing that it implied the future extension of hostilities into China. John D. Hickerson, U.S. assistant secretary of state for U.N. Affairs, had informed Sir Keith Officer, of the Australian delegation, that once the aggressor resolution had passed, the United States favored such action as the total severance of diplomatic relations with China, financial measures, trade restrictions and probably a blockade of the China coast. In addition, the Soviet Union would be exposed as the instigator of the aggression, he said.[80]

This explanation did little to ease the fears of the Commonwealth and European governments. Warren Austin, the American ambassador to the U.N., reported on December 30 that Britain and France were reacting vigorously against his suggestion that a resolution charging Chinese aggression against the United Nations be introduced, and they were urging "in [the] strongest terms [the] un-desirability at this stage of any UN action which would commit [the] UN to fight in Asia against Chinese Communists." Austin noted that some Asian and Latin American delegations had also stated that conflict with China would not find the support of public opinion in their countries.[81]

But despite the strength of the opposition to the aggressor reso-lution, the United States would not put it aside. Congressional pressure helped see to that: on January 19 and 23 respectively, the House and the Senate adopted their own resolutions branding the Chinese as aggressors. Acheson feared that if the United Nations did not soon follow suit, there would be demands for unilateral U.S. action. As it was, he said, the delay occasioned by allied and U.N. opposition had brought the U.S. administration "to the verge of destruction domestically."[82] General Bradley, in discussions with Sir John Slessor, Britain's air vice marshal, was adamant that the "strength of public and Congressional feeling in this matter" made it essential for the resolution to go through.[83] In sum, Acheson told Bevin, U.N. failure to recognize China as an ag-gressor would not only mark the beginning of the end of the United Nations as a collective security organization but also set off "a wave of isolationism [in the U.S.] which would jeopardize all that we are trying to do with and for the Atlantic Pact countries." For these reasons, Britain and the rest of Western Europe should support America in this matter, he said.[84]

Nevertheless, in order to gain a large vote in favor of the resolu-tion, the United States was willing to soften its position on future action against China. "Only practical steps would be taken," Acheson said; the administration would not contemplate asking the U.N.'s Collective Measures Committee to recommend any mili-tary operations against Chinese territory; would not ask for the severance of diplomatic relations with China but only for non-recognition of the PRC government by those who had not yet recognized it; and would accept a selective economic embargo ini-tially in order to "preserve the greatest possible degree of free world unity."[85] But this was as far as the United States was willing to go, and the Truman administration was still not certain of secur-ing the level of international support it desired.

China's New Year's Eve offensive had aided the U.S. position, and if, as a result of this offensive, the Chinese "volunteers" con-tinued into South Korea, the United States recognized it would then be easier for the various delegations to put aside their objections to the U.S. resolution. The Canadian ambassador, for example, gave his personal view that if the Chinese moved south of the parallel, "there would be very little choice anyone would have."[86]

Very shortly thereafter, as a result of the Chinese military thrust, the U.N. command abandoned Seoul. Despite this new turn in the military situation, the British tried one last tack to restrain the Americans: they suggested going ahead with the aggressor resolution, and then doing nothing further within the U.N. machinery. But the Truman administration, having made one important concession to the British—to authorize the Collective Measures Committee to defer its report of what action to take until the Good Offices Committee had reported on the progress of negotiations— now felt it could go no further. Indeed, Truman put it more forcefully at a cabinet meeting on January 26 when, with talk of British appeasement in the air, he told Acheson to "proceed with resolution as drafted and despite British opposition."[87]

That opposition was weakening anyway. The British were still worried about the military implications of the aggressor resolution, but many within the U.K. government believed as Bevin did, that in the end, they must support U.S. foreign policy positions: "We have to imagine what it would be like," Bevin said in mid-January, "to live in a world with a hostile Communist bloc, an unco-operative America, a Commonwealth pulled in two directions, and a disillusioned Europe which would be deprived of support in the form of American troops and American involvement in active European defence."[88] Perhaps more than any other, this statement epitomized the plight of such powers as Britain, which, following World War II, had been forced through military and economic weakness into a position of dependence on the United States. Given this assessment of America's world role, and the recognition of the asymmetrical nature of the relationship between London and Washington, it is not surprising that the United Kingdom accepted the U.S. amendments and voted along with 43 other nations in support of the February 1 resolution declaring China an aggressor in Korea.

CONSIDERATION OF RETALIATORY ACTION AGAINST CHINA

Undoubtedly, a strong connection did exist at one time between the resolution and possible military action against China. On December 3, at a meeting that discussed both the possible extension of hostilities and conditions for a ceasefire, Acheson had said: "If we must go ahead with hostilities against the Chinese . . . we must be forced out of Korea and therefore we must resist a suggestion of a ceasefire. In that case, we would have to try to get condemnation of the Chinese and have them branded as an aggressor."[89] The rather tortuous phrasing indicated at least some link between the aggressor resolution and an extension of hostilities into China. Clubb had also suggested that U.N. condemnation of China might make it possible to establish a naval blockade of the China coast.[90] And surely there must have been something behind the clearly stated beliefs of the British that the United States wanted first to "brand the Peking Government as aggressors," then follow this by "limited war" against China and the "general breaking off of relations with Peking."[91] In fact, shortly after China's massive intervention in Korea, various officials within the administration expressed a desire to retaliate in some way. Though it is necessary to emphasize that there was minimal support for a general war with China, less extensive options were not ruled out.

The most famous exponent of action designed to expand the hostilities was the U.N. commander, who was constantly referring to the "unprecedented restrictions" imposed on his military operations. In response to a new directive from the joint chiefs sent on December 29, requiring MacArthur to "defend in successive positions" and to determine the "last reasonable opportunity for an orderly evacuation" of Korea, he made a further impassioned plea: "Should a policy determination be reached by our government . . . to recognize the State of War which has been forced upon us by the Chinese authorities and to take retaliatory measures within our capabilities we could: (1) Blockade the coast of China; (2) Destroy through naval gunfire and air bombardment China's industrial capacity to wage war; (3) Secure reinforcements from the Nationalist garrison on Formosa to strengthen our position in Korea . . . (4) Release existing restrictions upon the Formosa garrison for diversionary action (possibly leading to counter-invasion) against vulnerable areas of the Chinese Mainland."[92] As if this were not extensive enough, MacArthur had also previously recommended the use of the atomic bomb. On December 24 he submitted "a list of retardation targets which he considered would require 26 bombs" and requested "4 bombs to be used on invasion forces and 4 bombs to be used on critical concentrations of enemy air power, both targets of opportunity."[93]

There were those among the general public and in Congress who would have agreed with MacArthur's request to use atomic weapons in China and Korea had they been aware of it, and many were ready to endorse MacArthur's other demands for an expansion of hostilities. Though all Truman's liberal supporters were against the extension of the war and were concerned about the future of Europe should widespread hostilities ensue,[94] louder voices criticized the "appeasement" of the Chinese and demanded tougher action, including the use of atomic weapons. The national commanders of the four largest veterans' organizations in America petitioned the president to give General MacArthur authority "to employ such means as may be necessary."[95] Bernard Baruch, former American representative to the U.N. Atomic Energy Commission, cited the widespread encouragement between December 4 and 8 for Truman to use the bomb, arguing that "it ought to be used if it can be used effectively."[96] There were similar demands in Congress, especially from Senator Owen Brewster and Congressman Mendel Rivers, of the Senate and House Armed Services Committees, who pointed to the effectiveness of its performance against the Japanese.[97]

Since battlefield events subjected administration officials to the same kind of emotional pressures as those experienced by the general public, it is not surprising that others, apart from MacArthur, seriously contemplated retaliation against China and nuclear warfare. Stuart Symington, head of the National Security Resources Board (NSRB), was the most extreme exponent in the administration of a complete ground-force withdrawal from Korea, to be followed by "an open and sustained attack upon lines of communication in China and Korea; and also upon aggression-supporting industries in Manchuria as considered militarily advisable." The United States should undertake this action unilaterally if necessary, he said, and deter future Soviet moves by announcing that any further Soviet aggression "would result in the atomic bombardment of Soviet Russia itself."[98]

Little support existed for either withdrawal from Korea or unilateral U.S. action, however, let alone for issuing threats of the kind Symington had suggested, which would closely identify the U.S.S.R. with events on the peninsula.[99] Acheson believed that the action Symington advocated would certainly bring about a third world war. As for threatening Russia with atomic bombardment, the secretary thought that the size of America's atomic stockpile was not sufficient to worry its enemies, but that the prospect would certainly "frighten our allies to death." And Marshall considered Symington's proposal so radical as to require the complete restudy of America's political, military, and defense mobilization policies.[100]

These comments effectively buried Symington's ideas. But he was not alone in considering the use of atomic weapons and an expanded war; some officials in the Defense Department were also willing to examine the question of undertaking atomic as well as conventional bombing operations against China. Several discussions involving the use of nuclear weapons had preceded Truman's unfortunate remarks at a press conference on November 30, in which he had implied that the use of the atomic bomb was under active consideration. On November 16 the Army's Plans and Operations Division, whose assistant chief of staff, Charles Bolté, was one of MacArthur's staunchest supporters, had recommended that the case for using nuclear weapons be reconsidered, and his request was granted.[101] On November 20, General J. Lawton Collins, the Army chief of staff, took the matter up with the other joint chiefs and advised making contingency studies on the use of the weapon. On November 28 the joint chiefs' secretary sent a priority notice to the Joint Strategic Survey Committee, asking for recommendations regarding the bomb's use against Russia should the Soviets intervene in Korea, and against China, given the fact of their intervention. That same day, Plans and Operations recommended warning Peking that if it did not withdraw its forces at once, the United States or United Nations would take appropriate military action against China. Noncompliance with this demand would lead to "air and naval attacks against those lines of communication and those military objectives and installations in Manchuria which are now being utilized to furnish military support to the Chinese Communist forces in Korea." The United States should also ensure that it was in a position to make "prompt use of the atomic bomb . . . as, if and when directed by the President."[102] On December 1 the division retreated somewhat from this extreme military posture, perhaps as a consequence of the military upsets at the end of November; it now advocated that the U.N. Command go on the defensive and not attack Manchuria with conventional or atomic weapons unless U.N. forces were faced with total disaster. Instead, the United States should initiate a campaign of covert operations in China "designed to harass, confuse, and inflict material damage on the Chinese Communists."[103]

Between early December and mid-January, the joint chiefs and their chairman, General Bradley, were also thinking in terms of some form of retaliation against China. There was real concern from the end of November that China would bring in its air force, which would, it was argued, if used on any scale against U.S./U.N. troops, make it impossible for them to remain on the peninsula.[104] At that point, the joint chiefs were not in favor of violating the Yalu border, primarily because U.S. airfields in Korea and Japan were crowded and thought to be vulnerable to counterattack. But as they realized the extensive nature of China's entry into Korea, as losses mounted, and as evacuation of Korea became a real possibility, the military chiefs came much closer to supporting retaliatory action in Manchuria. General Bradley, contemplating evacuation of Korea on December 3, asked how much the United States could afford to lose without further action against the PRC and suggested what sort of reaction would occur in Congress and among the armed forces if military action against China did not follow a U.S. withdrawal from Korea.[105] He sounded bitter: "We used to say that an attack on a platoon of the United States troops meant war. Would anyone believe it now if we don't react to the Chinese attack?"[106]

During a discussion between Truman and Attlee about possible action against China, Bradley again complained of the restrictions imposed on the fighting in Korea. The Chinese, he said, "were actually sending military forces against us and did not call it war, and yet if we drop one bomb across the Yalu they say we are making war against them."[107] Vandenberg shared Bradley's sentiments and argued that the proposed action against China would not affect America's capacity to defend Europe: "All we would need would be the naval blockade and the use of one or two air groups."[108] In the event of evacuation, the Navy and Air Force were absolutely clear about what had to be done. No one wanted a "complete war with the Chinese," but the two branches of the military believed that if evacuation did prove necessary, action should be taken—possibly to include a blockade and a concentrated air effort over the major Chinese cities—"to repay the Chinese Communists for their deeds."[109]

Discussion in the early part of December was mainly concerned with consideration of the course to follow in the event of evacuation from Korea, but a less prominent strain in the debate turned on the question of immediate retaliation against China. Plans and Operations had been in favor of some form of retaliation, and the assistant secretary of the Army advocated on December 5 the immediate use of Chinese Nationalist forces, a naval blockade of the Chinese coast, and the development and rapid execution of support to Asian non-Communists willing to initiate hostile operations against the PRC.[110]

On December 27 the Joint Strategic Plans Committee forwarded a series of recommendations to the joint chiefs for possible initiation if it should be tacitly agreed that a state of war existed between the United States and China. Navy and Air Force members of the committee recommended not only the stabilization of positions in Korea, to include the holding of selected bridgeheads, but also the intensification of air operations in Korea with future extension to China "as necessary"; use of Chinese Nationalist forces in Korea and assistance to their government in establishing an undeclared naval blockade against the PRC; and the initiation and support of guerilla activities inside mainland China. The Army members were less enamored of the idea of using Nationalist forces immediately; they recommended establishing a naval and air blockade of China with the forces then in the Pacific area, augmented by a submarine force. However, they did foresee a role for Nationalist troops in 6 to 18 months' time, in operations directed against the mainland and against the island of Hainan, off the south coast of China.[111]

On receipt of this report and in the light of MacArthur's December 30 telegram calling for intensified operations against China, the chief of naval operations, Admiral Forrest P. Sherman, stated his belief that it was "less than realistic to evade the fact" that open hostilities existed in Korea between China and the United States, and argued for the removal of certain restrictions that had been imposed on the prosecution of the war. The options he recommended for consideration, reflecting the influence of the joint chiefs' planning committee and of MacArthur, included a naval blockade of China as soon as the position in Korea was stabilized or after evacuation had taken place; the removal of restrictions on the operations of Chinese Nationalist forces and logistic support for their efforts against Chinese Communist troops; support for guerilla activities in China; aerial reconnaissance of Chinese coastal areas and of Manchuria; and the initiation of "damaging naval and air attacks on objectives in Communist China at such time as the Chinese Communists attack any of our forces outside of Korea." The establishment of the naval blockade was seen to require U.N. concurrence, but in Sherman's view, if the U.N. did not agree, "the time ha[d] come for unilateral action by the United States."[112]

These and other recommendations became the position of the joint chiefs of staff as of January 12, 1951, and were put forward for NSC consideration on January 17. At this meeting,[113] Acheson said that three aspects of the joint chiefs' proposals alarmed him: the naval and air blockade, the removal of restrictions on aerial reconnaissance, and Chinese Nationalist operations against the mainland. He doubted whether a naval blockade against China would be any more effective than U.N.-imposed economic sanctions, particularly if the British and the Portuguese (because of Macao) could not be induced to support it. As for the proposed use of Chinese Nationalist forces against the mainland, Acheson argued that so serious a step at least ought to be preceded by a detailed Defense Department study of its likely military effectiveness. Only then would the government be in a position to recommend for or against lifting the restrictions. Later on, he added that there was a problem in keeping a proper balance between U.S. national interests in the Far East and those in Europe, a "danger in centering all our concern on the Chinese."

Bradley responded somewhat defensively that the joint chiefs "never intended to advocate U.S. support of a large-scale invasion of the Chinese mainland." He did not think reconnaissance was a serious problem, since it "would not involve penetration into the interior of China." As for a blockade, Bradley did not believe British and American opinion to be "so very far apart on this." In any case, there was "heavy popular pressure for the United States to 'do something,'" unilaterally if necessary.

Secretary Marshall agreed with Bradley on this last point. He was considering what moves the country should make in defense of its national security. If the United States undertook unilateral courses of action, this would condemn the U.N. to a future as a "mere forum for debate. Nevertheless," he went on, "we must consider first of all the security of the United States." He seriously questioned whether America could afford to wait for an accord in the United Nations. Besides, he pointed out, there were numerous "Congressional inquiries and protests" taking place, many of which urged the administration "to get out of Korea . . . [and] before very long we should be hearing such questions as 'How much are we going to pay for Hong Kong?' 'What price Hong Kong?' 'Why do the British have so much influence on our policy?'" The United States had to consider its own interest in Korea and Japan, he said.

Robert J. Smith, attending the meeting for Stuart Symington of the NSRB, also countered Acheson's arguments. A blockade would be effective, he said, because China's internal communication system was "notoriously weak"; it would also impose "a heavy burden and drain" upon the Soviet Union. He went on to suggest undertaking aerial reconnaissance "well into the interior," since "many things were going on which we should know of." In his view, furthermore, the troops on Taiwan were the "best source of available manpower" and could create problems for the Communists.

Faced with these divisions among his principal advisers, Truman delayed a decision on the recommendations. He commended the value of both Smith's and Acheson's comments, though they were directly opposed, and returned the paper to the NSC staff for further consideration. It was a crucial turning point in the development of the administration's policy toward the war and toward China. Either there would shortly be a decision supporting expanded operations against China, or the United States would settle for a limited conflict.

These January recommendations of the joint chiefs were controversial and troublesome for still one other reason: that is, their prominence at the MacArthur hearings in May and June 1951 (discussed in detail later). On the basis of the joint chiefs' January 12 memorandum, General MacArthur argued at the hearings that his military superiors basically agreed with the policy recommendations he had made at the end of December. Marshall, in reply, disputed the general's interpretation of the memorandum and explained that it represented only tentative proposals that could be implemented if America came close to being forced out of Korea (which by May 1951 was very unlikely). But Marshall's explanation (subsequently endorsed at the hearings by Bradley and the joint chiefs) did not reveal the complete history behind the development of this memorandum. The joint chiefs' fears of an impending evacuation from Korea did influence their views, but the discussions within the department in December and January and the expressed opinions of the joint chiefs give support to MacArthur's argument that the Pentagon endorsed at least some of his December recommendations.

The fact that certain members of the Defense Department were in favor of a limited extension of hostilities to include action against China cannot be dismissed simply as the military's predictable bureaucratic response; other parts of the administration as well gave support to some of the Pentagon's suggestions. Acheson was instinctively against any expansion of the war to involve the Chinese, but some State Department personnel were not immune to the idea of punishing Chinese "aggression," and Acheson felt it necessary to represent their views.

According to Sir Oliver Franks, British ambassador to Washington, a "limited warfare" concept—that is, a controlled extension of the war into China—had originated within the State Department, and the British prime minister reported that Acheson had argued in its favor ("though with more eloquence than conviction") at the Truman-Attlee discussions in early December.[114]

The British delegates at the Anglo-American summit were concerned because, as they put it, they appeared "not to have convinced the Americans of the need to make a serious effort to reach a political settlement with the Chinese and not to have shaken them in their intention to undertake some form of 'limited war' against China."[115] When Lord Tedder inquired exactly what military action was contemplated, "Marshall, while emphasizing that the ideas were not fully worked out and that he was doubtful of their efficacy and success, said that they included a blockade of the China Coast, possible air action on certain points and covert activities in southern China."[116] Philip Jessup confirmed in late December that the Truman administration was struggling to establish a governmental military position on a limited war against China.

The Pentagon was not united on this, he reported, and there were doubts that bombings and a blockade could "actually defeat Mao's regime."[117]

It is clear, therefore, that officials within both State and Defense were considering the idea of a limited expansion of the war, and there may well have been a convergence of view between some members of the two departments during the period. Dean Rusk's preferred course of action, as he described it on December 27, was "to make it in the interest of the Chinese Communists to accept some stabilization by making it so costly for them that they could not afford not to accept." His main fear was that the United States was "not exploiting the situation as much as it should."[118]

Earlier in the month, on December 3, Rusk had suggested that America "could try to void China, making it hard for them to solidify their control and thus difficult to move into Southeast Asia."[119] He may have had an unlikely ally in George Kennan, recalled to the department for a few days at the beginning of December. Kennan argued that Peking had now committed an affront to the United States of the "greatest magnitude"; he probably expressed the attitude of many when he stated that the Chinese had done "something that we can not forget for years" and that they "will have the worry of righting themselves with us not us with them." In his view, the United States owed China "nothing but a lesson."[120]

Others in the State Department devoted less attention to the probable effects on China of bombing operations; they suggested "weakening, fragmenting and ultimately destroying the Chinese Communist regime" by supporting opposition forces within the country. Both Stuart and Clubb of the Office of Chinese Affairs believed it possible to use guerilla forces in southern China to this effect.[121]

Dulles also favored action along these lines to punish the Chinese, but he preferred to involve the Nationalists more directly by using Taiwan as a base for covert and even open activities against the mainland.[122] Shortly thereafter, selected U.S. embassies and consulates were instructed to collect "full and concrete information" on opposition groups in China.[123]

At this stage in December, there was little additional support within the State Department for the notion of undertaking direct attacks upon China. As a next step, Paul Nitze and Averell Harriman, for example, were in favor of blowing up the dams on the Yalu, but as of December 5 they do not seem to have supported Rusk, Clubb, Kennan, or Dulles further than this. Most officials were concerned that an expanded war would bring Moscow directly into the conflict. Only a few doubted such a result, but their views were of sufficient import to generate a debate regarding probable Soviet reactions to retaliation against China. The immediacy of events on the battlefield, longer-term assessments of Moscow's national interests, and the perceived degree and depth of the commitments Peking and Moscow had entered into all affected these estimates.

Assessment of Soviet Intentions and Reactions

No extensive efforts were made to ascertain why China had introduced its forces into Korea in such strength; the action was generally perceived as dictated by Soviet pressure, part of a "global Communist program." The CIA's explanation in December 1950 was that Moscow might be planning to bring on a general conflict in East Asia. Even if Moscow did not intend to do so immediately, it might be hoping to sap U.S. strength through involvement in a large-scale war of attrition in China, while the U.S.S.R. derived benefits for its policies in Europe, its primary focus of attention. Such a war would likely create dissension between the United States and its allies, and obstruct plans for the defense of Western Europe, it was argued. Whereas on November 9 the agency had concluded that limited bombing action by U.S./U.N. forces north of the Yalu would not influence the Kremlin's basic decision for or against war, by December 2 it was arguing that in the event of major operations against Chinese territory, Moscow would come openly to the military support of Peking under the terms of their treaty. It was "highly improbable" that the Chinese Communists would have accepted the risk of general war with the United States "without explicit assurance of effective Soviet support."[124]

Clubb agreed with this assessment. Throughout November he had pointed to the provisions of the Sino-Soviet alliance that would became operable in the event of Japanese aggression, and to Soviet propaganda emphasizing Japanese involvement in the fighting in Korea. All such statements should be seen, he argued, as a "Soviet design to lay the groundwork for citation of the provisions of the Sino-Soviet Alliance of February 14th 1950 in justification of Soviet intervention at some appropriate time."[125] In mid-November, the counselor at the Soviet Embassy in Peking had told K. M. Panikkar that if U.N. planes bombed Manchuria, the Soviet air force would attack them.[126] This information had more force in December, when the Soviet Union appeared to be fulfilling at least some of its material commitments by augmenting the Chinese air force to a degree sufficient to worry the joint chiefs; they feared that it would be used to devastating effect on U.S./U.N. troops evacuating North Korea.

Hence, retaliation against China had to be considered in the context of the Sino-Soviet Treaty of Alliance and the power of the Soviet and Chinese air forces. In late November and early December, the CIA, Acheson, Nitze and Clubb were instrumental in injecting into policy debates the possibly disastrous military consequences associated with the invocation of the Sino-Soviet treaty. On November 28, Acheson had stressed that air action in Manchuria (although it might be essential at some point in order to save U.S./U.N. troops) carried with it the real risk of Soviet entry into the hostilities. By December 1 he had elicited the admission from Generals Collins and Bradley that Soviet support for China would be so detrimental to U.S./U.N. positions as to require the threat or actual use of the atomic bomb.[127] But on December 3, Bradley put aside the fear of open Soviet entry into the conflict when he received another disturbing telegram from MacArthur: the commander reiterated that the U.N. was in an "entirely new war against an entirely new power of great military strength and under entirely new conditions." The prospects were, he said, "steady attrition leading to final destruction."[128]

Later that same day, perhaps under the increased stress this telegram invoked and the disastrous battlefield situation, Bradley advocated blockading the China coast, "bombing and a good many other things to bother" the Chinese.[129] Acheson tried to refocus Bradley's attention on the country that was the prime threat to America's security: "We are fighting the wrong nation," he said. "We are fighting the second team, whereas the real enemy is the Soviet Union."[130] Acheson reiterated that a war with China would have grave effects on America's ability to fight the Soviet Union, and that U.S. resources would inevitably be diverted from Europe toward Asia as a result. Already there were signs, he said, that a general lack of confidence in American leadership was halting European defense plans and promoting neutralist sentiment.

These attitudes created a continuing need for Acheson to keep alive the concern about Soviet reactions to retaliation against China, and to concentrate attention on global security policy. He did not always receive support from his State Department colleagues, however. Indeed, even the Soviet expert, George Kennan, helped to undermine the fear of Soviet intentions; he took direct issue with the CIA position that the events of the previous week were part of a Soviet master plan. World War III was not inevitable, Kennan said, and neither was another Korea likely to break out elsewhere.[131] At a meeting with State Department colleagues on December 5, he undercut Acheson's position regarding the Soviet response to attacks on China by stating that he did not think Russia would react militarily "purely because of our harassment of China." His only argument for avoiding such harassment was that it would tend to split the allies, which "the Russians would consider . . . a very favorable turn of events."[132]

After the successful evacuation of U.S./U.N. forces from North Korea at the end of December, Acheson encountered further resistance to his view that Russian air support of China was a factor to be feared in the war, this time from his two closest advisers in State. In response to Rusk's suggestion that punitive action should be taken against China to force acceptance of a ceasefire, Acheson asked whether in that case the U.S.S.R. would respond by bringing in air and sea power. Jessup "doubted that they would bring in air and sea power locally unless they were willing to do it generally because this would set off a major war." And Rusk went on to remind Acheson that the Russians could have dealt U.S. forces a heavy blow by air during the evacuation of North Korea. They had not done so, even though such action would have destroyed the U.S. ability to defend Japan. If the Soviets were interested in starting a general war, Rusk said, "this would have been a good way to do it."[133]

By the end of December, therefore, three reputable analysts in the State Department were beginning to argue either that the Soviets were not contemplating the initiation of a global war, or that limited harassment of China would not result in a major Soviet response. Walworth Barbour, of the U.S. embassy in Moscow, was even more precise: on January 15 his opinion was that air and naval activity directed against China would lead the Soviets to provide China with large-scale air defense but would not lead them to invoke the Sino-Soviet treaty or initiate anything other than "unofficial" Soviet military activity in Communist-held territory in Korea.[134]

A number of persons within the military supported this assessment, including General MacArthur. In urging the extension of military operations into China, he stated quite firmly that Soviet forces would not enter the fighting in Korea; he had "always felt that a Soviet decision to precipitate a general war would depend solely upon the Soviets' own estimate of relative strengths and capabilities, with little regard for other factors."[135] The Joint Strategic Plans Committee, which at the end of December had recommended intensified military activity directed at China, agreed with MacArthur's opinion that the U.S.S.R. would commit its own forces to the fighting only when it believed the time was right from its own standpoint. The joint chiefs' recommendations of January 12 did not include an analysis of possible Soviet response, presumably because they believed that operations against China would not greatly increase the risk of war with Moscow.

Others within the military establishment took a different tack in support of a policy of retaliation, attitudes that epitomized the Truman administration's approach to dealing with Communist regimes. On December 4 the three service secretaries argued for a policy of boldness in relation to China and for the need to overcome any feelings of timidity that the thought of Russian air force intervention might arouse: "Policies dictated by caution are as likely, or more likely, to involve us in war with Russia than those which indicate firmness of purpose."[136]

Clearly, there were sharply opposing viewpoints in the period from early December to mid-January with regard to Soviet reaction to any extension of hostilities involving China. Acheson, Clubb, Nitze, and the intelligence establishment considered it a strong possibility that such action would lead to the invocation of the Sino-Soviet Treaty of Alliance and to the onset of a large-scale war of attrition between China and the United States; the three service secretaries acknowledged Soviet entry as a risk worth taking, given the U.S. preference for boldness over caution; and the JSPC, General MacArthur, Kennan, Jessup, and Rusk argued variously that Soviet global security interests dictated noninvolvement in the war, that there was little evidence of Soviet intention to participate openly in the hostilities, and that noninvolvement might afford greater gains for Moscow than open intervention in Korea.

Seen from this perspective, it is perhaps surprising that in the period immediately following China's entrance into the Korean War there was not an extension of hostilities to include its territory. At the higher levels of the executive branch, the burden was almost entirely on Acheson to argue the case for restricting the conflict to Korea, and even he found it necessary to represent the case for a limited war against China in discussions with the British in early December. But in late autumn, the great uncertainty as to Soviet and Chinese intentions in Asia and the assessment that Moscow had dictated Peking's entry into Korea assisted his arguments against crossing the Yalu. Acheson also received support in December from CIA estimates indicating an increased Soviet readiness to risk global war; from the evidence that Moscow was augmenting China's air strength; and from Secretary Marshall, who was more cautious at that time than his joint chiefs.

The timing of Attlee's visit was also crucial in reminding the administration of the urgency of European needs during a period when attention was turned toward Asia. Although the whiff of "unilateralism" was in the air, an extension of the war without the support of the allies and at the risk of undermining European policy was not an attractive prospect. The British made it only too clear that they could not support an expanded war; in their view even a "limited war" against China as outlined at the talks would lead to conflict with the U.S.S.R., and a policy of harassment of China would not get America anywhere even if it were carried on for years. A withdrawal of British support for the Korean War effort was particularly undesirable at a time when U.S. military force levels in Korea were recognized as inadequate and General MacArthur's requested reinforcements could not be provided until early in 1951. The allied and U.N. reaction to "hot pursuit," bombing the Yalu bridges, and the aggressor resolution also indicated that the United States would gain little, if any, support for widening the war, and that the cloak of legitimacy the U.N. had provided to U.S. policy in Korea would be completely removed.

Another reason the concept of an expanded war against China did not receive the necessary support in December was that energies were taken up with developing plans to concentrate and possibly to evacuate U.S./U.N. forces. In addition, General Collins returned on December 8 from a visit to Korea, convinced that the troops were not in a critical condition and that a junction could be made between the Tenth Corps and the Eighth Army, leading to the establishment of a bridgehead at Pusan.[137] On December 11 the Tenth Corps began its evacuation from Hungnam, moving—without serious military loss—17,500 vehicles, 550,000 tons of bulk cargo, and 105,000 troops. (Truman described the news as the best Christmas present he had ever had.) The military situation, then, was less critical and more encouraging in mid-December, perhaps undercutting the arguments of those who advocated immediate retaliation against Chinese territory.

But as the new year opened, the Chinese launched a further offensive that pushed U.S./U.N. forces south of the 38th Parallel, and public opinion and attitudes within the U.S. bureaucracy hardened toward the Chinese. Admiral Sherman said that it was time to stop equivocating and to recognize the state of war that existed between China and the United States. Dean Rusk spoke of meting out punishment harsh enough to make the Chinese accept a cease-fire. The joint chiefs eventually presented a set of proposals to be considered once positions in Korea had stabilized or when complete evacuation had taken place. These included a naval and economic blockade of China, reinforcement and support of the Chinese Nationalists in operations against China, and an increase in covert operations against the mainland government. The discussion of this memorandum indicated that support was building within the administration for tougher action. Secretary Marshall spoke of the possibility of unilateral U.S. action; he and General Bradley reminded those present of the pressures to "do something" emanating from both Congress and the general public. The country seemed confused by America's involvement in a war it would not go all out to win. Truman appeared to find some merit in these arguments as well as in the opinions expressed by his secretary of state, but he refrained from making a decision beyond encouraging his officials to do all they could to "embarrass" the Chinese Communist government.

It became agreed policy to retaliate against Chinese air bases if Chinese air power was used to attack U.S. forces in Korea, outside of Korea, or in transit to or from Korea, but Acheson managed to block implementation of the other recommendations by suggesting further study of the role Chiang Kai-shek's forces could play in the conflict, and by raising questions about the relative efficacy of a naval blockade as compared with stricter economic measures.[138] A clear and strongly argued paper produced in the State Department also must have helped his case. The United States had assured its allies of its intention to localize the war in Korea, the document said; no U.N. approval for military measures against China would be forthcoming, and unilateral action would "confirm all the fears and suspicions about our motives and intentions which have been expressed by our enemies and thought by some of our friends." In addition, the unity among Western nations and their ability to defend themselves in the future would be jeopardized. Furthermore, U.S. leadership in and out of the United Nations would be compromised. The paper went on to ask whether there was any evidence that limited military action would deter China from further aggression or undermine Communist control: "After Korea," it warned, "the United States cannot afford a second military 'failure' against China."[139]

Points such as these had to be thought through before additional military measures could be taken against China. On January 17, Generals Collins and Vandenberg returned from Korea convinced that the military situation had greatly improved once again. This fact, combined with the considerations the State Department had raised, brought the Defense Department around to Acheson's position. On January 19, Acheson asked Vandenberg and Collins whether failure to breach the Yalu border was handicapping U.S./U.N. forces. Optimistic at that time, both denied that it was. Already it was apparent that the Chinese were suffering severe logistical problems as a result of U.S. bombing operations in North Korea. If the United States really wanted to go to the source of supply, it would have to go into Russia, Vandenberg said, and he was "not in any sense urging that [the U.S.] do this."[140] Shortly thereafter, the joint chiefs confirmed that conditions had changed in Korea; the prospect of being forced into a beachhead had influenced the views expressed in their January 12 memorandum, but they now agreed that a blockade of China should not be established unless U.N. troops were forced out of Korea, and it certainly should not be established unilaterally. As regards aerial reconnaissance, the U.S. military was "now respecting Chinese territorial waters and . . . not overflying Manchuria." From a military viewpoint, circumstances did not warrant the use of Chinese Nationalist forces against the mainland: "Our actions now are based on the premise that we should do nothing to spread the war outside Korea."[141]

Rusk agreed; his loyalty to Acheson reasserted itself in late January, and he dismissed the possibility of direct action against the PRC. In early February he argued that a blockade and the bombing of air bases in Manchuria would not have much effect anyway. Rusk also modified his opinion with respect to Soviet support for China: reflecting Acheson's views more closely, he said that a sea and air attack on China and support for Chiang Kai-shek's forces "would be inadvisable because of the great probability of direct Soviet intervention." Collins and Bradley were now willing to agree that such a course of action "would involve excessive risks at this time." In these circumstances, a better solution would be to work for a stabilization of military lines, a ceasefire based on the 38th Parallel, and a phased withdrawal of all foreign troops.[142]

A consensus had been reached, and the conflict in Korea remained confined to the peninsula during this most critical stage of the hostilities. A limited extension of the war had been seriously considered, however, and the notion of "punishing the Chinese aggressor" for American casualties remained a potent idea. Retaliatory action had so far been withheld chiefly because of divided views as to probable Soviet reaction to an attack on China.[143] In the light of this uncertainty, lack of allied support for an expanded war, and American political and military weaknesses, the Truman administration urged a negotiated settlement based on the prewar status quo.

[5]

Countercurrents, or the Relationship between Means and Ends: March 1951–February 1952

During the third phase of the war, the drawbacks inherent in a limited-war policy became more apparent and generated tensions in the policy-making body. The frustrations were deeply rooted and went beyond the immediate problem of Korea. The very concept of limited war, with no lure of outright victory, was alien to American experience. It required both the public and the policy makers to overcome the tendency toward impatience in foreign affairs, and to put aside the search for a decisive and recognizable end to the conflict.

There were compelling reasons for not going all out to win in Korea. The improved military position from mid-January 1951 onward, the return of U.S./U.N. troops to the 38th Parallel in March, and the opening of the armistice negotiations in July undercut the need and desire to consider removing geographical restrictions on the war. Policy makers therefore held fast to the consensus forged in February 1951: that an extended war involved excessive risk and would not occasion allied support. The relief in April of General MacArthur as Commander in Chief, Far East and as U.N. commander, and the publication of the major part of the testimony gathered in the hearings called to investigate the general's dismissal, also served to bolster support for a limited-war policy.

Yet there was a reverse side to these events: the opening of the truce negotiations raised the prospect that acceptance of the *status quo ante bellum* would not provide an opportunity to deflate the military prestige of the Chinese Communist forces; more important, it could mean that the United States would face a "stalemate" war, tying down indefinitely large numbers of American troops. Neither scenario guaranteed that a peace settlement in Korea could be concluded, or—if it could—that it would be adhered to.

THE SEARCH FOR A NEGOTIATED SETTLEMENT

The turn of the tide in the Korean fighting began with the failure of the Chinese offensive in late January. General Matthew Ridgway, who had taken charge of the Eighth Army after Lt. General Walton H. Walker's accidental death, was credited then and subsequently, with the success of the U.S./U.N. military operations that month. But the steady lengthening of Chinese supply lines also had an impact on the fighting—a significant factor when Washington considered whether to move north once again. The improvement in U.S./U.N. fortunes removed any remaining doubts regarding the ability to hold in Korea. Seoul was recaptured in early March, and toward the end of the month, U.S./U.N. forces were reestablished along the 38th Parallel. In the State Department's estimation, the U.N. Command should now stay put on that line because of "(a) the capability of the Moscow-Peiping axis to inflict a decisive defeat upon United Nations forces if they make the decision to do so, (b) the risk of extending the Korean conflict to other areas and even into general war at a time when [the U.S. was] not ready to risk general war, (c) the heavy additional drain on American manpower and resources without a clearly seen outcome of the effort, (d) loss of unity among [America's] allies and in the United Nations in support of the Korean effort, and (e) the diversion of additional United States effort from other vital requirements."[1] The statement represented a clear and forceful argument for accepting limited U.S. objectives in Korea.

Arrival at the parallel also held out the prospect that the conditions existed for seeking a ceasefire. On February 12, C. B. Marshall, of the Policy Planning Staff, had suggested to Paul Nitze that stabilization of the military line along the 38th Parallel would involve both American and Chinese concessions, thereby saving "two sets of faces."[2] Because of conversations he had held in January with a "Third Party" from Peking, Marshall believed that the Chinese really wanted a ceasefire. On January 30, Peking had attempted to get a letter through to the U.S. government, a gesture

that Marshall said ought to be taken with the "utmost seriousness"; the United States should suggest that Chinese and North
Korean armies withdraw north of the parallel and U.S./U.N. forces
come to rest at that point.[3] To Marshall, indirect contacts between
Peking and Washington (which were finally damaged by the passage of the "aggressor" resolution in the U.N.) indicated that the
Chinese—under the pressure of an internal crisis, rising tensions,
and divisions within their leadership—were hoping for a
ceasefire.[4] The CIA confirmed in March that the Communist
armies had suffered heavy losses, and that new Chinese troops
entering Korea were likely to be less effective fighters than the
previous forces.[5]

George Kennan favored working through Moscow to achieve an
armistice. He suggested in mid-March that the time had come to
approach the Russians informally and secretly, since there was "a
mutuality of interest" between the United States and the Soviet
Union "sufficient to make possible such an arrangement." If the
Russians replied that the Chinese should be in on the conversations, America should "play the role of the offended party," he
said, "insisting that the Chinese Communists were hysterical and
childlike and that it was impossible to do business with them,
whereas the Russians were responsible, businesslike and, after all,
the real power to deal with."[6]

Moscow had in fact been taking various soundings at the United
Nations in March. Foreign Minister Andrei Gromyko, for example,
had let the secretary-general know that the U.S.S.R. was interested
in initiating bilateral discussions with the United States in order to
negotiate a settlement in Korea, and Soviet ambassadors in London and New Delhi were hinting that the time had come to take up
the question of a ceasefire.[7] Charles Bohlen, then based in Paris,
was thus assigned to sound out Vladimir Semyonov, political ad-
viser to the chairman of the Soviet Control Commission in Germany, but he was rebuffed on this occasion: Semyonov asserted
that such matters should be broached with Gromyko.[8]

The rebuff may have been caused by General MacArthur's
March 24 statement to Communist military commanders. Indeed,
the manner and timing of MacArthur's intervention seriously
damaged Washington's ability to seek discussions with Moscow or
to pursue the suggestion of additional approaches to Peking. While
ostensibly pledging his readiness "to confer in the field with the

Commander-in-Chief of the enemy forces," MacArthur exaggerated the military success of the U.S./U.N. campaign and deni-
grated the capacity of the Chinese to conduct technologically advanced warfare: "This new enemy, Red China," he said, "of such
exaggerated and vaunted military power, lacks the industrial capacity to provide adequately many critical items essential to the
conduct of modern war." Additionally, he warned the Chinese of
the dire consequences of any extension of the war into their territory: "The enemy . . . must by now be painfully aware that a decision of the United Nations to depart from its tolerant effort to
contain the war to the area of Korea through expansion of our
military operations to his coastal areas and interior bases would
doom Red China to the risk of imminent military collapse."[9] It was
hardly the kind of declaration that would encourage an adversary
to begin negotiations, and it prevented Truman from issuing a
planned presidential announcement that held out the prospect of a
wider settlement of Far Eastern problems. MacArthur's unauthorized intervention was the final straw as far as Truman was concerned; an act so disloyal to the U.S. commander in chief convinced the president to remove the five-star general from his
command.[10]

MacArthur's statement may well have held up the peace process
for several more weeks, but his dismissal occasioned two major
foreign policy addresses by Truman and Acheson in April, in
which they both emphasized that the spread of hostilities in Asia
would risk a third world war, and that the United States was
seeking a peaceful settlement of the conflict in Korea.[11] The blunt-
ing of another Chinese offensive in May finally allowed this sentiment to be acted upon. At John Paton Davies's suggestion, Kennan
was asked to arrange a meeting with the Soviet ambassador to the
U.N., Jacob Malik, which took place at the end of May. At a second
meeting on June 5, Malik confirmed that the Soviet government
wanted a ceasefire in Korea at the "earliest possible moment."; he
suggested, however, that the United States should work directly
with the North Koreans and Chinese, since Soviet forces "were not
participating in the hostilities." Despite this disclaimer, it was Malik's radio address on June 23, in which he called for a "ceasefire
and an armistice providing for the mutual withdrawal of forces
from the 38th parallel," that prompted the formal start of armistice
negotiations on July 10th.[12]

Concurrently with the effort to open armistice negotiations, the Truman administration undertook a major review of Asian policy, culminating in the production of NSC 48/5.[13] This document specified that the current objective of U.S. policy was to seek the unification of Korea by political rather than military means. It meant, effectively, a return to the prewar position in Korea, since political discussions were not thought likely to be meaningful. Immediate objectives included the termination of hostilities under "appropriate armistice arrangements," the establishment of South Korean authority at least as far north as the 38th Parallel, and the withdrawal of non-Korean armed forces from the peninsula. While these objectives were being sought, the document advocated continuing "strong efforts to deflate Chinese Communist political and military strength and prestige by inflicting heavy losses on Chinese forces in Korea." The United States should also intensify activities designed to turn the Chinese people against their current leaders and to develop a new non-Communist leadership. Despite this proposed harassment of the Chinese, however, it was clear that the main goal now was to confine and terminate the conflict: the United States should "seek to avoid the extension of hostilities in Korea into a general war with the Soviet Union, and seek to avoid the extension beyond Korea of hostilities with Communist China, particularly without the support of [America's] major allies."

The U.S. government recognized that the war had seriously overstretched its military resources, rendering it even more problematic for America and its allies to withstand a general war. Whereas the availability of manpower to the Communist forces was deemed to be virtually unlimited, the U.N. Command was severely constrained in this respect. NSC 48/5 confirmed that "dependable South Korean units" were to be developed to take over the major part of the burden in Korea, but this was a long-term goal. In the meantime, ROK troops were not highly thought of as fighting material. In early May, in fact, General James A. Van Fleet, commander of the Eighth Army, had argued that until these troops had demonstrably competent leadership, "there sh[ou]ld be no further talk of the US furnishing arms and equipment for additional forces."[14]

Of greater concern to the United States than the comparative strengths of ground forces was the enhancement of Communist air power that had begun in the spring of 1951. Hoyt Vandenberg noted rumors of the formation of a Soviet "volunteer" air force, and Rusk reported that conversations in Russian had been intercepted between enemy planes and the ground.[15] Overall, national intelligence estimates at this time indicated that the Soviet Union had the ability to "(a) expel the US from Korea, (b) ensure successful defenses of the Chinese mainland against any force . . . (c) attain air superiority over Korea, the Sea of Japan, and probably Japan proper, (d) attack the Japanese main island with sufficient force to overrun Hokkaido and probably also Honshu."[16] In these circumstances, the retention of limitations on the scope of the Korean fighting and the efforts to achieve a peaceful settlement were deemed prudent and wise.

The emphasis in NSC 48/5 on the risk of precipitating general war if anything other than the present restricted course of action were followed in Korea provided a major plank of the administration's argument at the MacArthur hearings in May and June of 1951. These congressional hearings were held to investigate the dismissal of General MacArthur and, more generally, to examine the administration's Far Eastern strategy and conduct of the war. The Truman administration's two most central and powerful arguments were, first, that limitations on the scope of the fighting would give the United States time to build up its own strength; second, that MacArthur's extended-war program not only could not guarantee an end to the conflict but would very likely bring the Soviet Union directly into the hostilities, at the same time estranging America from its NATO allies.[17]

In an impressive show of solidarity, all the administration's main witnesses stressed that global war could well result if MacArthur's ideas were implemented. They all reported that U.S. capabilities were not sufficient to withstand a wider Far Eastern conflict, and that the allies on whom America depended would desert the United States if such action were undertaken. General Bradley, in testimony that was excised from the public record at the time, stated that the Soviet Union could easily establish air superiority in the Far East and given the size of its Far Eastern armed forces, could compel U.S./U.N. forces to evacuate Korea entirely.[18] General Vandenberg (also in excised testimony) emphasized the limited nature of U.S. air capabilities in that part of the world and elsewhere: "The air force of the United States . . . is really a shoe-string air force and these groups that we have over there now doing this tactical job are really about a fourth of our total effort that we could muster today, and four times that amount of groups in that area over that vast expanse of China would be a drop in the bucket." The Soviets, on the other hand, could launch 2,000 planes—"much more than I have."[19]

Bradley also argued that Moscow was intimately involved in the planning of the war. Korea was "just one phase of this battle" between Moscow and Washington, he said, and the conflict there should not be allowed to sap America's strength. MacArthur's plan might be acceptable if military activity in the limited Far Eastern theater were the sole consideration, but from the global perspective Bradley considered it wrong.[20]

Part of Acheson's testimony detailed the terms of the Sino-Soviet military alliance and the reasons why the Truman administration believed that Moscow would come openly to the support of Peking if Chinese territory were attacked. "Even if the treaty did not exist," he said, "China is the Soviet Union's largest and most important satellite. Russian self-interest in the Far East and the necessity of maintaining prestige in the Communist sphere make it difficult to see how the Soviet Union could ignore a direct attack upon the Chinese mainland."[21] And as Secretary George C. Marshall pointed out, there was already plenty of evidence of Soviet support for its Communist allies even at this level of hostilities: Soviet pilots were flying the MIGs, implementing ground-to-air communications systems, building up sophisticated antiaircraft protection, and providing the wherewithal for mining the east coast of Korea.[22]

Acheson also explained, for those interested in maintaining the allied coalition, his view of the requirements of a successful alliance. Given extreme allied reluctance to countenance an expanded war, an American decision to adopt such a course of action would shake confidence in the United States as a partner: "The power of our coalition to deter an attack depends in part upon the will and the mutual confidence of our partners," he said.[23] Admiral Forrest P. Sherman added that he considered solidarity with the allies essential to an effective naval blockade. The Soviet Union might disregard or forcibly oppose a unilateral American blockade; in his opinion, a U.N. operation would be the "only effective course."[24]

The joint chiefs pointed to the military benefits that U.S./U.N. forces were deriving from the preservation of the Chinese "sanctu-

ary" north of the Yalu; as Vandenberg put it, "the sanctuary business, as it is called, is operating on both sides."[25] There were many
other military actions the Chinese could undertake, Bradley warned, but "they have not used air against our front line troops,
against our lines of communication in Korea, our ports; they have
not used air against our bases in Japan or against our naval forces."[26] So why risk, Marshall asked, attacking their "scattered targets in Manchuria," thereby exposing America's "vulnerable" and
"highly concentrated" targets in Korea to retaliation?[27] Bradley
emphasized not only the risk but also the futility of extending the
war into China: the U.S. Air Force already had a supply line of
about 200 miles to work on, which could be subjected to concentrated attack. Extending this line another 200 miles into Manchuria
would merely thin out the bombing operations.[28]

A number of senators asked for an explanation of the failure to
implement some of the lesser courses of action that MacArthur had
proposed, such as the bombing of Rashin and the use of Chiang
Kai-shek's troops. Generals J. Lawton Collins and Bradley responded that the Rashin operation risked a Soviet reprisal; moreover, they said, it would not be effective because Rashin had no rail
connections to the south, and any supplies there could simply be
moved across the border to Vladivostock.[29]

The military also deployed some very strong arguments against
the proposed use of Chinese Nationalist troops in Korea. Marshall,
for example, feared they might not fight any better than South
Korean troops. Collins put it even more bluntly: "We were highly
skeptical that we would get anything more out of these Chinese
than we were getting out of the South Koreans, because they were
the same people that were run off China, in the first place."[30]

It was a well-orchestrated performance by the administration
and seemed to convince many of those with a genuine interest in
foreign affairs, apart from the diehard "Asia-Firsters," that Mac-
Arthur's recommendations stemmed from his preoccupations as a
theater commander. The united way in which its main spokesmen
explained the limited-war policy benefited the executive branch.
The published testimony of military personnel in particular did not
entirely reflect the views they had held in late December and early
January on such subjects as the naval blockade, the sanctuary in
Manchuria, and the plan to bomb Rashin—where, as late as February, Marshall had favored an attack—but it served in May and June

to convince the "weight of articulate opinion" and the liberal press that the administration's strategy was correct. Even Acheson's critics in the media complimented him on the quality of his testimony (though they tempered their praise by suggesting that he could now "resign with honor"). Among certain sections of the public, therefore, the administration's case for limited war had been sustained.[31]

FACTORS UNDERMINING THE LIMITED WAR POLICY

The results of the hearings were not all of positive benefit to the administration, however, nor particularly conducive to the maintenance of a limited-war policy. In the State Department's view, the concentration on America's China policy had heightened the general public's realization of the magnitude of the "loss of China" to Communism, and congressional criticism had served to undermine public confidence in the diplomatic establishment. In an April 1951 poll, the majority had favored bombing bases in Manchuria and assisting Chiang to return to the mainland; one-third had favored launching a general war against China. The hearings did little to deflect the general public from these views.[32]

Moreover, what the administration could not avoid, as it explained its case, was a decisive loss of flexibility in an already hardened diplomatic posture toward China. Although Acheson had restated on May 3 that he did not want America to be committed to "all-out and limitless assistance to Chiang Kai-shek,"[33] the ties between the United States and the Chinese Nationalist regime were bound ever more tightly during the hearings. General Marshall, for example, conceded that Taiwan would never be allowed to fall into the hands of the Communists, or the PRC allowed to assume a seat in the United Nations. These statements and others made in mid-1951 would mean, according to Warren Austin, America's U.N. ambassador, that if there were "no settlement in Korea, the public pressure to get peace or hit harder [would] increase." In Austin's view, the "toughened" policy outlined at the hearings had made a settlement more imperative but, at the same time, more difficult to obtain, since it "leaves us without a bargaining position."[34] Nor was it helpful to ceasefire efforts that the U.S. Military Advisory and Assistance Group, headed by

General William C. Chase, arrived in Taipei in May 1951 to help with the task of training Chiang's forces.

Furthermore, during that same month, Rusk and Dulles made uncompromising speeches against the government in Peking on the day that the U.N. General Assembly adopted a resolution recommending a total embargo on strategic goods to China and North Korea. Rusk's hard words seemed to rule out any future accommodation with the PRC: "The Peiping regime may be," he said, "a colonial Russian government—a Slavic Manchukuo on a large scale. It is not the Government of China. It does not pass the first test. It is not Chinese."[35]

It has recently been argued that Rusk's speech may have been designed to goad non-Stalinist Chinese Communists to act more like Chinese nationalists; in this respect, it could be regarded as a contribution to the previous efforts to drive a wedge between Peking and Moscow. It may also have been intended to protect the administration from rightist political attacks.[36] But at the time, few saw the speech in that light. Acheson needed to explain to the president, for example, that Rusk had not put forward any new policy toward China but had simply reiterated what had been said in the past.[37]

Despite this disavowal that the speech represented a change in policy, it caused considerable consternation within the State Department and in allied capitals. Acheson told Rusk that in the future he wanted all speeches on controversial subjects cleared with him personally.[38] But the damage had been done. The British ambassador expressed the view of many diplomats when he observed that the administration's Far Eastern policy seemed to be "drifting . . . in the direction of that espoused by General MacArthur."[39] The unrest was ironic in view of what the executive branch had been arguing before Congress, but explicable as a casualty of the domestic turmoil in which the United States formulated its foreign policy.

INCREASING MILITARY PRESSURE AGAINST CHINA

The hardened U.S. stance vis-à-vis the PRC conflicted with the administration's desire to begin truce negotiations with the Communists and with the attempts to build support for limiting the war to the Korean peninsula. So, too, did discussions and planning, both before and after the MacArthur hearings, that envisaged war with China under certain circumstances. This activity succeeded in bringing to the surface the tensions that underlay the eschewing of all-out victory in Korea.

One of the most emphatic statements MacArthur had made at the hearings was that the joint chiefs had supported his views on the need to expand the war into China, citing passages from the January 12 memorandum as proof of this contention. Though they disputed MacArthur's interpretation of this document (arguing that it was written at a time when the United States was likely to be forced into a beachhead or to evacuate Korea entirely), the secretary of defense and his joint chiefs did move closer to the general's position in their secret testimony before the joint committee. They agreed that it would be necessary, under certain circumstances, to reexamine the limitations imposed on the geographical scope of the conflict. They also revealed that MacArthur had been authorized to retaliate against China if its forces attacked U.N. troops outside Korea (that is, in Japan, Okinawa, or the Philippines); if the Chinese launched an air-sea attack against Japan; or if their air force launched a massive air attack on U.S./U.N. troops inside Korea. Under these conditions, Marshall told the senators, the U.N. commander had authority "to bomb airfields, air depots, and air generally in Manchuria and in Central China, in Shantung province in Central China in the immediate vicinity of Wei-hei-wei."[40] Bradley revealed less about policy and more about the military's attitude to the application of force when he commented that if the present limited-war policy failed to work, they might consider a MacArthur-style alternative: "Now, if . . . you cannot solve it . . . in a few months we may say, 'Yes, we cannot do it any other way, and now we will do these things.' "[41]

China's entrance into the war and the production of the January 12 memorandum had prompted the development of contingency plans and various feasibility studies in reference to an expanded war. As noted earlier, the joint chiefs had recommended in early January that preparations be made to impose a naval blockade of China, that air reconnaissance restrictions be removed, that the ban on Chinese Nationalist operations against the PRC be lifted, and that support for those efforts directed at the mainland be increased. They also recommended the provision of covert assistance to nationalist guerilla forces in China. Although consideration of this memorandum was terminated once NSC 48/5 had been accepted, some of the actions it recommended were implemented or examined in greater detail during the spring of 1951. In April, for example, the U.N. Command was given permission to conduct air reconnaissance of air bases in Manchuria and the Shantung peninsula, in view of the increase in Communist air capabilities.[42]

In addition, and as a result of the State Department's earlier query concerning the proposed use of Kuomintang (KMT) troops against mainland China, the military had undertaken a study of their likely effectiveness. The report was completed on March 14 and submitted to the NSC for consideration; it stated that Nationalist troops were "incapable of withstanding a prolonged and determined all-out assault by Chinese Communist forces," and only under certain circumstances involving U.S. assistance would they be able to "execute limited operations against the mainland." At the MacArthur hearings, the joint chiefs repeated that they were highly skeptical of the worth of Chiang's forces. What was left out of their testimony to the senators, however, was the observation made in March that assistance to Nationalist troops could have enormous potential benefits for U.S. policy goals in Asia, and that the provision of U.S. support could, in the joint chiefs' view, bring these forces to the point of efficiency equal to that of the average Chinese Communist soldier. KMT troops constituted "the only immediately available ground forces for use on the mainland of China, and their acceptance and use would inspire hope among millions of non-Communist Chinese on the mainland of China and non-Communist sympathizers throughout Asia. An increase in the tempo of guerilla activity and sabotage within Communist China would be promoted, while, at the same time, the threat of Nationalist landings on the China coast would prevent further CCF [Chinese Communist Forces] withdrawal from South China for transfer to Manchuria and Korea. Furthermore, this trend combined with possible large-scale guerilla activity in Kwangsi and Yunnan would materially reduce pressure on Hong Kong and Macao, and reduce support of the Viet Minh." Given the potential benefits, it is not surprising that the joint chiefs recommended U.S. involvement with guerilla warfare on the mainland as "a prelude to larger overt operations using Chinese Nationalist forces if such should appear practicable in the future."[43]

In support of these recommendations, and despite State Department fears, the joint chiefs approved MacArthur's request "to make a show of force" in the coastal regions of eastern and southern China and in the Taiwan Strait area in order to obtain photographic intelligence of those regions, including Hainan.[44] The mission was carried out on April 11 and 13 and also involved a visit to Taiwan by the new commander of the Seventh Fleet, Vice Admiral Harold M. Martin. It was a large and undoubtedly disturbing operation as far as the Peking leadership was concerned. The maneuvers undertaken on the 13th involved 20 American warships and 140 American aircraft.[45]

Concurrently with these attempts to increase military pressure on China, the State Department began a more systematic collection of information on guerilla activities on the mainland in order to promote what it called "third force" elements. O. Edmund Clubb proposed the formation of a State Department task force, involving himself, John Paton Davies, and Philip Sprouse[46] to work with and promote the activities of individuals such as Kan Chieh-hou as "third force" leaders. (Kan had once been a diplomatic representative for Li Tsung-jen, Chiang Kai-shek's long-time rival). Although "third force" activity was subsequently to prove abortive—because of the steady expansion of Chinese Communist control and fears that America's allies might see such activity as directed as much at Chiang Kai-shek as it was at the Communists—these undertakings increased interest in the possible political and military vulnerability of Communist China. On May 22 an intelligence estimate concluded that "covert US logistical support would substantially increase the capabilities of non-Nationalist and Nationalist resistance forces on the mainland, but not to the extent of posing a serious threat to the Chinese Communist regime or of precipitating full-scale war." Nevertheless, it considered that U.S. covert action would probably increase the problems of control in China (particularly in the south-central region), divert more of the government's resources to internal security problems, harass vital north-south communication lines, and weaken to some degree the regime's military capabilities.[47] For these reasons, and despite Chinese Communist political strength, covert operations still seemed worth expanding.

U.S. CONTINGENCY PLANS FOR A CHINESE EXPANSION OF THE WAR

While the Truman administration examined the feasibility of various covert and overt schemes designed to harass the PRC, it was also developing contingency plans to deal with any such increase in Chinese military activity as air attacks on U.S./U.N. troops, whether inside or outside Korea. It was agreed that in this eventuality large-scale naval and air strikes would be launched against China. If an air attack came in Korea, few saw any option but retaliation. Only Robert Hooker of the PPS argued that retaliation should not necessarily be automatic, "unless and until it has either been demonstrated that the offensive cannot be contained and defeated otherwise, or until the risk that we will be unable to defeat it is greater than we can afford to run."[48] But Hooker's voice seems to have been a lone one. Despite previously expressed fears that the Chinese and Soviets had the ability to attain air superiority over Korea, at this point it seemed that the absence of a Chinese air attack was all that kept the administration from an expansion of the war.

In February 1951 the Joint Strategic Planning Committee (JSPC) provided both political and military reasons why a Chinese attack outside Korea could not be dealt with by action inside Korea. There would be "no political choice other than to retaliate in China. . . . Aside from military considerations, no political party could retain the support of the people if it turned the other cheek." Besides, the committee argued, notable benefits could be derived from retaliation against China. Air attacks on the limited communication facilities of the Chinese would reduce their potential for operations in Korea and Indochina and against the regime's internal opponents. Additionally, this would intensify the economic strains the Chinese were experiencing and produce commensurate effects on the Soviet economy. U.S. bombing would also generate resentment against a leadership that had exposed its people in this way. Such retaliatory action might invite global war with the Soviet Union, but "inasmuch as the decision for Chinese attacks on U.N. forces outside of Korea would have been taken with the knowledge that retaliatory attacks were almost certain, it would appear that the USSR would have already made the decision regarding overt participation in the Korean war," thereby precipitating a world war.[49]

The JSPC acknowledged that the State Department would have problems in gaining allied support for retaliation against China if an air offensive were launched within Korea (although not if it came outside the country), and the Truman administration recognized that it must consult the other countries whose forces were fighting in Korea. To maintain the legitimacy of America's primary position in the U.N. Command, it was necessary to gain allied compliance with a retaliatory policy the United States regarded as essential. In early April, therefore, Rusk began to prepare the ground. At his regular briefing to the ambassadors of countries with troops in Korea, he warned that air support on a large scale might accompany the next Chinese offensive. The arrival of U.S./U.N. forces at the 38th Parallel appeared to be a mixed blessing, since it was just within range of the MIGs, he said, and in the event of a Chinese air strike, the U.S. Air Force must attempt "to meet it in every possible way."[50]

The allied response to this proposal caused much consternation in Washington and exacerbated State and Defense Department differences over this policy. The British were skeptical about the probability of a Chinese air strike. Why was it, the U.K. chiefs of staff asked, that if a massive air attack appeared imminent, no precautions were being taken against it? In their view, it was possible that the American administration "had considered that for military and domestic/political reasons authority to bomb Manchuria must be given and that enemy air attacks on a suitable scale would provide an adequate pretext."[51] (A suitable scale, according to Bradley, would be an attack by 50, 100, or 200 aircraft, but not by six.)[52]

The British insinuation annoyed the Americans, who saw it as a typical reaction from a power that, although now overshadowed by the United States, still saw fit to criticize American officials for what the British interpreted as their naiveté. But the dialogue on this question indicated how reluctant the U.K. government was even to talk about the possibility of an expanded war, whereas the U.S. administration wanted to face it as a serious possibility and next step. A further bone of contention between the two governments was the question of where the initiative for launching the attacks should lie. The British, above all, wanted to prevent leaving the decision in the hands of the UN commander, and they wanted time for the British cabinet to be consulted. But as Acheson argued in a personal message to the foreign minister, Herbert Morrison, (who was appointed to the post after the illness and death of Ernest Bevin), the U.N. Command "must retain the latitude to determine whether an attack requires immediate counteraction in order to preserve the safety of the forces."[53] In that case, Morrison replied, the U.K. government could go only so far as to agree "in principle" to be associated with the policy of counterattack; it would receive full British support only when the cabinet had been consulted at the time the emergency arose.[54]

It was not a wholly satisfactory outcome, and the issue of consultation with allied governments became a matter of contention between the State and Defense Departments, as well as between America and its allies. At a meeting of the joint chiefs and officials from the State Department on April 18, Vandenberg and Bradley strongly argued against waiting for allied views if an emergency arose. The British might be willing to sacrifice the brigade it had in Korea, but the United States could not sacrifice its nine divisions, Vandenberg said. Nitze, and the deputy undersecretary of state, H. Freeman Matthews, conceded that the United States should preserve its right to make the decision to counterattack, but they suggested that consultation should take place if possible. As Nitze said, it was "very important to have the U.K. with us, particularly if we get into a general war."[55]

On April 27 the question of consultation was again the main issue: General Ridgway, MacArthur's successor in Korea, requested that he be delegated the authority to decide to attack enemy bases in Manchuria and the Shantung peninsula following any major air attack from Manchuria or from behind enemy lines— a major air attack being defined as "a concerted effort by large numbers of enemy combat aircraft against our ground forces, rear bases, or fleet." The joint chiefs responded the next day that Ridgway was "hereby authorized at your discretion without further reference to the JCS or higher authority, to attack,"[56] although he should, if at all possible, seek the joint chiefs' advice before taking action. Acheson protested that this was not enough of a restraint, especially since the ambassadors of countries with forces in Korea had just been assured that the final decision on retaliation would reside in Washington.

In line with the method that had recently been developed for resolving serious interdepartmental disputes, Acheson and Vandenberg took the matter to the president for final decision. Truman approved the directive but added a final paragraph "which emphasized the vital necessity of informing Washington instantaneously if there were not opportunity for consultation with the JCS so that our allies could be informed and the risk of dissension on their part over the action would be minimized."[57] It was a decision that barely met Acheson's objections; as in a number of instances in the next few months, he had to modify his preferred course of action to accommodate military requirements.

PLANNING FOR U.S. EXPANSION OF THE WAR

Apparently, there were other disadvantages associated with regaining the 38th Parallel, apart from the danger of air attack. Despite its relief at having regained that position, the Pentagon perceived hazards in what they thought of as a "stalemate" war centering on that line. On April 5 the joint chiefs sent a memorandum to the defense secretary in which they reviewed U.S. military policy in Korea and cautioned that an armistice that left Communist forces in the country would be detrimental to the U.S./U.N.: "It would constitute an unwarranted drain on our military resources, and would keep our forces in Korea." The JCS therefore recommended continuing military action in Korea until an acceptable political solution for the country appeared attainable "without jeopardizing United States positions with respect to the USSR, to Formosa, and seating the Chinese Communists in the United Nations." This would require the gradual increase of dependable South Korean units (the "Koreanization" of the war), immediate preparations for naval and air action against the Chinese mainland, and an assessment of the degree and nature of support the United States could expect from its allies "if, while continuing our present military course of action in Korea, operations against the mainland of China are initiated."[58]

The memorandum was forwarded to President Truman by the secretary of defense on April 9 and to the NSC for consideration on April 10.[59] Marshall appeared favorably disposed towards the joint chiefs' recommendations, but the memorandum seemed to bemuse the State Department. One unidentified member of the PPS wrote on his copy that he did not understand the logic that had led to the reference to action against China.[60] Certainly, it was an imprecise document, but its subsequent consideration in the NSC 48 series may help to explain the somewhat equivocal position of NSC 48/5. Although the latter document has rightly been regarded as a major statement of America's limited-war policy at a time

[147]

when a truce appeared attainable, it did contain recommendations for naval and air action against China, and operational support for KMT troops if Chinese aggression should occur outside Korea, or in the event that U.S./U.N. forces were forced to evacuate the peninsula. It also spoke of the need to deflate the political and military strength and prestige of the Chinese by inflicting heavy losses on their forces.[61]

The document "brought the administration surprisingly close to MacArthur's recommendations just at the time it was seeking publicly to refute them,"[62] but the same kinds of contradictions had surfaced on other occasions following China's entrance into Korea. The tensions were present because of a basic desire to exact retribution for the killing of American soldiers, because of a wish to inflict total defeat on the enemy, and because of a more sophisticated awareness of the frustrations and strategic weaknesses inherent in fighting a protracted, limited war in an area of secondary importance and against what Acheson had earlier called "the second team."[63]

One corollary of this attitude was a need to end the war as quickly as possible—if not by political, then by military means. On May 29, for example, 12 days after the acceptance of NSC 48/5, Admiral Sherman said that he was "coming around to the view that an honest-to-God naval blockade would be advisable." Bradley thought the United States should attempt "to solve the problem the way we were" and as the NSC had so recently decided; however, he acknowledged that if those efforts proved ineffective, "additional measures might be necessary."[64] At the same meeting, Sherman also advocated ignoring the 38th Parallel and moving north if the opportunity arose: "There were plenty of indications that the Chinese had taken punishment," he said. Bradley appeared to agree: "If there [was] no nibble from the other side, then perhaps the wraps ought to be taken off." Some of those present were nervous about these suggestions, but did affirm that U.S./U.N. forces might move north to the Wonsan-Pyongyang area (the neck or waist of the peninsula). Beyond that would be too risky, however.[65]

These kinds of discussions indicated that not everyone in the administration viewed a limited-war policy centered on the concept of an armistice at the 38th Parallel as the only course of action to be considered in mid-1951. Even after armistice negotiations were finally under way, Defense Department discussion soon moved to a consideration of the courses of action to be followed if armistice talks should break down, or if it should prove impossible to conclude an armistice. On July 13 (three days after the start of the talks) the joint chiefs forwarded a memorandum to the secretary of defense recommending an increase in military pressure on the enemy in the event that armistice negotiations failed. Such pressure should take the form of increased military operations in Korea to the maximum consistent with the capabilities and security of the forces, permission should be given to advance north, at least to the neck of the peninsula (approximately the 39th to 40th Parallel), and restrictions should be removed on bombing Rashin and the Yalu River dam and power complex. The memorandum also recommended an extension of the war outside Korea—to include "hot pursuit" into Manchuria with "destruction of enemy planes after landing, and neutralization of opposing anti-aircraft fire"—as well as support for a "vigorous campaign of covert operations" through effective aid to anti-Communist guerilla forces in China and Korea, and disruption of enemy lines of communication. Further, the 16 nations with forces in Korea should be induced to support the implementation of additional political and economic pressures against China, a naval blockade of the country, and an expansion of the U.N.'s potential for military operations through the commitment of additional fighting units. In addition, and over the longer term, the "organization, training, and equipping of Japanese defense forces" and the development and equipment of "dependable" South Korean units should be speeded up to augment capabilities in the area.[66]

On July 18 the secretary of defense forwarded these recommendations to the president without comment, since—as he explained—his opinion had not been formulated at the time. However, the delay caused by Marshall's lengthy consideration of the document did not prevent the stepping-up of military operations in Korea in the meantime. Despite the continuing armistice negotiations, bombing operations in July and August became more punitive. Ridgway, for example, reported a plan to launch an air strike on Pyongyang using 140 medium and light bombers and 230 fighter aircraft, and on July 25 the JCS agreed, provided that no publicity be given to the "mass" nature of the raid.[67] At the beginning of August, Ridgway requested the removal of restrictions on the bombing of Rashin. General Bradley contradicted the testimony he had given at the MacArthur hearings by granting permission to bomb this target, requesting that the secretary of defense obtain the president's final approval. Whereas the military views of the joint chiefs had previously been overruled by considerations "advanced strongly by the Secretary of State," in August of 1951 Acheson conceded the case.[68]

The State Department would also shortly alter its position on other questions raised in the July 13 memorandum. In August the department produced a draft position paper covering action to be taken within the U.N. should an armistice agreement not be achieved. The draft outlined several possible enemy responses to a failure of the truce talks, from a de facto ceasefire to a massive ground and/or air offensive. The paper proposed that each scenario be related to a particular U.S./U.N. military response and stressed the need to consult the 16 nations participating in the Korean operations before initiating the courses of action the joint chiefs had envisaged in their policy paper.[69] Bradley and the JCS, however, regarded these refinements as "not only unsound but so dangerous militarily as possibly to jeopardize the security of the United Nations forces in Korea."[70] Since the considered views of the Truman administration were shortly to be placed before Morrison during a foreign ministers' meeting in Washington, it was essential that these differences between State and Defense be overcome.

Some of the differences were explored further at a State Department meeting with the joint chiefs on August 29.[71] As summarized by Bradley, the crucial differences were whether or not to let the enemy take the initiative in the war, and whether or not to undertake further military action without consultation with the allies. The prospect of long-drawn-out armistice negotiations in Korea frustrated Bradley. In his view, it was necessary to "solve the situation and bring it to a definitive end." If the truce talks failed, "we could not sit there to see what the enemy was going to do, as that might involve sitting there five years . . . that would not be supported by the public and it would be necessary to take positive steps, not just wait and see." Moreover, if negotiations ended and hostilities were renewed, "it would not suffice to slap the enemy on the arm instead of on the wrist; it would be necessary to knock him out."[72]

Rusk did not disagree pointedly, but he placed great emphasis on the need to consult with the allies before undertaking a naval blockade, "hot pursuit," or bombing beyond Korea's borders. Bradley demurred, arguing that air action involved only U.S. forces, not those of the allies. Rusk tried another approach by reminding Bradley that the contemplated retaliatory action might precipitate general war—in which case the country "would be in much better shape with [its] allies if [it] had taken them into confidence," he said.[73]

By September 8 the State Department had given some ground to the Pentagon, and a redraft of the State position paper supported many of the original JCS recommendations. An interim decision to press for a complete economic blockade of China, and for agreement within the U.N. or with as many countries as possible to prohibit their ships from calling at Chinese ports, helped resolve State-Defense differences over the blockade. It was also decided to reexamine the use of Nationalist forces in operations against the Chinese mainland.[74]

The same day this redraft was sent to the Defense Department, Acheson outlined to the U.K. foreign minister the course America planned to pursue if the armistice talks should fail. Reading from the position paper, he sought British reactions to such proposals as moving to the neck of the peninsula, attacking the Yalu River dams and power installations, training and equipping Japanese defense forces, and a total economic blockade of China. He did not refer to the decision to reexamine the use of KMT troops, nor did he mention proposed covert operations. In reply, Morrison restated the familiar British position: "The UK was anxious not to become involved in a mainland war with China" and did not want to retaliate unless there was really good cause; the British government was unwilling to take action that might further cement China's defensive union with Russia. Furthermore, in the British view, if the United Nations became more heavily involved in the Far East, "the Soviets would likely start trouble elsewhere." Morrison was also concerned about the prospect of training Japanese forces, and he raised some doubts about the effectiveness of a blockade against China. Nevertheless, and despite these cautionary comments, a measure of agreement was reached on the other courses of action Acheson outlined, and the British government imposed no formal restrictions on U.S. contingency planning.[75]

[151]

Subsequently, there were similar discussions with Canada, Australia, and New Zealand. Canada, too, reported "little basic difference between Canadian views and the general thinking of the United States government" on the question of action to be taken if armistice talks broke down. The Canadian General Staff was against a strategic advance to the neck of Korea because it would lengthen U.S./U.N. supply lines while shortening those of the Communists, but it recognized the need for tactical maneuvering. The government in Ottawa also reiterated its desire to be consulted prior to any advance. Both Britain and Canada had indicated their reluctance to provide additional reinforcements for Korea, as well as general concern regarding a blockade of China; overall, however, U.S. and allied views on how to respond to a failure of the armistice negotiations were seen to be "closely parallel."[76]

These discussions with allies were deemed essential in America because in mid-September the prospects for an armistice appeared "discouraging." (Negotiations had in fact been recessed since August 23 as a result of confirmed and alleged U.N. violations of the Kaesong neutral zone). Consequently, some members of the State and Defense Departments had come to believe that it would be better for the United States to break off (not simply recess) the negotiations, once it had been determined that a new and major Communist offensive was underway, than to wait for a Communist decision to stop the talks. Since this change of policy made it necessary to convince the public that the Communists were entirely to blame for the breakdown in negotiations, the State Department, in consultation with the Psychological Strategy Board, developed a plan—code-named Operation Broadbrim—designed to inform world opinion that the Communists had been trying to sabotage the peace talks. The plan was also aimed at enhancing covert operations to increase dissatisfaction inside China and promote discord between Peking and Moscow.[77] At this stage of the war, the administration appeared "more interested in preparing public opinion at home and abroad for the breakdown of peace talks than in building up support for a ceasefire."[78]

Fortunately, on September 20 the Communists proposed the resumption of truce discussions and thus, for the time being, prevented further discussion of terminating the talks. However, even after the resumption of negotiations on October 25, their slow pace continued to frustrate the Defense Department, which still felt that inconclusive military operations in Korea could lead to the steady attrition of manpower and materials. Before long, the department argued, U.S. public opinion would not support a policy that failed to bring about a successful military conclusion to the war.[79] For these reasons, the JCS again attempted to toughen U.S. activity at the forthcoming session of the United Nations. The American delegation, Defense officials said, should emphasize "the necessity of applying more decisive measures than heretofore." It should demand that a "total trade embargo be imposed immediately" and that arrangements for a naval blockade be worked out.[80]

The Pentagon was becoming so concerned over the prolongation of the negotiations that it next moved to consider the position to be taken should the armistice not be signed in the near future. Since lengthy discussions were providing the Communists with opportunities to build up their strength, particularly in the air, the joint chiefs proposed in early November that the U.S. Air Force should unilaterally bomb Chinese air bases whenever Chinese air activity was on such a scale as to jeopardize the security of U.S./U.N. forces. The State Department was fearful of this new suggestion, because now the military wanted permission to take the bombing decision before a Chinese air attack had actually occurred, and solely in response to an unspecified increase in air activity.[81] This, of course, contradicted the contingency policy that had been agreed upon earlier, that such action would be taken only in the event of a major Chinese air attack on U.S./U.N. forces and even then would require the U.N. commander to seek instructions from Washington if time permitted, thus allowing the United States an opportunity to inform the other participating nations.

Further changes in policy were proposed in November in response to the protracted negotiations. Some progress had been made on the question of the demarcation line between forces, but final agreement was delayed because of a disagreement between the U.N. Command and Washington. General Ridgway wanted to stand firm on the principle that the line of contact should be that which existed on the date of the final armistice agreement, whereas Washington was willing to be more flexible and accept the present line of contact, with the proviso that it would be renegotiated if other issues were not settled within a reasonable period—about one month. Washington's view finally prevailed, and the demarcation line was established on November 27. The 30-day time limit expired, however, with little further progress made—in Ridgway's view, because the UN Command had lost bargaining strength. In particular, it was proving impossible to resolve the question of inspection arrangements designed to prevent a violation of the armistice agreement. Some members of the Truman administration, notably Generals Ridgway, Vandenberg, John E. Hull, and Admiral William M. Fechteler (the new chief of naval operations) considered inspection so essential that they would be willing to risk terminating the negotiations on this point.[82]

The solution was found in arrangements to deter a truce violation; essentially, the United States decided to trade the issue of inspection for a warning that should fighting be resumed in the future, the hostilities would be extended in scope and location. It was thought essential to obtain allied, particularly British, agreement to this, and Acheson and Bradley attempted to do so in November 1951 in a meeting with Anthony Eden, the new foreign secretary of a Conservative administration in London.[83] Acheson explained to Eden that since adequate inspection arrangements were unlikely to be agreed upon at the truce talks, the United States favored letting the Communists know that drastic measures would be taken if a violation of the armistice occurred. This warning was to form the substance of the "Greater Sanctions" statement, to be issued at the close of the war by as many as possible of the nations fighting on the U.N. side.

In November and December, Acheson described in some detail the retaliatory action proposed: at the minimum, it would take the form of an attack on China's air bases and a naval blockade of the China coast. General Vandenberg affirmed that the air action would not be directed primarily against Manchuria, since there were no targets there that would make the outcome decisive. Instead, he recommended hitting Chinese supply lines (including food supply) and creating general disruption within China by destroying railways and ports, and mining rivers. Such attacks, he said, would be launched from Okinawa, Guam, the Philippines, and carriers at sea.[84] The British gave their support to the "Greater Sanctions" statement, but they were reluctant to be tied to specific courses of action against China if the statement's provisions came into effect.

By January 1952, when Eden and Winston Churchill, once again Britain's prime minister, arrived in Washington, Acheson had become more determined. He described the war in Korea as being at a critical point; either an armistice agreement would be obtained soon, or the fighting would shortly take a more serious course. If there were no armistice, he said, or if one were entered into and later broken, it would be essential to bomb military targets in China and to institute a naval blockade. Bradley stated, in response to a question from Churchill, that it was not the U.S. intention to use the atomic bomb, "since up to the present time no suitable targets were presented. If the situation changed in any way . . . a new situation would arise." What Churchill did not know was that the Army, with presidential approval, had carried out Operation Hudson Harbor in late September and early October; this involved several simulated atomic strikes in support of U.S./U.N. ground offensives in Korea and demonstrated that timely identification of large masses of enemy troops was a rare occurrence.[85]

The British were no doubt uneasy about the discussion of atomic weapons, visualizing opposition attacks in Parliament and the disapprobation of public opinion in Britain if they should be used. But in general, Churchill and Eden were much less obstructive than previous Labour ministers had been. Churchill went out of his way to support the U.S. role as "leader" in the Far East and affirmed that the U.K. would "do its utmost to meet US views and requests in relation to that area." He also expressed support for America's Taiwan policy, and Eden explained that the British government no longer believed that "Titoism" could be fostered in China or that policy should be based "on such a tenuous possibility."[86] Only in respect to a naval blockade were they energetic in voicing their opposition, arguing against it on the grounds of its ineffectiveness unless it included Dairen and Port Arthur, at the risk of Soviet involvement. (In this regard, the United Kingdom was to receive the wholesale support of Canada, whose foreign minister doubted that the effects of a blockade would be felt in China for weeks or even months.)[87]

Allied reluctance on the question of a blockade notwithstanding, there was much evidence to show a growing disquiet within the administration during the second half of 1951 as a result of the "stalemate" war. Indications that shipping continued to enter Chinese Communist ports irritated Admiral Fechteler. In October, he said he was thinking in terms of a "genuine naval blockade," except for Port Arthur and Dairen, and he asserted that he had the means to do it.[88] Vandenberg also appeared to feel the time had come to take decisive action. He recalled his testimony at the Mac-Arthur hearings and his statement that U.S. airplanes should not cross the Yalu: "I said we might change our mind in six months. It is now six months. In April our plane production will be better. The situation has entirely changed."[89]

PUBLIC AND CONGRESSIONAL ATTITUDES

The long-drawn-out negotiations similarly frustrated the general public, which might soon demand that additional steps be taken to end the conflict, some officials argued. Reflecting this militancy, a survey showed that nearly 60 percent wanted the United States to give Chiang Kai-shek's forces all the help they needed to attack the Chinese Communists; in October, 60 percent also urged the bombing of China's air bases. Truman's presidency remained unpopular, and the truce discussions were becoming increasingly so. State Department surveys noted that in March 1951 a majority desired a settlement of the conflict at the 38th Parallel, but by November they were beginning to have doubts about the armistice and believed that U.N. air and ground strategy would have to be reconsidered if negotiations failed. In addition, as it became clear that the talks were going to be difficult and protracted, the increasingly impatient public began to revert to its previous position of support for General MacArthur, and to criticize Truman once again for having relieved him of command. MacArthur's dismissal not unexpectedly caused an uproar also among Truman's political critics in 1951. Senator Robert Taft and Congressman Joseph W. Martin, among others, discussed Truman's possible impeachment and vigorously supported MacArthur's case as outlined at the hearings. Joseph McCarthy went so far as to suggest that it was the "midnight potency of bourbon and Benedictine" that had led the president to dismiss "the greatest American" the senator knew. In June, not long after Marshall's testimony before Congress, McCarthy launched into a harangue lasting two and three-quarters hours against the secretary of defense, whom he described (along with Acheson) as being part of "a conspiracy on a scale so immense as to dwarf any previous such venture in the history of man. A conspiracy of infamy so black that, when it is finally exposed, its principals shall be forever deserving of the maledictions of all honest men."[90]

General attacks on the administration's Korean War policy also contributed to domestic pressure to expand the conflict if talks failed, and helped diminish support for continuing the negotiations. Senator Henry Cabot Lodge joined those who advocated the employment of atomic weapons if they could be used "efficiently and profitably." Senator Taft said he was not interested in any truce at the 38th Parallel, describing it as an "appeasement peace."[91] Others reiterated familiar themes such as the need to bomb China, to use Nationalist troops, and so on. Soon after the start of the negotiations, the GOP complained that the Communists were using the talks simply as a cover for building up their military strength. During the winter of 1951–52, Senators Alexander Smith and Cain went to Korea. In Harry P. Cain's report to his Senate colleagues, he stated: "It is perfectly clear to anyone who visits Korea, that the Communists have increased their fire power by making available more artillery and ground forces. Worse than that, they have increased their air power by constructing airfields behind the Yalu and in North Korea, thus placing the position of the United Nations in jeopardy in the event the truce talks collapse." Smith, on the program *Meet the Press*, said much the same thing and advocated taking the "wraps off" Chiang Kaishek's forces, blockading the China coast, and bombing beyond the Yalu.[92] Former President Herbert Hoover was later to add to the feeling of uncertainty these statements had generated by warning in an address to the nation on January 27, 1952, that the Chinese had built up a great air force: "What the outcome may be we do not know."[93] And in December 1951, Senator William F. Knowland stoked an already intense hatred of China by releasing to the press the names of 32 American citizens imprisoned in China, a list that the State Department had provided him on a confidential basis.[94]

By the end of 1951, America lost what little flexibility it had had in its policy toward the PRC. For example, in an unsuccessful attempt to gain Senate confirmation of Philip Jessup's appointment to America's U.N. delegation, Acheson ruled out any future accommodation with the Chinese Communists. Furthermore, he asked Senator Alexander Smith to help combat the "persistent but baseless reports" that the U.S. government had ever favorably considered recognizing Peking, seating its representatives in the U.N., or allowing it to acquire Taiwan.[95]

Against this background and as a result of policy changes proposed or agreed upon in previous months, the executive branch undertook a review of Korean War policy in the late autumn of 1951, culminating in the signature of NSC 118/2 on December 20. As noted earlier, the joint chiefs had proposed bombing China's air bases if its air activity jeopardized the security of U.S./U.N. forces. Along with this recommendation, the joint chiefs' July 13 memorandum, prepared to meet the possibility that armistice negotiations might fail, was brought forward once more, although in slightly modified form. "Hot pursuit" was now to be abandoned, because it was considered too costly in terms of probable casualties without any compensatory advantages. The joint chiefs also dropped the requirement to move to the neck of the peninsula, leaving the timing, nature, and extent of the operations to the discretion of the U.N. commander. What they requested was consideration of two questions: first, to what extent U.S. forces should be committed to Korea to achieve U.S. objectives; and second, whether the concept of Chinese "volunteers" would still be accepted, "and, if not, whether restrictions regarding the expansion of the area of hostilities into Manchuria and China will continue in effect."[96]

These JCS comments, along with the modified July 13 memorandum, were incorporated into NSC 118/2.[97] The document was a major restatement of the limited-war objectives outlined in NSC 48/5 of May 1951, but the inclusion of the military's memoranda served to orient the paper toward action to be taken if armistice talks failed. In this event, military operations in the Korean area were to be intensified, consistent with the capabilities of the forces available to the U.N. commander; and restrictions were to be removed against advances or attacks in Korea, including those that had restrained bombing of the Yalu River dams and power installations. (Restrictions against attacks within about 12 miles of the Soviet border were to be retained, however.) A vigorous campaign of covert operations against China was also to be instituted, and enemy lines of communication were to be disrupted. Bombing the PRC's air bases was agreed to if Chinese air activity increased, but the president would have to authorize the action specifically. Acheson had also stated that if time permitted, his department should have the opportunity of informing key allies of U.S. intentions, while protecting the surprise nature of the operations. The question of imposing either a total trade embargo against China, which the State Department preferred, or a naval blockade, which Defense urged, was returned to the Senior NSC Staff for further study.

The staff study accompanying NSC 118/2 repeated the Pentagon statement that the immobilization of large parts of the U.S. armed forces in inconclusive operations might become intolerable. It repeated, too, the view that the American public might soon "demand the adoption of military measures adequate to achieve a political and military decision" in Korea if the negotiations failed. The study noted that China was continuing to increase its military power, thus threatening America's "basic security interests in the Far East." Therefore, it was definitely in America's national interest to attempt to reduce the power of the present Chinese regime and weaken its alliance with Moscow. Moreover, war with China would "provide a significant strategic opportunity, perhaps the last opportunity, for the United States to weaken and undermine the Soviet Union's principal ally." In the staff's view, the United States could exert its power much more effectively against Chinese air and ground forces in north China, Manchuria, and Korea than in south and central China, Burma, or Indochina.

Nevertheless, despite the attraction of this policy and pressure to adopt it, the desire to return to the priority of defending Europe and the Near East remained strong. The staff study reminded the administration that the allies were reluctant to apply additional measures against China and wanted an end to the fighting as quickly as possible. In a long discussion of the fundamental choices facing America, the study came out against a policy of attempting to achieve a military victory in Korea, and in favor of using political means to work for a unified and independent Korea. If minimum objectives were not achieved "after a reasonable period," however, then policy choices would have to be examined once again, and "expansion of hostilities into China [might] become unavoidable." Furthermore, if the Communists were found to be deliberately delaying armistice negotiations while building up their offensive capabilities, pressure would be increased on their forces by stages. The United States would, in that case, undertake the same expanded operations that were considered necessary should negotiations break down.

ASSESSMENT OF SOVIET INTENTIONS AND REACTIONS

If military operations were to be expanded as the result of failed or protracted negotiations, then estimates of Soviet reactions to an extended war had to be sought. Certain members of the Truman administration had asserted in late 1950 and early 1951 that Moscow would not honor its pledge to come to the assistance of Peking unless Moscow believed the time was right from its own standpoint. Influential figures such as Nitze and Acheson, and CIA estimates predicting a willingness on the part of the U.S.S.R. to intervene openly in Korea and risk general war, had helped to counter those arguments. And many officials who had insisted that America should not fear Soviet involvement in the war were expressing emotions of the moment rather than well-considered appraisals of the likely level of support that China could expect from its primary ally. In the spring of 1951, however, when the crisis atmosphere in Washington had abated, the "Soviet factor" was reexamined. This time, there was a longer period for careful investigation of Soviet motives and intentions regarding the war and for the development of the kind of detailed staff papers that had led to the production of the contingency plans described above.

One reason why fear of a possible Chinese air attack was strong in April was that a special intelligence estimate that month had stated that the U.S.S.R.'s air capabilities had increased sharply in the Soviet Far East; indeed, "strenuous efforts [had] been made to develop the area's economy, particularly for military purposes."[98] These activities suggested that Soviet air participation in the Korean conflict might shortly be increased, with serious consequences for U.S. ground forces. In May 1951, NSC 48/5 had surmised that this air power might be used against U.S. troops in Japan and Korea if the U.S. Air Force attacked Chinese territory;[99]

the State Department's Office of Intelligence Research was certain that the risk of global war would not deter Moscow "from what it considered to be necessary support of China."[100] The U.S. embassy in Moscow painted a ghastly picture of Soviet power harnessed to Chinese manpower in an effort "to expand the portion of the world's natural resources under their control through the conquest of underdeveloped areas of the Far East." The embassy forecast continuing turmoil in the Far East, instigated by Moscow in order to expel U.N. forces from Korea and to secure such major objectives as the conquest of Taiwan and expansion into Southeast Asia. The only hope of circumscribing such action was by continuing the steady rearmament of the United States and of the West, the embassy staff wrote, bringing the time nearer when the Soviet Union "must decide to take the full risks under this policy or alter it."[101]

Subsequent Soviet interest in a ceasefire in Korea, culminating in Malik's speech of June 23, held out the possibility that the Soviets had decided not to take any further risks, but for some time the Truman administration remained uncertain as to Moscow's reasons for initiating armistice negotiations. The first estimates of the Soviets' intentions tended to stress the possible aggressive motives behind their encouragement of peace talks. A CIA evaluation in early July, for example, regarded the move as designed primarily to achieve an indefinite and prolonged armistice and a military disengagement in Korea that "would permit utilization of Chinese Communist resources elsewhere in Asia and would free Communist resources generally for utilization elsewhere in the world."[102]

The Defense Department's Joint Intelligence Committee agreed that a ceasefire would allow the Communists "to regain the military initiative in Asia" and leave them free to proceed with preparations for further military action. The committee also believed that the ceasefire was probably intended to create dissension and disunity in the West, and to generate a false sense of security.[103] Molotov's speech in July 1951, in which he spoke of "growing inner antagonisms in individual countries" and "sharpening struggle between the ruling cliques of these powers," seemed to indicate that the Soviet leadership thought it was making progress along the former path.

Acheson was particularly concerned about the latter possibility. When Foreign Minister Morrison pronounced the British government "fairly well satisfied" that the Soviet Union genuinely desired a settlement in Korea, Acheson quickly reminded him that the purpose of initiating peace talks was to eliminate American and other Western influence from Korea, while "lulling us all into abandoning our defensive efforts."[104] The State Department's Office of Intelligence Research also concluded on July 16 that Moscow's primary aim in advocating negotiations was to frustrate Western rearmament efforts, and that if unsuccessful in this aim, it still might resort to military activity in order to improve its immediate strategic position.[105]

Only Charles Bohlen viewed the Soviet wish for a ceasefire as genuine, and as marking a retreat. In response to the redrafts of NSC 68 that were taking place (and which continued to press the theme that the Kremlin's objective was world domination), Bohlen argued that Soviet softness in Korea was not primarily motivated by a desire to lull the free world to sleep; it was "more likely," he thought, "that the Russians desire some alleviation of acute tension in specific spots, i.e. Korea, because they see in it the genuine danger of global hostilities."[106]

Although few within the administration agreed with Bohlen's description of Soviet motives, many did see the Soviet Union as an opportunistic power. As Acheson said, Soviet failure to halt Western mobilization might concentrate Moscow's attention on moves designed to maximize its readiness for general hostilities; nevertheless, it was possible that Moscow might not "feel up to" a showdown with the West, and thus a genuine Soviet retreat remained possible.[107] Continuing with rearmament efforts might make this retreat a reality, in his view.

Having suggested several probable motives behind the Soviet call for a ceasefire, the administration then turned to consider possible Soviet military activity within Korea or in support of China. As the weeks went by and the Soviet Union did not utilize its augmented Far Eastern capabilities, the Defense Department returned to its earlier view that Moscow did not intend to become openly involved in the war. As the Joint Strategic Survey Committee noted in August, there was no firm evidence—despite numerous reports—that a Soviet-bloc "volunteer" army was being formed to fight in Korea, and no evidence either of a Soviet intention to commit any regular units of the Russian army in the immediate future.[108] The JSSC thought it more probable that the Soviet

Union would provide assistance in the form of specialists: radio and radar operators, tank crews, ordnance technicians, and the like.[109]

The Joint Intelligence Committee agreed that the U.S.S.R. did not want to precipitate a large-scale war over Korea. "Even in the face of the initial North Korean defeat," the committee noted, Moscow "did not choose . . . to expand the Korean conflict into general war"; indeed, the Soviets appeared willing to "forego temporarily some of their original objectives in Korea rather than to commit the military force necessary to gain a clear-cut victory." A propaganda campaign was now likely as a substitute for the unsuccessful military operations.[110]

Like the Defense Department, the CIA reverted to its earlier view of Soviet intentions in Korea, even though it had argued as recently as December 1950 that Moscow would soon be ready for global war. At that time, the agency had believed Moscow would come openly to the military support of Peking if the U.S. Air Force attacked Chinese territory. But eight months later, the agency argued that Moscow was not willing to involve itself in Korea at the risk of expanding the hostilities into a general war; it was more likely to "attempt to prevent an extension of the area of conflict and, in recognition of internal strains in Communist China . . . endeavor to provide enough logistical and technical assistance to insure maintenance of Chinese Communist will and ability to continue military operations in Korea." As things stood in August, there was no evidence that the Communists intended to commit the air power that was at their disposal. Though there had been an increase in Soviet technical and logistical support in Korea and Manchuria, again, there was no evidence that the assistance would be "on such a scale as to increase substantially Communist capabilities in Korea, in the near future." There were reports that tanks and artillery were being moved into Korea, and there were unconfirmed rumors of Soviet troop concentrations in Manchuria but no indications that they would be brought into Korea or that a "volunteer" army had actually been formed.[111]

The significance of this August estimate is further enhanced by its being the CIA contribution to the debate concerning the possible military consequences of taking action against China following a failure of the truce negotiations. The report also examined probable Soviet reactions to a range of military actions against China.

Whereas in December 1950 the CIA had taken the Sino-Soviet Treaty of Alliance fully into consideration, this time Soviet support for China was reckoned to be more qualified. "Hot pursuit" across the Yalu border, for example, would occasion only Soviet diplomatic protests and intensified propaganda directed at the United States. Bombing attacks on military installations in Manchuria would lead to the air defense of Manchuria, but Moscow would avoid increasing the risk of general war by cloaking its defense units in the guise of Chinese and/or "volunteer" forces. A naval blockade of China would not lead Moscow openly to attempt to break it by force; instead, the Soviets would step up the flow of supplies to China overland and try to reduce the blockade's effects by escorting additional shipments through Port Arthur and Dairen. Chinese Nationalist raiding parties would not occasion any Soviet military reaction, since they were not likely to threaten the stability of the Chinese Communist government. Most ominous of all from China's point of view, the agency concluded that "if the UN/US were to launch a systematic strategic air and naval bombardment of Communist China," Peking would ask for increased assistance, but "so long as this bombardment did not jeopardize Communist control over Manchuria and North China, the Kremlin would probably restrict its assistance to the provision of air defense units." If the attack did threaten Chinese control, then the Soviets would intensify their aid, possibly through the introduction of "volunteer" forces.[112]

Moscow's contribution to China's security in August seemed, then, to depend on the deterrent value of Soviet air defense operations; "lesser" military activity by the U.S./U.N., such as a naval blockade, "hot pursuit," and Chinese Nationalist attacks, would not occasion a Soviet response of any real concern to the United States. The CIA estimate therefore gave support to those who thought it necessary to consider further military action against China if armistice talks failed. But the report also showed that attacks on China would be a viable course only if the United States could withstand the increased loss of aircraft that would result from Moscow's participation in the air defense of China.

At the end of the year, the CIA produced a further detailed study of the consequences of military action against China.[113] The study again examined possible Soviet reaction to a naval blockade, limited air expansion, sustained air attacks on Manchuria and North

Korea, the employment of Nationalist military forces and non-Communist guerilla units already operating in China, or a combination of several of these courses of action. Like the August estimate, it concluded that air attacks in the immediate vicinity of the Yalu probably would seriously impair Communist air capabilities and reduce Chinese ability to threaten U.S./U.N. forces from the air, yet Moscow probably would not openly invoke the Sino-Soviet treaty and would restrict its assistance to the provision of air defense units. "Sustained and unrestricted UN air attacks" in China and North Korea, combined with ground operations across the parallel, were also considered likely to weaken the Communists' ability to hold in Korea. In this case, Moscow would not commit its own ground troops or use its air force overtly over U.N.-held territory, but would covertly use elements of its air force in Manchuria and North Korea.

Intensified military activity in Korea plus bombing in Manchuria and interdiction of China's seaborne imports, if successfully carried out, was a combination considered to offer enormous potential benefits for the U.S./U.N., including the end of large-scale military operations in Korea, a substantial reduction in China's ability to intervene in Southeast Asia, and the draining of Soviet resources to the extent that its military capacity would also be reduced. In response, Moscow would expand its aid to China, it was thought, probably with additional air defense elements, and it would also consider introducing "volunteer" forces; however, "at every stage . . . the Kremlin would probably endeavor to keep open the possibility of ending the conflict by political negotiation if the global interests of the USSR would be served by disengagement."

The CIA admitted that it might be mistaken with regard to Soviet reactions, and that miscalculations leading to world war could not be discounted at a time of high international tension. Nevertheless, the agency believed it "unlikely that the USSR will deliberately choose to precipitate global war because of the implementation of the courses of action examined in this estimate," even if China bore sustained attacks on its territory, or if the U.S./U.N. reinvaded North Korea, inviting the prospect of a return to the situation that obtained in October 1950.

In considering the likely value of Chinese Nationalist forces in operations against the mainland, the estimate concluded that these troops would not be ready until mid-1952 at the earliest and would still require U.S. logistic, naval, and air support. But it was estimated that a lesser amount of preparation would ensure their effective use in Korea; "certain selected divisions could be made effective in a relatively short time for rotational service on the Korean peninsula."

The CIA study also contributed to but did not resolve the debate between State and Defense over the relative merits of an economic embargo versus a naval blockade. If effectively implemented, an embargo would intensify economic strains within the PRC but do little else; given the loopholes that would certainly be found, an embargo was unlikely, by itself, to reduce China's imports substantially. A naval blockade, on the other hand, could be more trouble than it was worth unless combined with other extensive military operations in Korea and China; on its own, it might well create incidents that would heighten international tension, but it would not force the Chinese to end their involvement in Korea.[114] The issue thus remained unresolved at the end of the year. As John M. Allison told Acheson on December 17, the discrepancy between the two positions was, anyway, "more a matter of tactics than substance." State thought it advisable to proceed from an embargo to a blockade, since pressing for a naval blockade immediately would only lead the Western allies (certainly the British) to reject it, thereby causing a delay "in obtaining agreement to the embargo which we believe is possible."[115]

The effect that these military policies would have on the U.S. strategy of detaching China from the Soviet orbit was less frequently examined, given the conclusion that Sino-Soviet relations were, for the time being, close. As the CIA put it in September, "While frictions may develop between the USSR and Communist China, and there remain long term possibilities of a major clash of interests, it appears unlikely that any serious rifts will develop in the next two years. Ideological affinity and mutual antagonism towards the West, as well as common fear of Japanese resurgence, probably dictate a continued close relationship, at least over the short term."[116] Increased pressure on China, however—whether military, economic, or political—could increase internal dissatisfaction with the leadership in Peking and/or with Moscow. The U.S. ambassador to the U.N., for example, raised the tantalizing prospect that retaliation against China might hasten a Sino-Soviet rift, since it would "make even more glaring the perfidiousness of the

Soviet Union if we should extend the war to China and [the USSR] then refused to come openly to China's assistance."[117] Another suggestion was that a naval blockade would increase Peking's dependence on Moscow, thus hastening China's disillusionment with Russian aid.[118]

Western and Communist Military Capabilities

The path by which the intelligence community in Washington came to the conclusion that Moscow did not then wish to risk world war involved several stages. Of greatest significance was the belief that the U.S. reaction to the outbreak of hostilities in Korea had given the Soviets some reason to pause, as had the growing pace of Western rearmament efforts, stimulated by the war.

Although the United States still considered itself at a military disadvantage in comparison with Communist capabilities in the Korean area, the outbreak of the war and the defeats suffered at the hands of the Chinese had galvanized the U.S. government into action. The Soviet leadership must have been appalled at the wave of military and diplomatic activity and planning to which the fighting had given impetus in 1951. U.S. armed forces were to be rapidly increased and modernized, particularly the Air Force, whose new equipment would bring Soviet industrial sites within range of the projected aircraft, even from bases in America. There was to be an intensive concentration of effort on building the hydrogen bomb. Five airfields were to be constructed in Morocco, and large bases were to be developed in Libya and Saudi Arabia. Air units in Germany and Austria were to be reorganized and strengthened, as was a strategic bombing force in Britain. The number of American divisions stationed in Europe was to rise to six; early in 1951, General Dwight D. Eisenhower had assumed command of NATO, and NATO headquarters was established; in May, the United States proposed that Greece and Turkey also join the Western alliance. Such concentration of effort on Europe appeared to be paying off, as Europeans began to grapple more seriously with the problem of German rearmament. Outside Europe, the United States signed a series of defense agreements with Australia, New Zealand, and the Philippines in September 1951, and—over Soviet protests—the Japanese Peace Treaty, which consolidated Japan's alliance with the Western defense system. Not surprisingly, in reaction to this activity, the Soviet Union was, and was perceived to be, on the defensive, and thus Moscow concentrated on its peace moves and on tempting Washington's European allies away from America's embrace.[119]

The passage of time had also affected U.S. intelligence estimates of probable Soviet foreign policy activity. For some months, there had been no indications of "any Soviet intention to participate in the Korean fighting on a large scale or in military operations elsewhere in the Far East."[120] The assessments may also have been influenced by an intelligence report acquired by the Far East Air Force: according to this information, Peking had informed the commander of the Chinese air force that Moscow would not permit offensive action from Manchurian air bases, and that Soviet equipment was purely for defensive purposes.[121] As Rusk had told the British ambassador in October, the Chinese seemed to be deliberately refraining from using their air strength: "They were now capable of using air power offensively," he said, "but for some reason chose not to do so."[122]

The Communists, in fact, did not attack any South Korean targets by air. As one analyst has since written, and as General Marshall acknowledged at the MacArthur hearings, Pusan, which was often well lighted at night, was a "virtually perfect military target," yet it suffered no attack by air or with mines. Neither did the convoys of trucks and trains carrying troops and supplies.[123] The official U.S. histories of the war have all noted Communist circumspection on the sea and in the air. One history of naval operations, for example, notes that the Communists made no effort at sea, with the single exception of the mining campaign, and no attempt to support their ground troops with air cover. A submarine offensive, he said, "would have changed the entire nature of the war," and a determined air offensive would have caused the U.S./U.N. grave problems.[124]

This demonstrated unwillingness (or inability) on the part of the Chinese and North Koreans to use their full military arsenal and the apparent desire on Moscow's part to initiate peace talks, to avoid overt involvement in the conflict, and to refrain from diversionary action elsewhere were sufficient evidence to convince Washington that Moscow was "probably not prepared to accept the risk of general war to achieve its maximum objectives in

Korea."[125] Washington determined at the end of the year that neither would America seek its maximum objectives in Korea. The pursuit of the unification of Korea by the application of military force was unwise, the NSC staff concluded, since the United States lacked the necessary military capability and would continue to do so well into 1952. In addition, the nation's major allies would still not support an unprovoked intensification of Korean hostilities; especially Britain, which Secretary of Defense Robert Lovett said was "in desperate straits," and France, which he described as "practically bankrupt."[126]

U.S. and Communist air capabilities were seen to be fairly evenly balanced at the end of 1951. Vandenberg, who had indicated he now wanted freedom to use his air power against China, admitted that not until spring 1952 would production of U.S. planes be sufficient to maintain air superiority. And an intelligence estimate had concluded not long before that if the enemy air buildup continued at the same pace, the Chinese and North Koreans—even without the participation of Soviet units—would be able to damage U.S./U.N. positions severely. This might render it impossible for U.S./U.N. forces to conduct offensive operations "except at prohibitive cost," it said.[127] If, as Rusk told the joint chiefs, the United States decided to expand the war and found it could not "carry it through," America would yet more speedily lose the support of the other nations fighting in Korea.[128]

By providing Peking with a sizable and relatively skilled air force, Moscow had helped deter America from expanding the war into China, at least until the U.S. Air Force had increased in size, if for no other, more pressing reason. It was accepted that Moscow did not want to go to war over Korea and would not support China openly even if its territory were attacked, but in other respects the Soviet Union had managed to enhance the security of its ally.

NSC 118/2 was therefore a reaffirmation of America's limited-war policy, since it rejected courses of action designed to achieve its maximum objectives in Korea. Nevertheless, the staff study that accompanied it did acknowledge that intensified military and other pressures on the Communists might prove necessary simply to achieve America's limited objectives: basically, an acceptable armistice agreement, a secure future for the ROK at least as far north as the 38th Parallel, and the gradual withdrawal of non-Korean armed forces from Korea. In the event of a failure to achieve an armistice and these limited goals, or a breach of an armistice agreement, the National Security Council members confirmed their intention to apply additional military pressure against China and North Korea. Moreover, if the negotiations became indefinitely prolonged, these new courses of action were to be applied in stages. The NSC referred to the CIA estimate of Soviet reactions, indicating that a third world war would not result even if these additional measures were implemented. But while it could not be guaranteed that U.S. force would prevail, the cost to the United States of such action appeared unacceptable in terms of the damage to America's support in the U.N. and among its NATO allies, and the overall depletion of its military resources.

Although the autumn of 1950 was bleak for the administration and it was seen to have blundered militarily, feelings of optimism resurfaced from late February 1951 onward. A truce on the basis of a rough parity of military positions looked possible, and signs were that the Soviets in particular, but also the Chinese, agreed that the time was right for talking rather than fighting. Having regained the parallel, major allies such as Britain, France, and Canada remained reluctant to support any activity that hinted at expanding the hostilities, or to consider large-scale operations above the 38th Parallel. Against this background, Truman was ready to grasp at what seemed a reasonably honorable way out of this unpopular and debilitating war. The revelations regarding policy in Korea and the conflicting appraisals of U.S. national security needs put forward at the MacArthur hearings may have confused the general public, but the bulk of "informed opinion," as the State Department termed it, supported the administration's case for a limited war and a negotiated settlement. When the truce negotiations finally began, a majority of the public favored America's attempts to bring them to an early and satisfactory conclusion.

But each factor that enhanced the prospects for an armistice and limited war was double-sided. The parity in military positions, return to the parallel, and opening of negotiations forced consideration of military actions that would be instrumental in giving America the kind of ceasefire arrangement it desired. At the MacArthur hearings, Bradley and the joint chiefs spoke of not being satisfied with a stalemate in Korea for long, and of lifting restrictions on the prosecution of the war if it proved impossible to conclude an armistice. There was also examination of possible action to be taken if an armistice were breached once entered into or—toward the end of the year—if negotiations seemed to be dragging on indefinitely.

During the course of these policy discussions, the differing approaches of the State and Defense Departments were illustrated quite starkly. On each occasion that policy making entered a new phase, State sought to ensure that the allies were informed of the policy, that their reactions were included in the policy assessment, and that they would be consulted before any new action was initiated. Defense, however, basically believed that the allies should follow America's lead. As the joint chiefs put it in November, "The United States is now the dominant power in the Western Pacific. Consequently, in any conflict of interest arising between the United States and other Western Powers which may affect the position of the United States in the Far East, the United States should in its own interest insist that United States security considerations in that area be over-riding."[129] The United States was not working in a coalition of equals, and its tradition involved taking unilateral action and using unrestrained force. For the Defense Department this tradition had merit and was beginning to reassert itself. For example, as Allison informed Acheson at the end of December, the Pentagon wanted it made "unmistakably clear that restrictions [associated with moving into North Korea] which have, in fact, resulted from previous governmental level decisions do not apply in case of a breakdown of armistice talks."[130]

Certain restrictions imposed on U.S. military operations in Korea and China were, in fact, removed in 1951. In April there had been a "show of force" along the South China coast and air reconnaissance over Manchuria. Approval was also obtained to bomb Rashin, and if the president assented, the U.N. commander could bomb Chinese air bases whenever enemy air activity was deemed sufficient to jeopardize the security of U.S./U.N. forces—a phrase never fully clarified. With regard to the additional military measures that might be applied should negotiations fail or a truce be violated, the Defense Department set the agenda and obtained governmental agreement. Thus, although there was no dispute that America's maximum objective of obtaining a military settlement of the Korean unification problem was too dangerous a notion to contemplate, these discussions indicated there was still the problem of obtaining compliance with America's limited aims.

Major American allies remained significant obstacles to any contemplated expansion of hostilities in Korea and China, since their economic and defensive needs were still great. In addition, Washington believed it likely that allied and U.N. support would fall away even faster if it turned out that the United States, having expanded the war, could not prevail militarily. But the allies did accept the need to issue a warning statement threatening expansion of the war if the enemy broke the armistice agreement, and they agreed that if there were no armistice soon, further measures might have to be taken. France, eager to obtain American help in its Asian colony, sought the same kind of automatic military response to any Chinese intervention in Indochina that the United States sought from its allies in post-armistice Korea. Britain's Conservative government, preoccupied at year's end by problems in Iran and Egypt, tried much harder than Attlee had done to come to terms with America's China policy. It would not support a naval blockade, primarily because of the threat that would pose to the stability of Hong Kong, but did agree to consider bombing north of the Yalu if armistice talks failed. As Churchill told his chiefs of staff at the end of November, "Russia would start world war III when she wanted to: she certainly would not do so merely to honour her pledge to China."[131]

Churchill's opinion regarding the Soviet reaction to the bombing of China coincided with the view held by some in the executive branch in Washington. The CIA produced in 1951 some of the most categorical reports on probable Soviet reactions since the outbreak of hostilities in June 1950. The Soviet call for a ceasefire, and the assumption that Western military rearmament was causing Moscow to switch from military to political weapons in the East-West conflict, influenced these assessments. Much of the Soviet Union's behavior toward the events taking place in Korea indicated that it did not intend to become openly involved in the fighting. There was evidence that Soviet technical personnel were in Manchuria and in North Korea and that the Soviet Union was contributing to a substantial increase in air strength in those areas, but the Russians were operating in a defensive and directive capacity and had not yet authorized the use of the augmented air power.

It was concluded therefore that Russia would not initiate a global war in response to an attack on China or stand openly beside its ally but try instead to keep the conflict limited. Nevertheless, though in this sense the Soviet Union had diminished in importance as a deterrent force in Korea since the end of 1950, the U.S. administration assumed that Moscow's covert assistance could tilt the military balance in the Communists' favor. The MacArthur hearings may have painted too stark a picture of U.S. military capabilities and "shoestring air force," but the production of vital jet aircraft was only 11 per month between July and September of 1951; not until April of 1952 would the production curve begin to go up.[132] Until U.S./U.N. air and ground force capabilities increased in Korea, an extension of hostilities would result in an "unsatisfactory deployment of US military strength."[133] Notwithstanding the stresses and strains of this policy, a limited war and limited objectives were still the prudent course to follow.

[6]

Military Force as an Instrument of Policy: February–December 1952

Despite the frustrations associated with the uneven progress of the armistice negotiations, there was some cause for optimism at the beginning of the new year. In early January 1952, Acheson thought an armistice agreement possible by the end of the month. Although this hope proved unrealistic, by the early spring the three remaining issues that had delayed agreement were close to being resolved. According to a State Department intelligence report, the U.S. delegation could feel reasonably sanguine about the prospects for a settlement. The past behavior of the Communists, it said, had indicated that they were willing to make significant concessions. They had already given way on the content of the agenda for the talks, agreed to drop the reference to the 38th Parallel as the final armistice line, and acquiesced in changing the site of the negotiations in October 1951.[1] In March a further compromise had been reached: the Communists would withdraw their demand for Soviet participation in the work of the neutral nations supervisory commission in exchange for a U.S. decision in favor of the rehabilitation of airfields.

Even the one remaining issue, the question of the voluntary repatriation of prisoners of war—which in February 1952 had become a fixed American objective for both humanitarian and propaganda purposes—seemed capable of fairly speedy resolution. On the basis of a U.S. prediction in April that about 116,000 of the 132,000 prisoners of war would accept repatriation, the Communists indicated their willingness to allow the U.N. command to conduct a poll of the prisoners to determine exactly how many would be willing to return to their place of origin.[2]

The U.S. estimate turned out to be wildly inaccurate: only about half the prisoners said they were willing to return to their homelands. Of the approximately 21,000 Chinese prisoners held, 16,000 said they did not wish to go back to the PRC (although the number was artificially high because of the influence of former Chinese Nationalist troops who were used as guards in the Chinese compounds).[3] Informed of these figures, the Communists totally rejected the concept of nonforcible repatriation, and from May 7 the negotiations at Panmunjom became deadlocked over this one issue. That same day, Truman made a statement to the press in which he gave his unequivocal support to the concept of voluntary repatriation.

This final stumbling block caused the war to continue for another 14 months, even though both sides at the talks and other nations working within the U.N. framework put forward various formulas for resolving the question. The seeming intractability of the problem contributed to the narrowness of approach adopted by the Truman administration, which favored military force over diplomatic compromise as a method of achieving a settlement on U.S. terms.

It was apparent that the 16,000 Communist Chinese POWs unwilling to return home were at the heart of the problem, since the Communist negotiators had implied that the Koreans could be dispersed as each side wished.[4] During the last seven months of the Truman administration, many State Department officials were willing to search for a compromise formula; they saw little point in risking a breakdown of the negotiations and an expanded war over this one issue. Arthur B. Emmons of Northeast Asian Affairs, for example, suggested several possible courses of action the United States could take, including presenting the case to the International Court of Justice; capturing more prisoners; juggling the figures; and working for a settlement outside the current negotiations. Others in the State Department considered a private appeal to the government of India to assume responsibility for the nonrepatriate Chinese, or supported the Mexican proposal for the immediate exchange of POWs who were willing to be exchanged and the dispatch of the remainder as political refugees to U.N. members willing to accept them.[5]

The Defense Department, however, supported by the president, would not consider any formula that did not provide a guarantee of free choice of destination for the prisoners after a specified and limited amount of time. Without this guarantee, Defense officials argued, the U.S. administration would be inundated with cries to "bring the boys home," while the Communists held on, strengthened their forces, and reopened the war. And Acheson, aware of the president's firm attitude, was not willing to stand up for a compromise formula to resolve the question. The resultant failure to make any progress on the issue during the last months of Truman's presidency brought to the fore the administration's belief in the value of force as a way of obtaining significant political concessions. Truman reflected this belief in his private diary, in which he periodically relieved his feelings; there, the president advocated issuing an ultimatum with a ten-day expiration date, informing the Soviet Union that the United States intended to blockade the China coast and destroy military bases in Manchuria. Unless Moscow changed its policies, he wrote, this would lead to "all out war. It means that Moscow, St Petersburg, Mukden, Vladivostock, Pekin[g], Shanghai, Port Arthur, Dairen, Odessa, Stalingrad and every manufacturing plant in China and the Soviet Union will be eliminated." Later on, he forecast either an end to hostilities in Korea or the complete destruction of China and Siberia.[6]

INCREASING MILITARY PRESSURE

Though Truman never formally proposed going to such extremes, other parts of the administration agreed that some kind of termination date for the armistice negotiations should be set. The Joint Strategic Survey Committee stated in April that a date should be decided upon whenever the joint chiefs were of the opinion that the Communists were protracting the negotiations "merely to serve their own ends." If no armistice agreement had been reached by the set date, the JSSC advocated the immediate initiation of the measures outlined in NSC 118/2: an increase in military operations in Korea, attacks on the Yalu River dams and power installations, air attacks on Chinese bases whenever they increased their air activity, an embargo or blockade of China, and a vigorous campaign of covert operations against the PRC government. Sensitive to the probable criticism these actions would invoke among NATO allies, the JCS planning committee suggested that the U.N. Command could soothe their feelings by placing the onus for the failure of negotiations on the Communists; this would render it politically possible to initiate a harsher military policy. The committee also recommended examining a number of additional military measures designed to force a settlement in Korea, including "tactical use of atomic weapons . . . commando operations and acceleration of guerilla operations, to include demolitions."[7]

The report further proposed that the United States consider introducing Chinese Nationalist forces in Korea. In February, General William C. Chase, head of the military advisory group in Taipei, had thought it a good idea for 30,000 to 40,000 Nationalist troops to be used in Korea to give them battle experience, help with their training, and develop their leaders.[8] The CIA had concluded much the same thing by the end of 1951. In April 1952 the Defense Department joined the chorus and proposed a more active policy in support of Taiwan. At an NSC meeting, the deputy secretary pointed out that America had too few assets in the Far East, and the Nationalists represented one that had not been developed to its full potential.[9] General Mark Clark (who replaced Ridgway as U.N. Commander on May 12, 1952) apparently thought so too: on May 27 he asked that two Nationalist divisions be sent to join his command immediately. This question then, along with that of the appropriate U.S. response to the long-drawn-out negotiations, which Clark and Admiral C. Turner Joy (the chief U.N. negotiator at the truce talks) had recommended be unilaterally suspended in May,[10] came under detailed examination from that time onward.

With negotiations at a stalemate over the POW question, the U.N. Command undertook large-scale bombing operations in Korea on a regular basis and heightened its harassment of the PRC. General Clark was a well-known supporter of the MacArthur strategy for ending the war in Korea; perhaps because of his assumption of the U.N. Command in May, all U.S. commanders engaged in fighting on the peninsula "recognized that they could now take more forceful action."[11] General Otto P. Weyland, commander of the Far Eastern Air Force, for example, described the new phase of activity as "a significant change in combat operations policy."[12] A detailed study of targets provided the background for a bombing campaign called Operation Pressure Pump, which began on July 11; "practically every operating air unit in the Far East was to have a part in the savage assault against 30 targets designated in Pyongyang."[13] The Air Force flew 1,254 sorties that first day, dropping

23,000 gallons of napalm. Pyongyang suffered its heaviest bombing on August 29, when 1,403 sorties were flown and nearly 700 tons of bombs were dropped. In a relaxation of the bombing restrictions near the Yalu River, the U.S. Air Force was given permission on September 1 to bomb an oil refinery at Aoji, only eight miles from the Soviet border and four miles from Manchuria; on September 30 a chemical plant right on the Yalu was destroyed in a bombing raid. The State Department agreed not to raise any objections to these activities provided that no immediate publicity was given to them, that approval was not taken to mean the rescinding of previous restrictions, and that Britain was informed. The British government was informed, but was no doubt alarmed when its representative in Tokyo reported that Washington had "accepted the probability that a few bombs may fall on the other side of the Yalu River."[14]

The most controversial bombings were the sustained attacks, starting in June, on the Yalu River power installations. Although there were few occasions (unlike the situation in Vietnam between 1964 and 1968) when the administration seriously sought to orchestrate its words at the truce negotiations with deeds on the battlefield, the June bombings were undertaken to induce a more cooperative attitude at the talks.[15] Not surprisingly, these raids were extremely popular in the United States, but they caused consternation in the capitals of allied and neutral states, and renewed fears that the United States had begun to implement a policy that would culminate in an extension of the war to China.

In early June, Clark had ordered attacks on all North Korean power installations except those located on the Yalu, previously designated forbidden targets. The joint chiefs seized the opportunity of extending Clark's plan to include the Suiho installation on the Yalu. As they explained their decision to the defense secretary, inasmuch as the Suiho installation was "the largest and most important of all Korean hydro-electric plants, it is believed necessary that this installation also be attacked in order to effectively neutralize the whole system."[16] The subsequent order instructing Clark to include this target advised him simply to take "reasonable precautions" to minimize the inadvertent bombing of Manchurian territory.[17] The first bombings on June 23 involved some 500 aircraft. This and subsequent raids caused a power blackout in North Korea for 15 days and resulted in the loss of 23 percent of Manchuria's power requirements for 1952.[18]

Acheson, in London at the time the first raids were taking place, apparently supported the operation but was unaware of the bombing schedule. The criticism that members of the British Parliament heaped upon him and the dismay of the Conservative government, whose minister of state for defense, Lord Alexander, had so recently been at General Clark's headquarters, forced Acheson to mount a strong defense of the bombings on the grounds of the strategic significance of the target. But despite Acheson's support for the military action, and his apology for the error—a "snafu" as he described it—that prevented the U.K. government from being informed of the intended operation, the raids undermined the Truman administration's credibility with its allies. The Foreign Offices of London and Ottawa were skeptical of the "snafu," believing instead that consultations had been deliberately omitted for fear that the allies would raise objections.[19]

These bombings also led to a resurfacing of the anxieties MacArthur had once generated: that the U.S. military was exercising too great an influence on policy. India's prime minister, Jawaharlal Nehru, was "disturbed at the thought that the future of the United Nations and of war and peace might be decided without proper consultations, and might ultimately depend on the discretion of military commanders who would naturally think more of local military objectives than of large questions affecting the world."[20] One outcome of the June bombing mission was that the British fulfilled a long-term aim to appoint a deputy chief of staff to Clark's headquarters. But in an atmosphere of tension, if not quite distrust, between the governments of the United States and the United Kingdom, the British feared that this appointment might give Clark the right to say the U.K. had been "consulted" about any military action. As a consequence, London felt it now had "more responsibility without more power."[21]

The British also questioned the legitimacy of bombing the power installations: Herbert Morrison, foreign minister in the previous Labour administration, had been told in 1951 that such action would be taken only in the event of a breakdown of truce negotiations. An examination of the minutes of meetings between Acheson and Morrison showed the U.K. government to be correct in this instance, and also confirmed that the United States had agreed to consult the British if it decided to bomb this target.[22]

What concerned New Delhi, Paris, Ottawa, London and others was that the U.S. attitude seemed to be hardening to a point where an expansion of the war into China would be inevitable if an armistice were not soon achieved. Furthermore, the attacks on the Yalu power complex, as the *Survey of International Affairs* produced by the influential Royal Institute of International Affairs in London put it, appeared to be an "attempt to provoke the Communists into launching a general offensive, in the hope that this would be bloodily repulsed."[23]

Provocation also seemed to be the main aim of the mock amphibious operation near Wonsan on October 15, involving several thousand U.S./U.N. troops; when the practice operation was officially acknowledged, the U.N. Command suggested that it might later become real.[24] And Chinese Nationalist "guerilla" forces launched the largest of several raids on offshore islands during this period, this time on Nanjih, off the southeast coast of China between Shanghai and Hong Kong. According to reports, the three-day operation involved 4,000 Nationalist Chinese; the British said these were regular troops, rather than guerilla forces, and interpreted American reluctance to discuss the raid as evidence that American advice had been available during the planning of the operation, in contravention of Truman's neutralization order of June 1950.[25]

This stepped-up harassment of China and North Korea indicated that, as NSC 118/2 had outlined, pressure would indeed be increased in stages if truce negotiations were not completed in the near future. Discussions regarding policy toward Indochina, undertaken in June 1952, reinforced the impression that offensive action against Chinese territory could now more readily be considered. If the Chinese intervened in Indochina in force, the United States would have to respond, Acheson warned the U.K. ambassador. The only way of changing the Chinese mind, he said, was by striking at the PRC "where it hurts" or by instituting a naval blockade.[26] It subsequently became U.S. policy, as outlined in NSC 124/2 of June 25, vigorously to oppose any overt Chinese attack on Southeast Asia by interdicting Chinese communication lines (including those inside China), establishing a naval blockade, intensifying covert operations against the PRC government, and using anti-Communist Chinese forces (including KMT troops) in military operations in Southeast Asia, Korea, or China proper. If the United States determined "jointly with the UK and France" that the situation required military action against China, America would take "air and naval action in conjunction with at least France and the

UK against all suitable military targets in China."[27] It was explained to the British that this action would go beyond those military targets immediately adjacent to the battlefront and would include mining rivers and bombing ports and supply lines. The pattern of retaliation against China had thus been set by mid-1952. The United States would avoid completely any involvement in a land war in China; it would concentrate on the use of naval and air power to achieve its goals.

There was further evidence later in the year that the United States planned to continue its tougher stance toward the Communists until an armistice was achieved. In August the State Department began work on a paper outlining action the U.N. General Assembly might take against China in the forthcoming session. The authors sought passage of a resolution supporting the UN Command's conduct of the negotiations and requesting the Communists to accept a settlement recognizing the principle of nonforcible repatriation. In the event of a negative response, the Additional Measures Committee would be called upon to recommend the imposition of a total embargo against China and North Korea, to request all states to "increase and intensify assistance to the United Nations action in Korea and in particular to contribute additional forces to the Unified Command," and to urge that all states "sever, limit or refuse to enter into diplomatic relations with the aggressors in Korea."[28] The paper echoed the courses of action originally thought necessary when the United States had prepared to label China an aggressor in Korea in the winter of 1950–51.

Little headway was made with this proposal, however. In informal discussions with Commonwealth governments, reactions were "almost wholly negative," particularly with reference to the total embargo. Clearly, it would take a major effort to push such a resolution through the General Assembly, and if the American delegation tried to do so, the attempt could lead to "the transfer of negotiations from the manageable Panmunjom forum to the unwieldy UN Assembly"[29]—a most undesirable loss of control as far as the United States was concerned.

Though forced to curtail its own U.N. activity, the U.S. administration still could not prevent other delegations from suggesting solutions to the POW issue. In early September the Mexican delegation had proposed resolving the POW question by granting refugee status to those unwilling to be repatriated. General Clark, the joint chiefs, and the secretary of defense were totally against this idea, arguing that a truce without settlement of the POW problem would remove the bargaining weapons needed to force a decision on the final status of the prisoners. But as Acheson said, the Mexican proposal had been made, and some kind of response had to be given to it. Acheson recognized that in order to maintain some credibility with U.N. members and demonstrate that America really desired peace in Korea, it was essential to prove that the government "had exhausted every reasonable effort to obtain an armistice." Moreover, he said, "unless the G[eneral] A[ssembly] was satisfied that all reasonable proposals had been made there would be strong efforts difficult to resist to have the UNC put forward such proposals or in some manner transfer the negotiations from Panmunjom to the General Assembly." If the Communists rejected the Mexican resolution, or one based on it—and Acheson thought the chances of their accepting it were "about one in a thousand"— the United States would have built the "best possible platform" for bringing about a "unilateral recess" in the negotiations.[30]

The Defense Department remained unconvinced; it was secure in the strength of the U.S./U.N. military position in Korea and thus regarded any further concessions as unnecessary and undesirable. It was necessary to solve the issue of the prisoners once and for all while U.S. troops were in Korea in force and could keep bombing North Korean territory in an attempt to gain a settlement.

In view of the importance of this disagreement, the matter was taken to the president for resolution.[31] The outcome was already heavily loaded against the secretary of state: two days prior to the meeting between the State and Defense Departments, Secretary Robert Lovett and the joint chiefs had put the military case to the president and obtained his full support. In addition, the country was in the middle of a bitter election campaign, during which a constant charge was that Truman administration officials were Communist "appeasers."

At the meeting on September 24, it was apparent that Truman remained unmoved by Acheson's arguments. The question was, the president said, should the United States "do anything in the world to get an armistice in Korea?" He was not willing to get an agreement "just for the sake of an armistice," especially if it left China in a position to renew the fighting. In explaining Defense Department views, Acting Secretary William C. Foster advised the president that America should increase the military pressure "until a real armistice" was obtained. This could be accomplished by "more intensive bombing, further expansion of the ROK Army, use of Chinese Nationalist forces, and amphibious landings in Korea." In the department's opinion, the U.N. Command's chief negotiator, now General William K. Harrison, should state the final U.S./U.N. terms and give the enemy ten days to think them over. If the Communist delegation rejected the terms, the United States "should indefinitely recess the negotiations, at the same time increasing military pressures." The CIA director, Walter Bedell Smith, wanted to go even further. In his view, "a mere armistice would not solve the real problem," because peace in Asia could not be guaranteed as long as the Chinese had the "potentiality for further devilment." Increased military pressure should be put on the Chinese Communists. Nationalist forces were a "pistol at the head" of the PRC; they should be used, he said, to interdict Chinese coastal shipping, for example. Admiral William Fechteler, chief of naval operations, confirmed that the U.S. Navy could enforce a blockade of China if called upon to do so, and the undersecretary of the Air Force said that an expansion of the air war was possible, "not on a sustained all-out effort, but effectively nonetheless."

Truman decided in favor of using greater force to achieve U.S. aims in Korea. He rejected Bedell Smith's suggestion of American support for a KMT naval blockade because of its effect on the presidential election campaign and within the U.N., but he did agree that Nationalist troops were valuable in the threat they posed to Shanghai and the China coast. In a restatement of the military's position, he supported the idea of a ten-day period for Communist acceptance of U.S. terms on the POW issue; if they rejected the proposal, the United States would declare an indefinite recess and "be prepared to do such other things as may be necessary."

Even before the president's decision had been made, the joint chiefs had cabled Clark on September 23 that he should prepare to take certain measures in the event the armistice negotiations were considered to have failed. These actions might involve the "removal of all restrictions [except for] attacks on the USSR proper [and the] use of atomic or chemical weapons." They informed Clark that the detailed courses of action being considered included amphibious, airborne, or ground offensives to increase the pressure on the Communists and possibly to secure the waist of the Korean peninsula; air attacks on aerodrome complexes; the naval blockade of the Chinese mainland with coordinated air attacks on transportation centers; and the bombing of communication centers in north and central China and in Manchuria.[32]

Clark was more than ready to support these proposals, and he minimized the risks attached to them. On October 9, a day after the armistice negotiations were indefinitely recessed in response to the Communist rejection of General Harrison's final proposals, Clark sent a personal letter to the Army chief of staff. He reported that he was sending a team of staff officers to Washington to present a plan "designed to obtain a military victory and achieve an armistice on our terms." Although he had not envisaged the employment of atomic weapons in the operation, he felt it would be advantageous if he were granted authority to consider their use "against appropriate targets including those of opportunity."[33] General J. Lawton Collins had reported in July that the United States had tactical atomic weapons available for use,[34] and presumably Clark had this development in mind.

General Clark's plan (OPLAN 8-52), forwarded to the joint chiefs on October 16, comprised a drive to the waist (sometimes called the neck) of Korea, major amphibious and airborne assaults, and air and naval attacks on China. To accomplish it, he would require three additional U.S. or U.N. divisions, plus two from the ROK army and two from Nationalist China. He also requested 12 battalions of artillery and 20 antiaircraft weapons. In addition, he recommended that plans be made for the use of atomic weapons.[35] On November 7, General Collins informed Clark that his plan was under consideration, intimating that the main problem with it was the force requirements at a time when American worldwide commitments were "extremely heavy."[36]

The heaviness of America's global obligations and the level of reinforcements Clark required to force a military conclusion to the conflict in Korea were major constraints in considering the spread of hostilities outside Korea. But less extensive actions could be undertaken to increase the pressure on China and North Korea in the meantime, as the bombing policy in North Korea, the mock amphibious landing at Wonsan, and the increase in guerilla raids had all shown. In addition, discussions were initiated in October concerning the possible deneutralization of Taiwan, a proposal that was causing new difficulties between State and Defense. Acheson was convinced that it was not the time to discuss deneutralization with America's allies, especially while the Truman administration was seeking U.N. support for its negotiating position at Panmunjom. Others within the administration, however, found irksome the restraints the allies imposed on the use of Kuomintang troops. Both the CIA and the Defense Department were in favor of using Chiang's forces in some capacity, and the new director of the Office of Chinese Affairs, Walter F. McConnaughy, proposed keeping the deneutralization question under constant review.[37]

Activity at the United Nations during the winter of 1952 showed even more starkly the pressure being exerted on Acheson. In early October the United States had gained the support of 20 other nations to cosponsor a resolution reaffirming the inviolability of the concept of nonforcible repatriation of prisoners of war. However, when India's foreign minister, Krishna Menon, introduced a resolution suggesting that nonrepatriates be left for an unspecified period in the hands of a commission that would decide their future, support for the 21-power resolution began to crumble. In order to prevent a total loss of support for the American position, Acheson put enormous pressure on the British and Canadian delegations, in particular, to reject the Indian proposal. The secretary of state's demands on Foreign Minister Anthony Eden and, as Eden himself described them, the "undignified and personal attacks on Selwyn Lloyd" of the U.K. delegation indicated to the British that Acheson was being pushed by the Defense Department. Indeed, Eden dubbed Acheson "more Royalist than the King" in representing the views of the joint chiefs. The secretary of state tried various ploys to convince the U.K. government that its support was vital, not only from Washington's point of view but also from the British standpoint. The incoming president, Acheson said, "would be surrounded by people who wished to extend the war into China." The allies would need "all the levers" they could get with the new administration, and one way to ensure this was to show how consistently they had supported the United States in its Korean War policy. If London did not stay with Washington on the resolution, Britain would lose its chance of "restraining the new administration from a 'get tough policy' with China." Moreover, he warned Eden that "divisions among us on this essential matter would bring grave disillusionment in the United States regarding collective security, which would not be confined to Korea but would extend to NATO and other arrangements . . . of the same sort."[38]

Acheson tried one other effort to force Eden's hand on the U.S. resolution: he confided that if the armistice talks broke down over the POW issue, America had plans for a major offensive. To this admission an alarmed Eden retorted, "But you haven't enough troops." Acheson replied, "We have four divisions we could send." The secretary of defense, Robert Lovett, also made it plain that if an "honorable armistice" could not be achieved, there was "a strong probability" that a military solution would be sought.[39] Rumors that the United States intended to expand the Korean hostilities circulated widely at the U.N. that autumn, and the secretary-general, Trygve Lie, was told that the American military were not interested in the resumption of negotiations, "because they were all set now for a big offensive, especially an air offensive, which they thought might end the war."[40]

The winter of 1952 was a dangerous and unpredictable phase of the conflict. Fortunately for the Americans, the Soviet Union harshly condemned the Indian resolution that had been introduced in the U.N., and this led the Indians to compromise and agree to the U.S. suggestion of a 90-day time limit for the retention of those prisoners not wishing to be repatriated. Without that compromise, America might not have found the common ground with its allies it was searching for. Neither would it have been able to stave off a serious political defeat in the United Nations. A different outcome would have made it difficult for Truman to resist the domestic pressures to give up both the search for a negotiated peace and his attempts to work within the U.N. framework.

U.S. MILITARY CAPABILITIES IN 1952

The four divisions that Acheson spoke of to Eden probably comprised two from Nationalist China and two from South Korea. On November 26 the joint chiefs had finally decided that two Nationalist divisions should be used in Korea. And after the Republican Party exploited the issue of the ROK army's expansion rate, Truman advanced plans to increase its size. General James A.

Van Fleet, the commander of the Eighth Army, announced on November 11 the mobilization of two new ROK divisions, plus six infantry units.[41] Previous doubts about the reliability of South Korean troops appeared to have been overcome, and thereafter there was a rapid expansion of the army.

These additions to the ground forces in Korea, however, still did not satisfy the requirements of Clark's military plan or markedly reduce the demands on America's military obligations elsewhere. The reaction of Secretary of the Army Frank Pace to OPLAN 8-52 mirrored his comments on the outbreak of the Korean War, when he had been reluctant to consider the commitment of ground troops in South Korea. In 1952 he warned again that military action requiring the extensive use of ground troops in Korea would "not only prove unrealistic when measured against the availability of additional UN forces, budget requirements and our present mobilization base, but any prospect of implementing such a plan prior to 1954 is simply out of the question." And as previously noted, General Collins's first reaction to the U.N. commander's plan had been to remind Clark of America's heavy global commitments.[42]

It seems likely, however, that the Army background of Collins and Pace influenced their thoughts on the future course of the war and increased their reluctance to place ground troops in the forefront of a new and more dangerous offensive. Compared to its capability prior to June 1950, the United States was in a far stronger position. In the review of NSC 68 undertaken in August 1951, it was reported that by June 30, 1952, Army units would be "fully equipped" as regards "initial equipment," and "substantially but not fully modernized." The naval buildup was also "proceeding substantially on schedule" and "actual forces" would be "in place and operational by July 1, 1952." The 95-wing program of the Air Force would be reached about the same time, although not all wings would be equipped with the latest model of aircraft. Total military strength had been set at 3.62 million troops for June 1952, which represented a gross input of 1.55 million men during the year. Any deficiencies reported were in the accumulation of the minimum level of war reserves needed in the event of world war, production difficulties in acquiring all the military equipment thought necessary, and the delay that Korean requirements caused in sending military aid to Europe.[43] Of course, these were serious deficiencies, but less so when considered against the background of administration estimates that the Soviet Union was not prepared to risk global war over the Korean situation and had made no attempt to use the war as an opportunity to initiate hostilities or tension elsewhere.

Probably the strongest arm of the military in 1952 was the U.S. Air Force. The F-86 Sabre jet was introduced into Korea in considerable numbers that year, and the U.N. Command was able to augment its overall air strength. In February the U.N. commander had requested additional numbers of F-86 aircraft, and these were promised for delivery by October. In addition, the joint chiefs reported that 65 F-86s and 175 F-84s would be diverted from commitments in other areas, which would bring Far East Air Force wings to full strength, with a 50 percent theater reserve.[44] Until the Sabres began to appear in Korea, the MIG 15s "rendered obsolete every American plane in the Far East."[45] Hence, bringing these wings to full strength represented a significant advance in the U.S. position.

The production of aircraft had also increased substantially by July 1952. In a discussion of America's dominance of the air war, the secretary of defense, Robert Lovett, recorded monthly aircraft production figures of 838 planes, "more in one month than total Korean losses since the beginning of the war." Lovett also testified to the efficacy of the F-86 jets; the Communists were taking an "awful pasting," he said. The score was "about eight to one in favor of our Sabre-jets vs. the MIGs . . . If we keep on tearing the place apart we can make it a most unpopular affair for the North Koreans."[46] In addition, there was some reason to think that the caliber of Communist pilots was going down in September, since a conventional U.S. fighter had succeeded in destroying the superior MIG in aerial combat.[47]

Compared with conditions a year earlier, therefore, the U.S. Air Force in Korea was in a much improved military position and, according to the secretary of defense, able to maintain the military pressure there indefinitely.[48] Nevertheless, it was recognized that intensified ground operations designed to force a settlement would require additional troops and would result in more casualties. The joint chiefs had already decided that Chinese Nationalist troops should be brought in to augment Clark's ground forces, which betokened a willingness to contemplate an extension of ground warfare in the near future. But this was a decision taken on the eve of a new administration. President-elect Dwight D. Eisenhower had already indicated that he had ideas of his own about acquiring additional forces; he had asked about the feasibility of equipping additional ROK divisions by using light artillery ammunition manufactured abroad, possibly in Italy.[49] If for no other reason, timing dictated that Clark's military plan could be taken no further in the last weeks of the Truman administration.

THE DOMESTIC POLITICAL SETTING IN 1952

Inevitably, election year led to heightened Republican Party criticism of the administration's Korean War policy and to a spirited defense of it, especially by Truman. There was little in 1952 for the Democratic Party to be optimistic about, however, a fact that no doubt contributed to Truman's decision not to run for office again. At the beginning of February, the *New Republic* had urged the president to retire, stating that he was "a spent force politically." The journal reflected the opinions of most liberals that the administration had become "tired and ineffective."[50] Whatever optimism had led Acheson to predict a settlement in Korea by the end of January—which would have improved the Democrats' electoral chances—had been demolished by the impasse over the POW issue.

The continuing failure to find a way out of an unpopular war contributed to a further fall in Truman's popularity in March, when 62 percent of those polled said they disapproved of his leadership, and a majority thought that entry into the war in Korea had been a mistake.[51] Paralleling the frustrations expressed privately in all parts of the administration, the State Department's survey of public opinion revealed a strong sentiment for increasing the military pressure, breaking off negotiations, and bombing air installations across the Yalu.[52] Public opinion surveys in June and July showed that 61 percent then favored a policy of bombing in Manchuria, and 53 percent felt that the United States should "stop fooling around and do whatever is necessary to knock the Communists out of Korea once and for all."[53] This opinion was not always reflected in American editorial comment; "opinion spokesmen," as the State Department termed them, continued to support the limited-war policy. For example, the *Christian Science Monitor*, commenting on the militant mood of the general public, reminded them that an expanded war would mean greater U.S. casualties. "Perhaps the greatest lesson to be learned from the present situation," it said, "is that America cannot expect to have it all their way in Asia any more than the Chinese can be allowed to have it all their way". Hanson Baldwin of the *New York Times*, writing on the second anniversary of the outbreak of the war, also demonstrated this circumspect attitude toward the conflict. But though these newspapers were influential, other sections of the media countered their views: State Department surveys of the press showed that calls for patience were being overshadowed by charges that the Truman administration had "no policy in Korea" and by demands that the U.S./U.N. "fight to win or pull out." *Time* magazine, for example—whose editor, Henry Luce, was a vigorous supporter of Chiang Kai-shek—bluntly remarked that failure to bomb air bases in Manchuria was "stupid and dangerous," as was the reluctance to use Chinese Nationalist forces as a "threat to Red China's flank."[54]

The GOP capitalized on the dissatisfaction of the public. In a blatant appeal to the chauvinist sentiment of the electorate, Republican Congressman Gordon L. McDonough of California asserted that "never in the history of our Nation have our Armed Forces suffered defeat in war. Never has the United States set out to gain an objective through armed conflict and abandoned that objective before the battle was fought and decisively won. Never, that is, before Korea." Everywhere that Senator Robert Taft went, he accused the administration of not wanting to win in Korea, and the platform statement at the Republican convention in July 1952 accused the Democrats of waging war with "no hope for victory."[55] From the beginning of the year, the party had encouraged the public distrust of the truce negotiations by emphasizing that the Communists were using them as a screen to cover a massive military buildup above the 38th Parallel and behind the Yalu. The Republican strategy for ending the war contained no new ideas, however, beyond those MacArthur had advocated in 1950 and 1951. Some did favor substituting Asian for American troops, either Nationalist Chinese or South Korean. Eisenhower seized on this popular suggestion, too, declaring on October 2 that if there must be a war in the Far East "let it be Asians against Asians, with our support on the side of freedom."[56]

One potentially bright spot that the Democrats hoped to capitalize on was the economy: with increased governmental spending and employment opportunities, living standards were again on the rise. But the GOP could turn even the improved economic health of the nation against the Truman administration by charging that the "prosperity had at its foundation the coffins of the Korean war dead."[57] Attempts were made to kindle feelings of guilt within the electorate: Republican Senator William Jenner of Indiana declared "every Fair Deal dollar" to be "dripping with the warm blood of 1,037,513 American casualties in World War II and 109,000 casualties in the Korean police action. The Republican Party doesn't want or believe in that kind of 'prosperity.' "[58]

The economic theme was developed in another direction detrimental to the Democrats in speeches by Dulles and Taft (among others) that prophesied financial exhaustion as a result of the Truman administration's limited-war and containment policies. Dulles had broken his links with Truman in early 1952 in a bid to obtain the post of secretary of state in a new Republican administration. In May he published a detailed statement entitled "A Policy of Boldness," in which he castigated current U.S. foreign policies as "negative" and incapable of ending "the type of sustained offensive which Soviet Communism is mounting." These policies, he said, would "never end the peril nor bring relief from the exertions which devour our economic, political and moral vitals." They were "treadmill policies which, at best, might perhaps keep us in the same place until we drop exhausted."[59] Dulles's remedy was to use the threat of atomic weapons coupled with strategic air and sea power to discourage any aggressor. It was the most extensive exposition to date of his "more bang for the buck" philosophy, which allegedly would solve two problems at once: cutting military budgets, and deterring any potential act of aggression by the threat of instant and massive retaliation.

One issue subject to bipartisan agreement, however, was the U.S. position on the voluntary repatriation of prisoners of war. In February about 60 senators, led by William Jenner, considered introducing a resolution in Congress opposing the forcible return of POWs.[60] Truman's early, instinctual reaction against returning unwilling prisoners, and his administration's final decision to stand firm on this issue at the truce talks, avoided problems with Congress, was praised in newspaper editorials, and found support among the general public. The Democratic candidate, Adlai Stevenson, also affirmed that he would never force unwilling prisoners to return home, as did General Eisenhower. These domestic attitudes reinforced the decision to maintain a hard line on this question at the negotiations. Only the Progressive Party, led by Vincent Hallinan, suggested a solution to the POW issue much like Mexico's proposal. But neither formula sparked much interest, and President Truman subsequently vetoed similar ideas.

"No more 'appeasement' of Communism" was a central message of the campaign. Republicans hammered away at related accusations that Acheson and his department had failed to "save" China, had invited the Korean War, and had shielded traitors who engineered these events. The "sell-outs" at Teheran, Yalta, and Potsdam were also repeatedly referred to, and these subjects were prominent in MacArthur's keynote address to the Republican convention. Senator Richard Nixon made some of the most extreme speeches about Truman's foreign policy record, accusing the president of "losing 600 million to Communism." He and McCarthy also charged that Stevenson was "soft on Communism" and a friend and defender of Alger Hiss; he was dubbed "Adlai the appeaser."[61]

In fact, Stevenson was an ardent Cold Warrior who believed firmly in the military containment policies of Truman and in the duplicity of the Soviet Union. Acheson made two speeches on the Democratic nominee's behalf, both of which fiercely attacked Moscow and emphasized the administration's tough stand against Stalin—sentiments that Stevenson endorsed. In proving his anti-Communist credentials, Stevenson (among other Democrats) was even willing to follow McCarthyist tactics in speaking out against "the Communist conspiracy within the United States" and "the sleepless concern of the responsible governmental agencies."[62] With both Democrats and Republicans fighting to show their uncompromising attitude toward Communism, it is difficult to see how the impasse over the issue of voluntary POW repatriation could have been broken in the summer and autumn of 1952.

One way for the Republicans to distinguish their policy toward the Communist world from that of the Democrats was to contrast the "offensive" nature of the Republicans' "liberation" strategy with Truman's "defensive" containment strategy. Despite certain misgivings, Eisenhower was willing to campaign on this stand in order to separate himself from the policy of an administration with which he had had close association, and to help heal the rift between the eastern and Taft wings of the GOP. After beating off Taft's strong challenge for the nomination, Eisenhower realized that he needed Taft and his many supporters to campaign on his behalf. As a bid to breach the divide, speaking before the American Legion convention in August, he called on U.S. citizens to join him in "rolling back the Communist tide in a great moral crusade." In September the Republican nominee finally arranged a meeting with Taft in which he hoped to work out their differences on foreign and domestic issues. Agreeing almost wholly on a statement Taft had drafted, they struck a bargain, and thereafter the senator publicly gave unequivocal support to Eisenhower's presidential bid.[63]

Eisenhower was willing to make other compromises to satisfy the conservative wing of the party. Appearing on a platform with McCarthy in Milwaukee, he declared that "national tolerance of Communism had 'poisoned two whole decades of our national life' and insinuated itself in our schools, public forums, news channels, labor unions, 'and—most terrifying—into our government itself.'" He also agreed to remove from his speech a favorable reference to General Marshall, whom he greatly admired, on the grounds that it would be seen as an "unnecessary rebuff to McCarthy and might jeopardize Republican successes locally and nationally."[64] His demonstrated willingness to engage in political compromise was a mark not only of Eisenhower's campaign but also, later on, of his period in office.

Throughout the autumn, and as a result of private polls indicating that Korea was a matter of grave concern to the electorate, Eisenhower moved to make the war a crucial part of his campaign. Where Stevenson commended the administration's hard stand at the truce talks and the moral correctness of its position on the POWs, Eisenhower criticized the decision to enter into truce negotiations, which he described as a trap. And he repeated a familiar GOP theme: the Truman administration had invited the war by its long-term mismanagement of Far Eastern policies.

Eisenhower's most valuable card was his ability to portray himself as a person of international and military experience; he had been involved in far greater conflicts than Korea, from which he and the country had emerged victorious. When Gallup asked

voters which candidate could "handle the Korean situation best,"
67 percent said Eisenhower; only 9 percent gave Adlai Stevenson
the benefit of the doubt.[65] Eisenhower's pledge on October 24 that
if elected, he would go to Korea was electrifying in its appeal and
equivalent for many Americans to his saying that he would end the
war. All he had promised to do, as he explained later, was to visit
Korea and "find out from those on the spot what more could be
done to improve our situation and what could help bring that
tragic war to an end at the earliest moment compatible with the
honor of the United States."[66] Despite this disclaimer of his ability
to find an easy solution to the Korean conflict, Eisenhower's experience and all the discussion of "liberation" and going on the offensive raised the expectation that he would find some way out of the
impasse. Indeed, whatever course of action Eisenhower might
have proposed as a method of ending the war would probably
have been endorsed by a majority of the voters in 1952.

ASSESSMENT OF SOVIET INTENTIONS AND REACTIONS

Eisenhower made no explicit reference in his election campaign
to the likely Soviet reaction to an expansion of the Korean War,
though he did question whether the spread of hostilities could
guarantee an end to the conflict. His prospective secretary of state,
however, made clear in major foreign policy addresses his belief
that the threat of instant retaliation would deter the Soviet Union
from further military moves, perhaps even from actions in support
of its Chinese ally. Members of the Truman administration had
also arrived at the conclusion that Moscow would not undertake
activity that risked global war, though they got there by a different
route from the one taken by Dulles.

They also foresaw the possibility that the war, and the Soviet
desire to maintain a limited role in it, could create tensions between
Moscow and Peking. New life was breathed into the "wedge"
strategy in 1952 through suggestions that enforced dependence on
Moscow would soon lead Peking to see the disadvantages of that
relationship, and Moscow to see the debilitating effects of supporting its ally's material needs. One official in the State Department's
Far Eastern Affairs Division, urged the United States to maintain its
military and economic pressure on China and not to relax or soften

its attitude. Sterner measures would, he said, "more speedily bring to a climax strained relations with the USSR forcing the Kremlin to reveal more fully and ruthlessly its plans to make Communist China a satellite." George Kennan, who had become ambassador to the Soviet Union, advanced the other side of the argument in August during Chou En-lai's visit to Moscow. Increased attempts to frighten China, he argued, might lead Peking to step up its demands on Moscow, thus introducing new stresses into the relationship.[67] Kennan's suggestion obviously appealed to the Truman administration and to the U.N. Command in Tokyo, who agreed that everything should be done to increase China's demands for Russian supplies. Consequently, the United States launched its heaviest bombing campaign of the war against Pyongyang at this time, and shortly it was confirmed that the "relentless continuation of [the] program of destruction" was "frightening" the Chinese, as their radio broadcasts indicated.[68]

A national intelligence estimate also concluded that despite a community of interest between Peking and Moscow based on "close ideological ties, common objectives, and common fears," there still existed "latent sources of friction and even of conflict" between the two powers, which the war had exacerbated.[69] The circumscribed nature of Soviet support for its ally was likely to strain these common interests, which for the moment prevented an open rift between the two Communist states. Soviet relations with North Korea had also been damaged, it was thought. As the State Department explained, Moscow's limited role in the war was contributing to the demise of Soviet influence in Pyongyang, to Peking's advantage.[70] Thus, in the department's opinion, the conflict might be leading to a diminution of both the political and the military strength of the U.S.S.R.

CIA estimates maintained the position that the Soviet Union did not want to precipitate global war, and that Moscow was fearful that the extent of its material and physical support for China and North Korea would be challenged. A national intelligence estimate of July 30, for example, had recognized that a de facto air war existed over North Korea between the U.S./U.N. and the U.S.S.R., but that Moscow was unlikely to take the grave risks associated with committing Soviet aircraft over U.N.-held territory. Furthermore, the CIA continued to believe that Moscow would not make the effort required to win the battle in Korea, because such action would risk world war; rather, the agency argued, the Communists really wanted an armistice, would continue with the negotiations, and would "not take the initiative to break the present military stalemate." Soviet feelers at the U.N. and the temporary encouragement Peking gave to Indian efforts to break the Panmunjom deadlock indicated that both major Communist governments wanted to find a solution to the POW issue. Despite the Kremlin's equipping of the Chinese air force, it had still sought "to limit its own role in the Korean war and has not sought to use the war as an excuse for initiating broader hostilities."[71]

Why the Soviets should be so concerned about the prospects of world war was explained in another intelligence study at the end of 1952. Moscow "almost certainly estimates," it said, "that global war would involve at a minimum widespread destruction to the USSR and the risk that its system of control would be destroyed"[72]—a conclusion that demonstrated an awareness of the superiority of America's atomic capabilities. Indeed, the nineteenth Party Congress in Moscow in August 1952 made it clear that the Soviet Union recognized America's technological lead. While the Soviet Union would still work to dampen the pace of Western mobilization, the main task was to strengthen its domestic economy so that it could concentrate resources on military-related scientific and technological research.[73]

Few within the American military disagreed with these estimates of Soviet intentions in Korea, and they were prepared to support their views publicly. General Bradley, for example, in a speech in March, had explained Soviet reluctance to start a general war as a consequence of America's expanding atomic stockpile, the growth of the U.S. Air Force, and the rehabilitation of Western Europe.[74] And many went on to link this assessment of Soviet intentions to policy deliberations concerning the possible extension of the war to China. In August, a memorandum to the undersecretary of the Army, Karl Bendetson, from Special Consultant Ralph J. Watkins made this connection clear. Watkins, fresh from a trip to Japan and Korea, wrote: "In all my high command policy conferences there appeared to be the same view of Soviet intentions as we have expressed here, namely, the belief that the Soviet would not be 'provoked' to initiation of a full-scale global war by any United Nations Command retaliation against Communist China—unless the Soviet had concluded that the time was right for striking and they all doubted that Soviet calculations could lead to any such conclusion now." In addition, Watkins disputed any notion of the invincibility of Soviet air power in the Far East, reporting that the realization of the U.S.S.R.'s vulnerability in that area and the increase in U.S. air capabilities had assuaged General Weyland's fears of a Soviet air attack upon Japan. Frank Pace, in a letter to President Truman that accompanied the Watkins report, said that the document was "quite in line with the policy decisions reached at the White House conferences."[75] What little contemporary evidence we have of Truman's thoughts on Soviet intentions in Korea seems to confirm the validity of Pace's remark. As Truman told the Chinese Nationalist ambassador, Wellington Koo, in November, he "did not believe the Soviet Union would want to extend the war" in Korea.[76]

General Clark, who recommended expanding hostilities into China in order to obtain a settlement of the Korean conflict, also connected the evidence of Soviet self-interest and caution with a denial of the risks of launching attacks on China. In his reply to the joint chiefs' memorandum of September 23, in which they had asked for comments on their possible future orders requiring the removal of most restrictions on the prosecution of the war, Clark was certain such action would not cause Moscow to enter the conflict: "The USSR has no qualms about dishonoring pledges such as may be included in the Sino-Russian mutual assistance pact. The USSR needs no excuses for her acts. In fact, the UNC has already been accused of countless alleged violations of the Manchurian border and attacks on Chinese territory. . . . I believe that World War Three will not be brought about by action on our part, that conflict will commence only when the USSR so determines on her own appraisal, unaffected by US or UNC actions, and that therefore any so-called extension of the Korean op[eratio]ns presents little risk in so far as precipitating World War Three is concerned."[77] All but one of the commanding officers in the Far East agreed with General Clark that the Soviet Union would not enter an expanded conflict, despite its treaty obligations. In their view, Moscow preferred to fight by proxy rather than risk involvement in a wider war.[78]

Acheson and other members of the State Department began to express the same kind of certainty. Furthermore, they were now very explicit about the circumstances under which the U.S.S.R.

would give full support to the PRC. In February 1952, at tripartite meetings held in Washington with the Canadians and British, Paul Nitze, H. Freeman Matthews, and John M. Allison listed two conditions under which they assumed the Sino-Soviet treaty would be invoked: if the overthrow of the Chinese Communist government appeared imminent; if some point in China close to the Soviet border were attacked. The State Department was proceeding on the hypothesis that Russia would not intervene if attacks delivered against the PRC were "strictly in connection with the Korean operations"; in Nitze's view, the Soviets would be prepared to see the Chinese take a "lot of punishment" before going to their assistance. In an alarming revelation of department practices, Nitze stated that in fact "there were so many unknown factors affecting relations between China and Russia that the State Department was inclined to exclude consideration of the possible effects on Sino-Soviet relations in making up its mind about the course of action to be adopted in the Far East."[79] Whatever else such a statement indicated about the quality of State Department advice on China and Russia, it showed that the alliance between Peking and Moscow did not expressly deter Washington when its officials considered military action beyond the Yalu.

The hypothesis concerning the conditions under which the Sino-Soviet Treaty of Alliance would be invoked appeared to hold firm for the State Department throughout 1952. In June, during ministerial talks in London to examine policy in the event of Chinese aggression in Indochina, Acheson stated that the United States was thinking in terms of "a blockade of the coast of China, combined with air action designed to upset the economy of mainland China and to lessen the will of the Chinese Communists to continue their aggression." Great efforts would be made to avoid the sensitive border areas of the Soviet Union, he said, but the United States was "of the opinion that the Soviet Union would probably not enter the conflict if it understood clearly that we had no intention of attempting to overthrow the Chinese Communist regime by force."[80] State Department officials had taken longer than others to reach this assessment of Sino-Soviet relations; thus their acceptance of this point of view represented a significant new stage in U.S. policy. No longer would Acheson argue that an expansion of hostilities into China risked world war. In a sense, he had reverted to his pre–Korean War position, that the "basic interests" of Moscow conflicted with those of Peking.

This, then, was the dominant view within the Truman administration regarding the likely Soviet reaction to a direct attack on Chinese territory. It should be acknowledged, however, that the occasional remark seemed to contradict this assessment. For example, at the close of Truman's tenure of office, Secretary of Defense Lovett discussed China's acquisition of jet bombers, which could only be "knocked out by bombing across the Yalu River," he said, but "if we do that it might be world war III."[81] This cryptic remark may have meant that Lovett believed Moscow would give its support to China if the United States bombed Chinese air bases, or that he thought any extension of bombing operations was likely to get out of control, leading first to a general war in the Far East and then to global conflict. Although some recent analysis argues that Lovett's statement demonstrates why the administration refused to sanction such bombing tactics,[82] much else that administration spokesmen said in 1952 denied that an expanded war would lead to World War III. Despite residual fears regarding Soviet reactions to an attack on China, the dominant view was that Moscow would not come openly and extensively to the support of China unless it appeared that the PRC government was about to fall as a consequence of U.S. bombing activity, or unless bombing operations strayed close to sensitive Soviet border areas. Perhaps Lovett made a statement that bolstered the concept of a limited war in an attempt at the close of the Truman administration to reaffirm what had been a central component of the public argument against an extended war. Perhaps he made it realizing that it was impossible anyway, at that stage, to initiate any new courses of action; the mandate had passed to a new administration.

That Truman should finish his political career with an unresolved Far Eastern conflict as its epitaph invites comparison with another Democratic president 16 years later. Other aspects of their conduct of these Asian wars also ran parallel, including their use of bombing operations in an attempt to force compliance from Communist negotiators. Given earlier concessions made by the Communist side, the Truman administration initially thought it would win on the POW issue.[83] It was in an attempt to ensure success that Truman sanctioned devastating air operations in North Korea, the bombing of installations on or near the Yalu, and increased harassment of the Chinese Communist government.

Members of the State Department again suggested various ways out of the impasse on the issue of the nonrepatriates at the close of the Truman administration. Charles C. Stelle of the Policy Planning Staff, for example, considered presenting the Communists with a *fait accompli* by reclassifying those prisoners refusing repatriation as political refugees, and then handing them over either to the South Koreans, or—in the case of the Chinese—to countries of their choice. Others within the administration suggested releasing the nonrepatriates unilaterally. But the possible repercussions from such courses of action were recognized to be so great that they could not be initiated during the last weeks of Truman's administration.[84]

The only course Truman could see to follow was to increase steadily the military punishment inflicted on the Communist forces, which might have culminated in an extension of the war to the Chinese mainland through a naval blockade and bombing activity. Whether Truman would ever have got to this point, we do not know. Probably he should be given the benefit of the doubt, and it should be assumed that he would have maintained a limited-war policy at the same time that he meted out ever greater punishment. But the augmentation of U.S. air strength encouraged those who were in favor of an expanded war, as did Moscow's persistent efforts to keep its material and physical involvement hidden and limited.

The allies—especially the British and the Canadians—did impose some constraints on a geographical extension of hostilities. Acheson consistently emphasized the value of international support for U.S. policies and continued to press for time to gain allied compliance with U.S. military and political activity, or at least for time to inform other governments of intended U.S. action. The British government's response to the bombing of the Yalu power installations demonstrated only too clearly the disruptive effect of an information failure on U.S.-U.K. relations, and the damage that could be done to the image of a strong and united Western bloc. The secretary of state's response to the Mexican proposal demonstrated once more the premium he placed on maintaining unity with U.N. members in order to retain the aura of legitimacy that the United Nations gave to U.S. activity in Korea. He was also aware that the U.S. role as UNC negotiator would be undermined if America did not appear to consider with some seriousness other governments' proposals for resolving the POW question. And he recognized that the U.S. position would be seriously damaged if

Truman sanctioned an expanded war over this particular issue, after all other important aspects of the armistice agreement had been concluded.

Nevertheless, though Acheson remained responsive to allied and neutral opinion, the Pentagon became less so during 1952. Because the burden that U.S. forces bore in Korea was irksome, relative to that of other countries, and their entanglement in Korea appeared likely to be long term, the Defense Department resented the furor the Yalu bombings caused, the private British protest regarding the use of napalm, and the unwillingness of the allies to consider a total economic embargo against China when Peking's forces were killing American servicemen. With Truman's consent, it gradually loosened the restraints on military operations and controls over the U.N. commander. As Mark Clark later reported, in 1952 he had "developed the procedure of just notifying Washington what [he] was going to do." Each day he was thinking up new schemes for hurting the Communists,[85] one of which involved a plea to consider the use of atomic weapons in order to end the war on U.S. terms. The joint chiefs were also considering the removal of all restrictions on the prosecution of the war except for attacks on the U.S.S.R. proper.

The Defense Department under Secretary Lovett apparently increased its influence with Truman in the last months of his administration. General Marshall's appointment as Secretary of Defense in September 1950 had undercut Acheson's preeminent position within the bureaucracy, as had the subsequent elevation of Marshall's deputy to that post. In a sense, Lovett wore the mantle of Marshall; he had enjoyed the general's confidence and thus gained the confidence of Truman also. More significantly, Truman appeared to want a clear-cut victory over the issue of the nonforcible repatriation of POWs, since victory on the battlefield had been denied him. U.S. willingness to consider the Mexican proposal seriously, for example, would have made it appear to the general public and to the Communists that the administration was willing to compromise on this issue. Acheson's arguments, primarily designed to maintain unity with U.N. members, thus had no influence on the president in September 1952. As a result, Acheson soon abandoned this tactic; at the U.N. in November he was tough and uncompromising in attempting to force allied compliance with U.S. goals.

By the end of the year, given the predominance of the Defense

Department in the decision-making process, allied opinion and projected Soviet reactions carried less weight in preventing an extension of the war into China. Moreover, U.S. capabilities within the theater improved during this period. But it was not until autumn that the F-86s became available in greater numbers and not until November that some additional ground forces could be found. An increase in ground troops was considered vital, because any intensification of operations to include attacks on China would also involve a movement into North Korea. Whereas the bombing of Chinese air bases and communication and supply lines probably would be effective only in the long term, the psychological blow of a loss of North Korean territory in combination with widespread bombing was thought likely to force concessions at the negotiating table. Hence, ground forces were an important requirement and as yet not available in the numbers General Clark thought necessary to carry out his plan successfully.

In addition, an extended war that would involve an increase in U.S./U.N. casualties and further drain U.S. military resources was difficult to justify; its sole warrant would have had to rest on the failure to resolve the issue of voluntary POW repatriation. The Communists provided no overriding military reason for expanding the war; U.S./U.N. ground troops had not been subjected to air attack despite the growth in Chinese air power. As the secretary of the Air Force, Thomas K. Finletter, revealed, the ground forces had been "free to move at will" because the Communists had "never taken the offensive in the air." And the Communist response to the stepped-up bombing activity in 1952 was circumspect to say the least; even when U.S. aircraft bombed the power installations, the stiff aerial opposition they expected never materialized.[86] The Antung air complex was only 35 miles from the Suiho power complex, but the MIGs located at Antung did not challenge the operation. Without any evidence of harassment from the air, it would have been difficult to establish the legitimacy of a decision to attack China.

By the time the United States was beginning to feel the strength of its military position in Korea, the country was in the throes of an election. Truman was so wholly identified with a limited-war policy that to extend the hostilities at that stage would have led to the charge that he was simply "electioneering." The GOP would also have criticized him for failing to follow MacArthur's lead nearly two years earlier. As General Clark's plan for an expanded war was being considered, Eisenhower became president-elect, winning 55 percent of the popular vote. Such momentous decisions as sanctioning intensified military operations or letting loose those prisoners unwilling to return home could not be taken by an outgoing administration.

Analysis of the 1952 vote has shown that the war did have a significant negative impact on Truman's popularity.[87] The Democratic administration went out of office partly through the force of a powerful alliterative slogan—Korea, corruption, and communism in government—coined by Republican opponents who were willing to sanction McCarthyist tactics in villifying the Democratic nominee.[88] But Eisenhower's pledge on October 24 to go to Korea and see what could be done to end the war, uttered by a man with his military reputation, was decisive in electoral terms. The frustrations at the military "stalemate" in Korea reflected in domestic opinion were relieved by a presidential candidate able to convince voters that he could break the deadlock.

[7]

The Strategy for Ending the War: January–July 1953

There were areas of continuity between Truman and Eisenhower administration policy toward the Korean War, despite the advent of a new executive with a fresh mandate and some new perspectives and personalities. The joint chiefs and General Omar Bradley stayed in their posts until August 1953, and Truman's director of the CIA, Bedell Smith, became undersecretary of state, working closely with John Foster Dulles. Their continuing presence ensured the maintenance of certain policy calculations about the most productive way to end the conflict. It was Eisenhower rather than Truman who took the decision to terminate negotiations if no further concessions were forthcoming from the Communist side, probably because the policy reassessments undertaken at the close of the Truman administration did not come to fruition until the winter of 1952 and spring of 1953. Acheson's comment that the November election did not allow the Truman administration enough time to do the job of "convincing the Chinese and North Koreans to bring the Korean war to a close"[1] reflected the overlapping views of the two chief executives.

Eisenhower's presidency did differ from Truman's in that Truman had encountered growing hostility, whereas the general enjoyed the confidence of the public; this fact removed some domestic and congressional restraints on Korean War policy. In addition, Eisenhower had built up the expectation that he would end the war soon; thus a decisive act on his part was both looked for and possible. Moreover, there appeared to be a significant change in attitude to the potential role of nuclear weapons. Though members of the previous administration had been constantly alert to the targets and situations that, from their point of view, might have made the use of such weapons profitable, Dulles and Eisenhower, unlike Acheson and Truman, frequently discussed these weapons as though they were just like any other except more powerful. These shifts in attitudes and improvements in conventional military capabilities implied that Eisenhower was free to conduct the fighting in ways as yet untried.

BREAKING THE STALEMATE: THE BUREAUCRATIC DEBATE

Eisenhower's visit to Korea in December 1952 raised a number of expectations, not least in the mind of U.N. Commander Mark Clark, who believed an expansion of the conflict would shortly be sanctioned. But to Clark's chagrin, Eisenhower at that time did not question how much additional effort it would take to win in Korea, or undertake a detailed discussion of the general's plan.[2] The president-elect preferred to leave the discussion of future policy until certain designated cabinet colleagues could come together, such as John Foster Dulles (State), Charles E. Wilson (Defense), and George M. Humphrey (Treasury). Meeting on board the USS *Helena* en route to Pearl Harbor, Eisenhower and his advisers agreed that any further delay in the truce negotiations could not be tolerated and that the United States "would have to prepare to break the stalemate." In their view, the only way to end the conflict "was to make the other side want to end it."[3]

Although Eisenhower strongly preferred to attempt a peaceful conclusion to the conflict in Korea, he was willing to consider ending the stalemate by going over to a major offensive, to involve—as stated in his memoirs—"strikes against the supporting Chinese airfields in Manchuria, a blockade of the Chinese coast, and similar measures." In addition, both U.S. and ROK force levels were to be built up in Korea, as were ammunition stocks. To prevent an expanded war from becoming "overly costly," Eisenhower was prepared to use nuclear weapons on "strategic targets in North Korea, Manchuria, and on the Chinese coast."[4] Like Truman, he did not believe that anything other than unrelenting military pressure would bring an end to the war. Soon after his return from Korea, he stated: "We face an enemy whom we cannot hope to impress by words, however eloquent, but only by deeds—*executed under circumstances of our own choosing*" (original emphasis).[5]

Some detailed and exhaustive assessments of the military action required to end the war were available to the new president. In December 1952, MacArthur had presented Eisenhower with his revised plan, which the president later suggested had influenced his thinking on the need to use nuclear weapons.[6] Of greater significance were the deliberations of the Joint Strategic Plans Committee, which in October 1952 had been instructed by the joint chiefs to reexamine the conclusions of NSC 118/2 and to advise courses of action that might lead to an armistice agreement on U.S. terms. These deliberations took some time, however, and the final report was not ready until March 23rd.[7]

Soon thereafter, the JCS sent it to the secretary of defense. It began with a familiar statement, that one of the basic reasons for the failure to achieve an armistice was insufficient military pressure on the enemy, then listed six courses of action that might be taken to force a settlement. For each course, it explained the objectives, military advantages and disadvantages, force requirements, internal and external political repercussions, and so on. It reviewed arguments for and against the use of nuclear weapons, potential allied and enemy reactions to their use, and the possible role Chinese Nationalist and South Korean troops could play in an expanded war. This report represented the most detailed discussion that had so far been undertaken of the options open to the United States, but it made no recommendations; that assignment was reserved for the National Security Council.

In April the NSC Planning Board circulated the report,[8] which it had made more comprehensible by listing the six courses of action in order of increasing severity. In the board's view, it was "hopeless" to continue the search for an acceptable formula on the POW issue; therefore, it was now considered necessary to examine seriously the six military options available, with a view to their future implementation.

Course A suggested a further buildup in South Korean forces in order to effect a limited redeployment of U.S. forces from Korea; course B, intensification of military pressure in order to make hostilities so costly that the enemy might agree to an armistice on U.S. terms; course C, maximum destruction of enemy forces and materiel in Korea through a series of "coordinated ground operations along the present line, followed by a major offensive to establish a line at the waist of Korea." Courses D, E, and F, however, involved an expansion of the war into China; they were described in NSC 147 as follows:

Course D—Extend and intensify military pressures on the enemy by stages, including air attack and naval blockade directly against Manchuria and Communist China, and, if required, increase ground operations in Korea, with a view to making hostilities so costly to the enemy that a favorable settlement of the Korean war might be achieved.

Course E—Undertake a coordinated offensive to the waist of Korea, and a naval blockade and air and naval attacks directly against Manchuria and Communist China, with a view to inflicting maximum possible destruction of enemy forces and materiel in Korea consistent with establishing a line at the waist, and to achieving a favorable settlement of the Korean war.

Course F—Undertake a coordinated, large-scale offensive in Korea, and a naval blockade and air and naval attacks directly against Manchuria and Communist China, with a view to the defeat and destruction of the bulk of the communist forces in Korea and settlement of the Korean war on the basis of a unified, non-communist Korea.

In outlining some of the military operations to be considered, the NSC Planning Board utilized the conclusions of a CIA report that estimated the likely effects of actions designed to impede the internal and external commerce of the PRC. The CIA study looked at three courses of action: a total embargo; naval blockade alone or combined with the "bombardment of transportation facilities in Communist China"; and blockade and aerial bombardment by the Chinese Nationalists.[9] None of these would certainly induce the Communists to agree to a settlement at the truce talks, in the CIA view; however, they would progressively reduce China's economic and military capabilities. In this respect, they retained some appeal for the NSC Planning Board, especially if they could be combined with other military activity.

In the light of Chou En-lai's conciliatory statement on March 30, indicating a desire to find a solution to the POW question and endorsing an earlier U.N. Command proposal to exchange sick and wounded prisoners, the NSC did not immediately take up the planning board's recommendations. Further delays in the talks, however, resulted in a directive from Wilson to the joint chiefs requesting them to forward their opinions on the six courses of action proposed by the NSC Board. The Joint Strategic Plans Committee (JSPC) carried out the preliminary analysis of NSC 147 for the joint chiefs, and because of a disagreement among the three branches of the armed services (the Air Force wanted air and naval operations to be combined with a ground offensive "as required";

the Army and Navy favored a coordinated offensive of all three branches), it declined to single out one course from the six, preferring instead to recommend a combination of courses D, E, and F. The joint chiefs accepted this conclusion and reported to Wilson on May 19. Such a combination would be "the most effective and the most economical in the long run for the United States to pursue in Korea," they said.

The three courses were thus condensed as follows and presented orally to the NSC meeting on the following day:

> Extend and intensify military action against the enemy, to include air and naval operations directly against China and Manchuria, a coordinated offensive to seize a position generally at the waist of Korea and be prepared for further operations as required in order to:
>   *a.* Destroy effective Communist military power in Korea.
>   *b.* Reduce the enemy's capabilities for further aggression in Korea and the Far East.
>   *c.* Increase possibility of enemy acceptance of an armistice on U.S.-U.N. terms.
>   *d.* Create conditions favorable for ROK forces to assume increasing responsibility for operations in Korea.

In order to achieve these objectives, U.S. and ROK force levels would have to be increased, and the U.N. Command should be prepared to launch an air offensive against Communist air complexes and other targets north of the Yalu; initiate air and naval attacks against Communist lines of communication in North Korea, China, and Manchuria; establish a naval blockade and conduct a mining campaign. It should also be ready to engage in mock airborne and amphibious raids to draw the enemy out into the open, conduct an aggressive land campaign to seize a position at Hungnam-Sinanju, and support Chinese Nationalist diversionary operations.

The joint chiefs also made it clear that these combined courses of action (in fact, all of them except course A and possibly B) would require the employment of atomic weapons "on a sufficiently large scale to insure success." They were convinced that piecemeal or limited implementation of these plans, "including extensive strategical and tactical use of atomic bombs," would not do if there were to be "maximum surprise and maximum impact on the enemy, both militarily and psychologically." General Nathan F. Twining told the president that success would require the complete destruction of the Chinese Communist air force.[10]

President Eisenhower voiced his anxiety about the possibility of Soviet retaliatory attacks "on the almost defenseless population centers of Japan" but agreed that the "quicker the operation was mounted the less the danger of Soviet intervention." Beyond this one anxiety, there was very little inclination at that meeting to challenge the joint chiefs' recommendations. Eisenhower therefore quickly announced that if the NSC members agreed, he wanted it recorded that "if circumstances arose which would force the United States to an expanded effort in Korea, the plan selected by the Joint Chiefs of Staff was most likely to achieve the objectives we sought." His statement was duly noted in the council's minutes.

Various activities would need to be undertaken immediately if the United States were to be ready to mount the operation within a year, at the latest. For example, the ammunition program for NATO forces had to be cut back, and additional stocks made available in Korea, and ROK and U.S. force levels had to be augmented. General Clark was instructed to revise his OPLAN 8-52 to meet the new objectives and the decision to employ nuclear weapons. In addition, the allies were to be apprised of the possibility of a military campaign to end the war. And hints were to be dropped in certain quarters: Dulles informed Nehru, on the assumption that it would be relayed to Peking, that "if armistice negotiations collapsed, the United States would probably make a stronger rather than a lesser military exertion, and that this might well extend the area of conflict."[11]

Concurrently with these deliberations, the U.N. Command had been inflicting more extensive military punishment on the Communists. In the largest attack for more than a year, ten American B-29s dropped 100 tons of high explosives on Communist frontline positions on February 2, only hours before President Eisenhower announced in his State of the Union message that the Seventh Fleet would "no longer be employed to shield Communist China." In May, the U.S./U.N. undertook the destruction of irrigation dams and rice fields. The aim of these bombing operations was to wash out enemy lines of communication, such as railways and roads, but also to destroy the rice crop, thereby increasing unrest in the countryside and ultimately causing famine.[12]

This campaign was coordinated with new instructions to the

U.N. delegation at the truce talks. On May 23 the joint chiefs sent Clark the administration's final position on the question of the voluntary repatriation of prisoners of war. The U.N. negotiator was to explain to the Communist side that this position was "final," but it was not to be presented in the form of an ultimatum. A one-week recess was to follow. If, during this period, the Communists rejected the U.N.'s final terms, the negotiations were to be not simply recessed but terminated—in which case, the joint chiefs informed Clark, they would "be prepared to act expeditiously." As General Clark later explained, this meant he could launch "conventional attacks on bridges across the Yalu and on bases in Manchuria" as soon as the negotiations officially ended. Specifically, the joint chiefs authorized him to step up air and naval operations, continue heavy bombing of North Korea, increase guerilla operations, deneutralize the Kaesong zone and bomb the area, and set free those prisoners unwilling to be repatriated. In the longer term, however, the more extensive courses of action recommended at the May 20 NSC meeting would be implemented.[13]

The decision to bring the negotiations to a head reflected the preferences of both the president and his secretary of state. Indeed, Dulles appeared to dislike the whole notion of the truce negotiations. On April 8, during an NSC discussion, he stated that he thought it "questionable whether [the U.S.] should feel bound by the other provisions in the armistice which we had agreed earlier," and that it was "now quite possible to secure a much more satisfactory settlement in Korea than a mere armistice at the 38th parallel." Although Dulles recognized that there would be allied objections to reopening discussion of the agreed-upon provisions, and subsequently he did very little to achieve new armistice terms, what he really wanted to say to the Communists was that unless they agreed to divide Korea at the waist, the United States would call off the armistice.[14] At a dinner in Washington on April 6, Dulles had explained to newspaper correspondents why a division at the waist would be advantageous: it would give Syngman Rhee's government 80 percent of the population of the country, plus valuable industries to supplement the agriculture of the South. With misguided self-righteousness, he added that if the Communists refused a truce along this line, the United States would take it as a sign that they were not acting in good faith.[15]

Eisenhower appeared to agree with his secretary of state. In March he had asked Robert Cutler, special assistant for National Security Affairs, to study what it would cost to reach the waist of Korea while doing the maximum damage to Chinese forces. At the end of the month, he spoke of the possibility of using nuclear weapons in order to "achieve a substantial victory over the Communist forces and . . . to get a line at the waist of Korea."[16] But whereas the president was considering various formulas designed to bring the negotiations to a conclusion, Dulles at times seemed more interested in devising schemes to justify calling off the talks. Later in April he provided further evidence of his disinclination to continue with the negotiation process when he told Robert Murphy, the U.S. ambassador in Tokyo, that Washington felt the talks would soon "prove to be a booby trap, enabling increased communist build-up to our disadvantage." The Communists, he said, had had "nearly two years to think over every aspect" of the settlement, and if they were really serious in this regard, "it should only be a matter of days" before they shifted their position on the POW question.[17]

In addition to proposing harsher settlement terms and being anxious to bring matters to a head, Dulles also seemed to be in favor of breaching the armistice agreement unless it was quickly followed by a permanent political settlement leading to a unified, "democratic" Korea. The president supported this position, and the NSC agreed that "the United States interprets the purpose of the armistice to be the achievement of a political settlement in Korea and that, if this purpose is not achieved within a reasonable time, the armistice may be voided."[18] As the exchange of sick and wounded prisoners was taking place between April 20 and May 3, Dulles's willingness to see this exchange as a hopeful sign was conditioned by his desire to prevent the conclusion of an armistice agreement until better terms had been extracted.

Not everyone in the State Department agreed with him. The push to move the permanent line to the waist of Korea and the threat of "voiding" the armistice seriously disturbed a number of lower-level officials. Kenneth T. Young and Charles Ogburn (Northeast Asian and Far Eastern Affairs, respectively) considered these suggestions both dangerous and unrealistic. They may have been as uncompromising as Dulles on the question of voluntary repatriation, but widening the war to achieve different armistice terms did not interest them. Indeed, Ogburn was so out of touch with Dulles's thinking that he even recommended reducing the military pressure on China and "talking peace instead of talking war. . . . As far as possible," he said, "consistent with our obligations and commitments, we should give the Chinese Communists as little reason as possible to find the U.S. an implacable and belligerent antagonist." In this way, China "would have a chance to begin perceiving the essential differences between its interests and those of the Soviet Union."[19]

Thoughts such as these were considered "disturbing" elsewhere within the department,[20] but they had little influence on Dulles, who was keen "to keep the Chinese under maximum pressure" and undermine their military prestige. In March, the speech writer, Emmet Hughes, asked whether the United States would "be glad—or—sorry if *tomorrow* the Communists *accepted* the Indian compromise" resolution, which had recommended a maximum of three months' retention by an international commission of those prisoners resisting repatriation, and which the General Assembly had accepted by a vote of 54 to 5 in December 1952. Dulles replied: "We'd be sorry. *I don't think we can get much out of a Korean settlement until we have shown—before all Asia—our clear superiority by giving the Chinese one hell of a licking*" (original emphasis).[21]

As recommended by the JCS and accepted by the administration, such a "licking" would have involved the use of atomic weapons. The "swift rethinking" of nuclear policy by the joint chiefs in the new administration may have been dictated by the successful detonation in mid-January of an atomic warhead of a size suitable for use as a tactical battlefield weapon.[22] But the joint chiefs' own explanation for their shift of position referred more to the surprise element associated with the weapons' use, the speed at which they could destroy enemy bases, and, in general, their ability to achieve greater results at less cost to the United States. It was not so much that weapons development served to provide the military with new options—although the atomic stockpile had grown larger— but simply that in the early Eisenhower years, at least, there was an expressed willingness to regard nuclear weapons as being like any other weapon of war. Their only distinction was that they had the power to bring a conflict to an end much faster and at less cost in terms of casualties when compared with the delay and expense of augmenting conventional forces.

Such thoughts about the role of nuclear arms pervaded the Eisenhower administration. They were reflected in the logic behind the "massive retaliation" strategy and the defense budget adjustments from 1953. Both Eisenhower and Dulles spoke of atomic weapons as though they represented a quantitative rather than a qualitative difference in methods of destruction. At an NSC meeting in February, Dulles emphasized the need to make their use more acceptable: he "discussed the moral problem and the inhibition on the use of the A-bomb, and Soviet success to date in setting atomic weapons apart from all other weapons as being in a special category. It was his opinion that we should try to break down this distinction." Also during this meeting, Eisenhower suggested that the United States should consider the use of tactical atomic weapons on the neutralized Kaesong zone, which General Clark said the Communists were using as an advanced military base, since it "provided a good target for this type of weapon."[23] In March both Dulles and Eisenhower were "in complete agreement that somehow or other the tabu which surrounds the use of atomic weapons would have to be destroyed."[24] In discussions at the end of the year with the British foreign minister, Anthony Eden, Eisenhower was certain that an adverse reaction from the American public was not to be feared: "The American public no longer distinguished between atomic and other weapons," he said, adding, "nor [was] there logically any distinction."[25] The president expressed a similar willingness to employ these weapons in the spring of 1955, when he said that "where these things are used on strictly military targets and for strictly military purposes, I see no reason why they shouldn't be used just exactly as you would use a bullet or anything else."[26] The president was committed to using tactical nuclear weapons whenever they were deemed militarily appropriate. He did not wish to see their "possibilities neglected."[27]

One question that has concerned analysts of this period of the war is whether the Eisenhower administration would actually have used atomic weapons if conventional means had not brought about a settlement of the Korean conflict. Or was the executive branch engaged in an elaborate bluff? We shall never know, of course, since even when policy makers indicate a firm intention to take a particular course of action under certain circumstances, they often do otherwise when those circumstances arise.[28] But despite this ultimate uncertainty, there is now extensive documentary evidence to show that the use of atomic weapons became an integral part of the planning designed to force a military solution in Korea. At a special NSC meeting in March, for example, Eisenhower remarked that though "there were not many good tactical targets . . . he felt it would be worth the cost" if their use led to a substantial victory over the Communists and a line at the waist of Korea.[29] At a meeting on May 13 called to discuss NSC 147, he pointed to the dollar savings that might accrue if nuclear rather than conventional attacks were mounted against enemy dugouts.[30] And in his memoirs he repeated the conclusions reached at the NSC meeting on May 20, that in order "to keep the attack from being overly costly," these weapons would be needed.[31]

Sherman Adams, assistant to the president, has reported that atomic missiles were moved to Okinawa in the spring of 1953,[32] and in December 1953, Dulles confirmed that it had been America's intention to use these weapons against Korea and China: at the Bermuda meeting in December with British and French ministers, the secretary of state said the United States had been "prepared for a much more intensive scale of warfare." He added, "It would not be improper to say at such a restricted gathering that we had already sent the means to the theater for delivering atomic weapons." Dulles also made it absolutely clear that if there had not been an armistice, the United States would have initiated a geographically expanded war. Under those circumstances, he said, "we would expect to attack with the most effective means the air bases the enemy was using for his effort in Korea. We would implement the doctrine of hot pursuit without being limited by the boundary between North Korea and Manchuria. We would expect to take such action as seemed best to us to achieve a decisive result in Korea." Nowhere did Dulles even suggest that the administration had been bluffing; rather, he concluded, "It was the knowledge of the [U.S.] *willingness to use force* that had brought about an end to hostilities" (italics added).[33]

The courses of action the joint chiefs outlined on May 20 described the form and method of expanding the war, and subsequent NSC decisions reaffirmed that the May 20 discussion continued to represent the considered view of the Eisenhower administration. Should an armistice agreement be breached and the conflict renewed, the "Greater Sanctions" statement was to be invoked and then followed by the combined courses of action the joint chiefs had outlined in May. As Eisenhower told congressional leaders, the plan was "to hit them with everything we['ve] got."[34]

EXTERNAL POLICY CONSTRAINTS

The decision to bring the armistice negotiations to a head was not made until late May because of constraints imposed by both internal and external forces. The death of Stalin on March 5 raised the expectation among America's allies and within the U.S. administration that the U.S.S.R. might adopt a more conciliatory stance in its relations with the West and, more parochially, might leave the Chinese and North Koreans with greater freedom to make concessions at the peace talks. Chou En-lai's radio address on March 30, followed by the exchange of sick and wounded prisoners, indicated that a shift of position was near. As Robert Cutler put it at the time, it would be premature to decide on an alternative method of prosecuting the war "in view of the new possibility that the Communists were really prepared to enter into an armistice in Korea."[35]

It was also acknowledged that the allies were, in Dulles's words, still "desperately anxious to see the fighting stopped."[36] The administration was aware of the growing feeling in Canada, Britain, the Netherlands, and India, for example, that America was not doing all it could to achieve a ceasefire, and that these states believed their level of participation in the peace negotiations should be increased. (In Britain, 77 percent of those surveyed thought that other nations should be involved in the truce talks.)[37] The Indian and allied governments considered the Chinese and Americans to be so close to agreement on the POW issue in May that they could see no reason why the discussions should reach a breaking point, or any grounds for an indefinite adjournment of the talks.[38] A U.S. decision in May to amend its negotiating position, even though it would differ from the compromise Indian resolution that America had endorsed in March 1953, caused such "anxiety and concern" among the allies that protests and criticism came from Britain,

Canada, Australia, Belgium, New Zealand, and Italy, as well as from neutral states such as Burma and India.[39] Indeed, the U.K. government was becoming so wary of what it saw as the increasingly harsh and uncompromising stance of the U.S. delegation at the peace talks that it wanted to withdraw its acceptance of the "Greater Sanctions" statement. Dulles warned Eden that if Britain went ahead with that, a serious crisis in relations between the two countries would result. Furthermore, under those circumstances the United States would reexamine the terms of the armistice agreement decided so far.[40]

The British government backed down on this issue, but the new tone of the U.S. administration continued to cause alarm. Eisenhower's announcement on February 2 that the Seventh Fleet would be removed from the Strait of Taiwan startled Britain and other governments, since it implied a newly aggressive stance toward the PRC. Although Dulles rushed to London with reassurances that America had no aggressive designs (the Eisenhower administration realized that Chiang could not accomplish much even when "unleashed"), Eden was not convinced; he told the British House of Commons that the change of policy might have "unfortunate political repercussions without any compensatory military advantages." In Nehru's view, it "intensified the fear psychosis of the world." The Canadians also found it a cause for regret.[41] Overall, on this and other issues, allied reactions indicated that the United States would have little if any support for breaking off armistice negotiations and expanding the war.

The susceptibility of Eisenhower to allied opinion might have been expected to be high. The president was an internationalist who recognized the primacy of Europe in America's defense strategy. As the first supreme commander of NATO, he had been sensitive to European political and economic difficulties but convinced of the need to persist with efforts to build a strong coalition of Western nations. Moreover, one of his major reasons for seeking the Republican presidential nomination in 1952 had been to keep Taft out of the race, since the senator's victory might have meant the triumph of isolationism. In May 1953, Taft made a speech that struck a chord in those nostalgic for an era when America was seemingly free of foreign entanglement: the United States, he said, "might as well abandon any idea of working with the United Nations in the East and reserve to ourselves a completely free hand."

Two days later, Eisenhower gave an unequivocal response: "No single free nation can live alone in the world," he said. "We have to have friends. These friends have got to be tied to you, in some form or another. We have to have that unity in basic purposes that comes from a recognition of common interests."[42]

Eisenhower's statements thus implied a rejection of unilateral action in Korea. But there were limits to the restraints that close ties with the allies would be allowed to impose. NSC 147 had spelled out quite clearly the disadvantages of an expanded war against China in terms of America's relations with its allies. Apart from the South Korean and Chinese Nationalist governments, which would welcome an extension of hostilities, principal allies and majority opinion in the United Nations would "strongly oppose" the action the document outlined. A U.S. decision to initiate the military activity described in courses D through F "would severely strain and possibly break the Western alliance" unless such action followed "a large-scale Communist ground offensive in Korea or coordinated and large-scale air attacks." The Political Annex to NSC 147, produced on June 4, estimated that "neutralist sentiment" would increase throughout Europe; in the key country, Britain, Bevanite forces on Labour's left wing could gain many supporters. Whereas the French attitude was modified by the possible linkage between the Korean War and China's support for Ho Chi Minh or intervention in Indochina, concerns similar to those Britain had expressed motivated the Canadian, Australian, and New Zealand governments.[43]

Despite the prospect of such negative reactions, the NSC nevertheless decided in May that if a breakdown in negotiations occurred, attacks on China would probably be required to bring the conflict to an end. Of prime importance to the United States was the decision that the talks could not be allowed to drag on any longer. The president, for one, did not think that the damage done to allied relations would be permanent. In his memoirs, he acknowledged that the spread of hostilities would have disrupted relations with Western governments; but if the all-out offensive were "highly successful," he thought "that the rifts so caused could in time be repaired." The acting secretary of state, Bedell Smith, agreed; rapid success, he stated on more than one occasion, would mean that "many of our friends who had fallen away at the outset would climb back on the victorious bandwagon."[44] And ultimately, Eisenhower's position may have been one of defiance: in the event of allied objections to American use of atomic weapons against Kaesong, he once suggested, "we might well ask them to supply three or more divisions needed to drive the Communists back."[45]

It has been noted that Eisenhower had great confidence in his ability to handle difficult situations and personalities, and that he had been successful in getting others to cooperate with him.[46] Perhaps the president's confidence, along with the dominant role the United States held in the Western alliance, led him to assume that allied criticisms could eventually be overcome. Without someone in his administration like Acheson, who had made such painstaking efforts during the Truman years to avoid an open breach with the NATO powers, Eisenhower was willing to demonstrate that Washington would not subordinate its interests to the cause of complete solidarity with London, Ottawa, or Paris. As has previously been noted, Dulles's "frequent trips abroad were more often occasions for cajolery or self-justification than for a genuine exchange of view. Nor did the administration hesitate to apply pressure publicly on allies when it seemed necessary."[47]

Besides, the allied arguments against action in China had already been weakened. The British, for example, while refusing to support a naval blockade, had expressed willingness to contemplate air action against China if there were no armistice, as Churchill reaffirmed in a meeting with Eisenhower in early 1953. And the French were aware that Korean War policy had benefited them in terms of military aid both in Europe and Indochina. Moreover, they had secured U.S. agreement to a statement linking peace in Korea with nonintervention by the Chinese in Indochina: on March 28 a joint French-American communiqué stated that if the Chinese Communists took advantage of an armistice in Korea "to pursue aggressive war elsewhere in the Far East, such action would have the most serious consequences for the efforts to bring about peace in the world and would conflict directly with the understanding on which any armistice in Korea would rest."[48] In return, the French government was no doubt expected to increase its level of support for U.S. action in Korea, even if that included an expanded war.

The Eisenhower administration also threatened its major allies with congressional retribution in the economic sphere if they did not support U.S. policy in Korea, as the president made clear in a letter to Prime Minister Churchill.[49] And there is evidence that the United States also would consider using economic weapons to enforce allied compliance with U.S. goals. At an NSC meeting on July 2, called to discuss U.S. policy immediately following an armistice in Korea, Eisenhower stated that the United States was in a position to bring "terrific pressure" against the allies should they seek to relax trade controls with the PRC, and he hoped the administration would be "quite heavyhanded in exerting such pressure." Subsequently, it was agreed that the government should "make an inventory of economic measures we would take, if necessary, to induce our allies" to support the continued diplomatic and economic isolation of China.[50]

Allied attitudes did place constraints on U.S. actions in Korea and China and did help to preserve the limited-war policy, but the greater willingness to acknowledge the asymmetrical nature of the relationship between the United States and its allies circumscribed the effects of their opinions.

PUBLIC AND CONGRESSIONAL OPINION

In contrast with Eisenhower's approach to other Western governments, where he appeared willing to dominate and expected acquiescence, as president he was well aware that his popularity with the American public "was essential to his ability to exercise influence over other leaders."[51] He was receptive, therefore, to public opinion and mindful of pledges made during his election campaign. At that time he had emphasized his ability to find an honorable end to the conflict in Korea; once elected, he recognized on more than one occasion that the general public wanted to end the fighting, not extend it. In December 1952, during his visit to Korea, Eisenhower said he sympathized "militarily" with Clark's plan to force a military conclusion but felt he had "a mandate from the American people to stop this fighting."[52] When Dulles proposed in April 1953 that the United States attempt to secure a better agreement than one based on the 38th Parallel, the president said he thought it "impossible to call off the armistice now and to go to war in Korea. The American people would never stand for such a move."[53]

Nevertheless, though opinion polls confirmed Eisenhower's perception that the majority of the public wanted an end to the war, there was confusion as to how best this could be accomplished. A State Department survey of press, radio, and congressional opinion revealed that most did not believe the Communists would yield on the nonforcible repatriation issue, but where this left the U.N. Command delegation, few were prepared to speculate. In public opinion surveys, 39 percent of those polled favored increasing military action as a next step, compared with 27 percent who favored holding the line and 23 percent who wanted the United States to pull out of Korea. Toward the end of March, 62 percent were ready to contemplate taking "strong steps" in Korea—if necessary, without the support of the allies—and 47 percent of the sample thought there was not much risk attached to increased action.[54]

These attitudes were confirmed in the comprehensive NSC Planning Board document, NSC 147, which reported that support for "vigorous action" to bring about a settlement in Korea was "widespread" but that there was no strong demand for any particular course of action. The report concluded that should "the president decide to initiate a more punitive policy, there was "a strong probability of predominant public support, particularly since surveys indicate great public confidence that the President will take the best possible steps to end the conflict." But if, on the other hand, "the President were to conclude that more forceful action at this time is unwise, his explanation of that situation would be likely to receive predominant public acceptance."[55]

The malleability of public opinion gave the Eisenhower administration considerable freedom to explore alternatives in Korea. Certainly Eisenhower did not experience the kind of protests and public demonstrations against his punitive bombing policy—which included irrigation dams and rice fields—that Lyndon Johnson encountered during the Vietnam War. And as he told Eden with reference to atomic weapons, he was certain the American public would not object to his authorization of their use, either. He may have been right. At the end of the war, for example, when the question was asked, "If truce talks break down, would you favor or oppose the United Nations using atomic artillery shells against Communist forces?" 56 percent of those polled said they would favor their use; only 23 percent disapproved of the suggestion.[56] Political consciousness was not as high then as it was in the late 1960s, and this fact, coupled with the singular confidence in

Eisenhower's judgment in 1953, gave the executive branch a relatively free hand.

Eisenhower's election victory had also secured Republican dominance in both houses of Congress, but this did not mean that those who had all along been vocal in their criticisms of Korean War policy would now be silent. Although the Republican majority was very slim—only a one-seat lead in the Senate and eight seats in the House—the vociferous group that had been calling for the unification of Korea and an expanded war against China now came into positions of prominence. It included Senator Taft, Senator Knowland (acting Senate majority leader during Taft's terminal illness), Congressman Dewey Short (chairman of the House Armed Services Committee), and Speaker of the House Joseph Martin, who continued to urge their own solutions for ending the war. Knowland wanted to terminate the negotiations and repudiate the Indian U.N. resolution that America had amended and voted for in December 1952.

When Dulles made it known that the United States was considering a move to the waist of the peninsula, the announcement generated both support and criticism from members of the Republican Party: support because such a move would involve an intensification of military action and the prospect of inflicting a defeat on China, and criticism because it also implied the permanent division of Korea. Senator Ralph E. Flanders, an ally of Knowland's, proposed in March a plan to unify Korea that included elections under U.N. auspices, and a neutral zone along the Yalu River to be inspected and administered by a commission made up of representatives from neutral Asian states. This plan was to be regarded as either the basis for a peaceful settlement or a necessary prelude to expanded hostilities to force a victory. According to Eisenhower's administrative assistant, the president was interested in this suggestion and talked about extending the neutral zone idea throughout the world.[57]

Congressman Short and Senator Knowland also made it known that they favored organizing a naval blockade of China. Short told newspaper correspondents that all his committee members concurred, and he implied agreement with the statement made by Admiral Arthur W. Radford (then chief of the Pacific Fleet) that such a step "was not likely to provoke serious consequences, such as enlarging and aggravating the war."[58] Key Republican members of the Congressional Atomic Energy Committee were also reported to have assured Eisenhower of their support if he decided to use atomic weapons to end the war in Korea.[59]

Senator Alexander Wiley, chairman of the Senate Foreign Relations Committee, was the most prominent Republican to counsel a cautious approach, but even he responded to the president's decision to "unleash" Chiang Kai-shek by declaring that the order "would open the way for Nationalist Chinese bombing of 2,000 miles of railroad running from Manchuria to Canton, the South China Sea, and French IndoChina." Taft was willing to support both a blockade and air attacks on China. In a radio broadcast in February, he said that "since the United States was already 'at full war' with Communist China, the bombing of Manchurian supply bases or the blockading of the China coast would not extend the war. 'A war's a war—it could be no worse than now.'"[60] Taft had lost the Republican Party nomination in 1952, but until his death in July 1953, he was still a force to be reckoned with in the party, especially in his role as Senate majority leader. Thus his views, and pressures emanating from other influential sections of the GOP, had an impact on the executive.

Still, there was the question of financing such operations. When Dulles warned the cabinet in March that a continuing stalemate in the negotiations could erode the administration's support in Congress, thereby endangering Eisenhower's whole legislative program, he was also aware that the economic cost of an expanded war would be great and therefore ultimately unpopular—particularly in the Taft wing of the GOP. As Dulles pointed out, forcing a military victory in Korea "would cost a tremendous sum threatening new inflation and necessitating new economic controls."[61]

The economic effect of an expanded war was a subject close to the heart of a fiscal conservative like Eisenhower. The main topic of conversation when the president-elect met with his cabinet designees after his trip to Korea had been governmental, especially defense spending.[62] On the first day of his presidency, he and Budget Director Joseph Dodge discussed general downward revisions in the budget in order to put the country on what Eisenhower regarded as a stronger financial footing.[63]

But the problem of paying for the Korean conflict cut two ways: on the one hand, expanded hostilities would be costly; on the other hand, the administration was tired of the war's drain on U.S. resources. And as Treasury Secretary George Humphrey pointed out on May 1, if Eisenhower was really serious about getting tax relief and a reduction in the budget deficit, "you *have* to get Korea *out of the way*" (original emphasis).[64]

To accomplish that, the administration was willing to prepare for the courses of action the joint chiefs had recommended, even though doing so would temporarily enlarge the defense budget and have serious logistic and mobilization implications. In particular, it would delay the shipment of items allocated for the Mutual Defense Assistance Program and increase the stress on the South Korean economy. Nevertheless, expansion of the ROK army continued at a rapid rate: on April 22, Eisenhower had approved the activation of two further divisions, and on May 13 he ordered Clark to activate the remaining four required to bring total army strength to the authorized 20 divisions. It was also estimated that the following forces could immediately be made available to carry out an offensive: the Eighty-second U.S. Airborne Division, one reinforced Marine division with an air wing, one Marine Corps amphibious troop headquarters, two medium bomber wings, and two troop carrier wings. A fighter bomber wing and three fighter interceptor squadrons were also ready for immediate use, though they had been scheduled for transfer to Europe or North Africa in May or June 1953.[65]

NSC 147 had stated that for the implementation of course D (that is, air and naval attacks on China and increased ground operations as required), the bombing of air bases could be undertaken immediately and the institution of the blockade within two to four weeks. If courses E and F were to be initiated immediately, without the gradual increase in pressure assumed in the less severe courses of action, the operations could commence within nine to twelve months of the date of decision.[66] Given the administration's preference for "maximum impact" and "maximum surprise," it was clear that the United States was attempting to have everything assembled and ready by May 1954.

Assessment of Soviet Intentions and Reactions

Following the decision to break off negotiations, the U.S. government knew that its plan to apply additional military pressure if necessary would put the Sino-Soviet alliance to the most stringent test it had yet faced. Truman administration officials had concluded that only if Communist rule in China were threatened as a result of U.S. bombing activity, or if bombs were dropped close to sensitive Soviet border areas, would Moscow enter overtly into the hostilities. Given the continuing influence of bureaucratic officials who had not changed their arguments, the Republican administration saw little reason to challenge this assessment in March and April 1953. Moreover, the recent Soviet Party Congress had reaffirmed the doctrine of peaceful coexistence and the need to stabilize the international situation. Moscow realized that if it came openly to the support of China under any but the most extreme circumstances, U.S. gains in Western Europe and Japan would be further consolidated, again heightening the perceived threat to Soviet national security.

The Joint Strategic Plans Committee had utilized CIA estimate SE 37 to assess the probable Soviet (and Chinese) reactions to attacks in North China and Manchuria. Basically, the estimate of March 9 corresponded closely with the conclusions reached in SE 20 of December 1951. As a response to a naval blockade of China, the 1953 estimate predicted Chinese attacks on the blockading forces, with covert Soviet aid. It was again presumed that Moscow might try to escort merchant ships into Port Arthur and Dairen and, in an intensification of its assistance, might try to force the blockade at other points. The estimate concluded, however, that Russia "would be unlikely to initiate general war solely because of incidents arising out of attempts to force the blockade." In response to a blockade coupled with "large scale and sustained" air and naval action against transportation lines in China, the agency expected Soviet air units to participate covertly in the air defense of China, particularly in Manchuria. As had been concluded during Truman's time in office, only in the "unlikely event" that this action threatened the maintenance of the Communist government in China would the Soviets increase their aid, "possibly even to the point of openly committing Soviet forces against US forces in US/UN-held territory and adjacent waters in the Far East." But the study's authors believed that without threatening the Chinese government's existence, such extensive action could "sharply reduce" China's military capabilities, seriously affect its economic potential, and increase the problems of control in the country.[67]

The NSC Planning Board had utilized Special Estimate No. 41, dated April 8, when it considered possible Communist reaction to courses D through F. This intelligence study added certain refinements to the CIA document cited above: for example, if U.S./U.N. air operations threatened to destroy the Manchurian industrial complex, the Communists might be "willing to sacrifice some of their interests in Korea to obtain a cessation of hostilities." The estimate also introduced into the analysis Communist reactions to air attacks in China in conjunction with an advance into North Korea. In these circumstances, it was thought possible that the Communists, "while seeking to negotiate an armistice that secured continued Communist control over a substantial portion of North Korea, might commit Soviet air units over UN-held territory and might introduce Soviet ground forces in Korea." The prospect of direct contact between Soviet and American troops would previously have been thought so dangerous as to rule out entirely any course of action that might bring that contact about; however—as the paper made clear in a new development of the argument with regard to the Soviet response—the onus for identifying such a confrontation as an act of war against the United States would lie with the Eisenhower admininistration: "The USSR would, in any event," it said, "leave to the UN/US the responsibility for recognizing the commitment of Soviet forces as a *casus belli*."[68] Another intelligence estimate produced at that time reiterated a more familiar position: aggression in Korea had "involved, throughout, an inherent risk of general war," yet Moscow continued "to limit its own role in the Korean war and has not sought to use the war as an excuse for initiating broader hostilities."[69]

Despite the intelligence community's sustained belief in the cautious nature of Soviet behavior, it was apparent that the joint chiefs and the president wanted to give serious consideration to the possibility of overt Soviet intervention in the hostilities. The contemplated use of nuclear weapons and the intention to destroy completely the Chinese Communist air force introduced major new elements into the equation. The joint chiefs' May 19 memorandum to the defense secretary, therefore, stated that NSC 147 did not clearly emphasize the risks involved in expanding the conflict. They thought it necessary to stress that expansion might involve the United States in a larger, longer, and more costly war with the PRC and could lead to an Asian war with the Soviet Union or, worse still, spark the outbreak of World War III. In May, they were being much more cautious than they had been over the previous months when they and their committees had pressed the State Department to toughen its stance. Now that the United States was on the brink of expanding hostilities, they were forced to contemplate the "worst case" before making a final decision.

The president contemplated it, too, but believed that the speed of the operation would lessen the risk of Soviet intervention. With seemingly little guidance from Dulles, who in April had seen the Soviets as being on the defensive, given America's "much greater power and the Soviet Union's much greater weakness concurrently,"[70] it was left to the Policy Planning Staff to prepare a more detailed analysis of the likely Soviet reaction. In the PPS view, if Moscow knew that the purpose of the action was limited, its response "would be commensurately tempered"; however, if the various feints and diversions convinced the U.S.S.R that the overthrow of the Chinese Communist government was the primary objective, then its reaction would be that much more severe. Though it was still believed that the Soviet Union "would not consciously decide to embark on general war," in these latter circumstances it might nevertheless intervene directly in air and sea operations. At the minimum, it could make Soviet airfields available to the Chinese; if it decided to go further, it might utilize Soviet air "volunteers." Outside the Far East, Moscow could take advantage of the strain in the Western alliance by increasing pressure on West Germany, particularly in Berlin. But the PPS still saw a ray of hope: knowledge of the U.S. buildup, rather than leading to Soviet military involvement, might persuade Moscow to agree to terminate the Korean hostilities.[71]

Despite the serious nature of the joint chiefs' recommended courses of action, the U.S. administration still maintained the belief that Moscow would try to avoid general war, would probably attempt to continue the fiction of its noninvolvement or "volunteer" involvement in the hostilities, and would in any case increase the level of its intervention only if it believed the destruction of the Chinese Communist regime was being attempted. The fears associated with possible Soviet involvement were much greater in May 1953 than they had been in previous months, yet were apparently insufficient to prevent the decision of May 20.

During the Truman and Eisenhower administrations there had

developed an assessment of the U.S.S.R. as an aggressive but not necessarily reckless power. As the CIA explained in its assessment of Stalin's leadership after his death on March 5, 1953, he was an "autocrat who, while ruthless and determined to spread Soviet power, did not allow his ambitions to lead him into reckless courses of action in his foreign policy."[72] The new Soviet leaders provided no indication that they were about to alter this course.

The intelligence agencies believed that the unequal distribution of the war's burdens was creating strains in the Sino-Soviet relationship, but as in the previous administration, they did not believe the frictions and conflicting individual interests were seriously hampering the effectiveness of Communist wartime cooperation. What the strains might be doing, however, was to accelerate a Soviet desire to end the Korean conflict. After Stalin's death there were a number of indications of a desire to improve Soviet-American relations. At the end of March, Ambassador Henry Cabot Lodge, who now led America's delegation to the U.N., reported "another indirect approach" for talks between Eisenhower and Malenkov. As in October 1950, the Norwegian official Hans Engen was singled out, first for a response to Chou En-lai's March 30 statement, and then for Norwegian views regarding a Soviet-American meeting. The Soviet official Vassili Kasaniev indicated that bilateral discussions might involve questions on the control of atomic energy and disarmament.[73]

The Soviet press printed in full Eisenhower's "Chance for Peace" address, given on April 16 to the American Society of Newspaper Editors, and produced lengthy editorial comments. To George Kennan (now at Princeton University), the editorials revealed "clearly that the present Soviet leaders are definitely interested in pursuing with us the effort to solve some of the present international difficulties." The message they were trying to put across with respect to Korea was, he thought, that progress could not be made on an armistice agreement while Washington persisted "in acting as though the Chinese were [Moscow's] helpless puppets." Kennan worded the Russian lament as follows: "Do you not see that it is *their* forces, not ours, that are engaged in Korea and must do the ceasefiring? Do you not understand that someone must pay them a price to induce them to accept the humiliation of losing their p.o.ws? Why should we pay them that price? Why should you at least not share it?" In the Soviet view, Kennan said,

Dulles was asking for unconditional surrender, but Moscow believed "the Chinese aren't that weak."[74]

This Soviet refrain regarding the independence of Russian and Chinese action in Korea was repeated on other occasions. For example, a U.S. embassy official in London was informed by his Soviet counterpart that an armistice agreement in Korea would soon be reached because the conflict benefited no one. When the American official suggested that it would be helpful to have Soviet assistance in persuading the Chinese of that fact, the Russian replied that the "Chinese people were very difficult people to influence."[75] And Soviet Foreign Minister Molotov told Charles Bohlen, the U.S. ambassador to Moscow, that the "outcome of these [armistice] talks does not depend on us."[76]

These kinds of statements probably derived in part from a Soviet desire to demonstrate its peripheral role in the conflict at a time when signs were that the war was about to be expanded. Charles Bohlen, still an influential figure within the Washington bureaucracy, remained convinced that the Soviets were fearful of a general war and wanted an armistice. When Bohlen presented his credentials in Moscow on April 20 (after an inordinately long delay caused by his controversial confirmation hearings in Congress), he proposed making a settlement in Korea a "litmus test" of American faith in Moscow's gestures of conciliation. He reported back that the Russians were "eager to support his statement regarding the importance of an armistice in Korea."[77]

The Soviets' conciliatory gestures, studied detachment from the events taking place on the peninsula, and disavowal of their ability to influence the course of the negotiations contributed to the Eisenhower administration's assessment that the Soviet Union did not want to participate openly in the hostilities and would be reluctant to increase the level of its support to its ally. When U.S. officials considered driving to the waist of Korea and initiating naval and air attacks on China, they did so with these Soviet attitudes in mind. Moscow had undoubtedly increased the vulnerability of Peking and Pyongyang.

Even without increased Soviet participation in the hostilities, however, an expanded war would still carry with it the risk of attrition of U.S. forces and a significant increase in the number of casualties. These facts were sufficient to cause the administration to move cautiously toward its May 20 decision, even while assuming that these losses could be minimized by taking advantage of the surprise and destructive effects of nuclear weaponry.

Eisenhower came into office with a clear mandate to end the war in Korea, and he was presented with a detailed assessment of what it would take to do so. Pledges made during the election campaign influenced his thinking when the administration began to consider an expansion of hostilities, yet he left a divided legacy in several areas.[78] He spoke of finding an honorable end to the Korean conflict, but in private he talked readily of using nuclear weapons in Korea and China. Like Dulles, he appeared to disagree with the moral inhibitions that others had placed on their use. The outcome in Korea and, in 1954, the rejection of atomic weapons in the defense of Dien Bien Phu have contributed to the image of Eisenhower as a president who won the peace and did not make war. But the outcome could have been very different in 1953. It was his administration's decision to present the U.N. Command's final position at the truce talks; it was the unanimous recommendation of his joint chiefs (which was not the case in 1954) that nuclear weapons be used in China and Korea to force a decisive victory, and he concurred.

A number of factors brought the administration to this decision. It had been agreed that it would be fruitless to continue much longer with the negotiations. In addition, Korea was seen as a drain on U.S. resources, preventing a restructuring of the defense budget and a reduction of the deficit. It was obvious that further military activity would immediately increase that budget, besides requiring some diversion of equipment from NATO's requirements and causing further deaths and casualties. But intensified military action, if successful, held out the prospect of fewer demands on U.S. military assistance in the future and a return to concentration on the defense of other, more vital areas.

Military success was also considered essential in order for the United States to ride out the storm of allied criticism that a spread of hostilities would cause. Eisenhower seemed confident that he could win allied support for the military action his administration contemplated, even if he had to exert political and economic pressure to attain it. As for Moscow's response to a wider war, Eisenhower concluded that as long as the Chinese Communist government remained intact, Soviet actions would remain carefully controlled. Like Truman before him, he believed that Moscow would prefer to maintain an indirect role, thereby avoiding any risk of a general war. Thus, though possible allied and Soviet reactions were constraints that influenced the administration's discussion of its options in Korea, the perceived need to "get Korea out of the way" diminished their impact.

Movement in the truce negotiations in March and early April delayed further study of the joint chiefs' recommendations. But on May 25 the U.N. Command put forward its final negotiating position and was given permission to break off the talks if agreement were not forthcoming. Clark would then be able to step up the bombing campaign as a preliminary to the spread of hostilities into China. Concurrently, Bohlen was authorized to explain to Molotov in Moscow the "seriousness and importance of this [U.S.] step." On June 3, Molotov assured Bohlen that the outcome of the negotiations did not depend on the Soviet Union, but he held out the prospect of a settlement by stating "that the path to the successful conclusion of the armistice talks has been mapped out."[79]

The next day, following a postponement requested by the Communist negotiators, the Chinese and North Korean delegations indicated their acceptance of the UNC's proposals. On June 8 the prisoner-of-war question, the issue that had held up the conclusion of the talks for so long, was resolved; by the 17th a revised demarcation line had been established. In all probability, Moscow, Peking, and Pyongyang thus averted a Far Eastern war of major proportions, since the Eisenhower administration did seem prepared to adopt a harsher policy to end the stalemate. The standard explanation for the Communist capitulation in early June is that the Chinese and North Koreans were intimidated by the threatened use of atomic weapons and weary of the heavy bombing raids. Unless Chinese or North Korean records are opened, we will never be able to ascertain the effectiveness of the administration's threats and actions,[80] although shortly thereafter, China did begin its nuclear weapons development program.

With the terms of the agreement basically mapped out on June 17, Syngman Rhee attempted to scotch the chances for a final settlement: he ordered South Korean guards at the POW camps holding North Korean prisoners to release those unwilling to be repatriated, and 25,131 prisoners escaped. By the afternoon of June 18, only 971 had been recaptured, and at the end of June only 8,600

North Korean nonrepatriates remained in U.N. hands. U.S. troops were not used to prevent this outbreak because Clark was unwilling to countenance the loss of life that he thought would occur if they acted to stop the guards.[81]

Not surprisingly, the Communists broke off the talks at this point but did not rescind their agreement to the terms that had been settled. On June 24 they launched another offensive, directed at ROK positions. Despite the provocation of Rhee's action and the U.S. failure to do much about it militarily (although not politically, since the administration contemplated the removal of Rhee), Dulles toyed with the idea of some kind of military reply, telling General Collins that "it would be unfortunate if this offensive was the last word." He thought the psychological effects of the final battle were "very bad" from the "standpoint of prestige and morale in that area." But in Collins's view, the overall loss of terrain was likely to be insignificant, and any counteroffensive not worth the casualties.[82] What Collins did not say, although it was evident, was that the United States had obtained the agreement it wanted at Panmunjom, and there was no point in jeopardizing that.

The armistice agreement was finally signed on July 27, but the general relief associated with the end of the fighting and prevention of further deaths was tempered by the release one week later of the "Greater Sanctions" statement. The war was over, but the threat of expanded hostilities was still not far below the surface.[83] The statement read in part: "We affirm, in the interests of world peace, that if there is a renewal of the armed attack, challenging again the principles of the United Nations, we should again be united and prompt to resist. The consequences of such a breach of the armistice would be so grave that, in all probability, it would not be possible to confine hostilities within the frontiers of Korea."[84]

[8]

Conclusions

Throughout most of the Korean War, America perceived the U.S.S.R. to be intent on remaining remote from the hostilities and eager to convince the United States of its desire to support a negotiated end to the conflict. The Soviet diplomat, M. S. Kapitsa, argued in 1969 that Russia had been prepared to send five divisions to North Korea during the war if the country appeared likely to be overrun by U.S./U.N. forces. And he has pointed to Truman's memoirs as evidence that the "mighty Sino-Soviet alliance" deterred Washington from expanding the war.[1] But the president's memoirs do not reveal the shades of the debate in his administration concerning the relationship between the two Communist powers or how circumscribed Soviet support for China was seen to be. Neither do they indicate how frequently the question of an expanded war was considered, nor how often the probable Soviet reaction to an attack on China was assessed. The result of these deliberations was that, except for a very short period and only under the most extreme circumstances, no significant figure within the Truman or Eisenhower administrations believed that Soviet armed forces would enter directly into the fighting, or that Moscow would openly invoke the Sino-Soviet Treaty of Alliance and stand beside its comrade-in-arms on the peninsula.

Even before the Chinese crossed the Yalu, it had become apparent to the U.S. administration that Moscow regretted its so-called probe to test the resolve of Washington and was seeking to extricate itself from any association with the war. Its failure to make any of the expected military moves before U.S. forces crossed the 38th Parallel helped convince Washington it could "roll back" Communism in an area of strategic significance to the U.S.S.R. with no real

Conclusions

military risk. Moscow's reluctance to issue any threats as U.S./ U.N. forces swept up the peninsula suggested to Washington that Peking would also remain uninvolved in the fighting. Since Russia was at the core of the Truman administration's thinking about Korean War policy, no major effort was made to ascertain whether U.S. entry into North Korea would challenge Chinese interests. The U.S.S.R., therefore, by remaining aloof from the conflict and by not voicing threats commensurate with its apparent strength or interest in the area, contributed to the rout of the North Koreans and to the precipitation of a bloody conflict between Chinese and American forces.

The start of the truce negotiations reinforced the view that the Soviets wished to appear detached from the fighting. Moscow was seen then as being engaged in a political propaganda battle to lull the West into a false sense of security; launching a peace campaign could accomplish this goal, and Korea was an obvious place to start. Russia's motives therefore were still highly suspect to Truman and Acheson, although Soviet actions implied only limited objectives in Korea. With this evidence, Washington began to discern a pattern to Soviet behavior; with the confidence the pattern generated, the United States began to relate the various military, political and economic actions it could take against China to specific Soviet responses. These responses, it was thought, would be predominantly covert and defensive, rather than open and offensive at the risk of precipitating a third world war. As throughout the long history of Sino-Soviet dealings, Moscow's actions would make plain that its national interests dominated the fraternal relations between the two Communist states.

In a limited sense, there were certain parallels between the perception of qualified Soviet support for its ally and pre-Korean War analyses of Sino-Soviet relations. Prior to June 1950, Acheson in particular had been keen to emphasize that there were latent and actual conflicts of interest between the two Communist states; and though China's entrance into the war pushed this consideration of a probable breach in relations into the background, American estimates of Soviet behavior during the war still indicated that Washington viewed Moscow as a very different power from Peking. The Soviet Union was recognized as a world power with global concerns. Moscow, like Washington, regarded Europe as the primary area of conflict between the Communist and Western worlds, and the impact of the war in that region mattered more to Russia than the activity taking place in Korea. Because of these wider concerns, it was surmised, the Soviet Union would not risk its global interests in order to provide China with the full level of support required to deter U.S. military activity—unless the Chinese government's very existence proved to be in danger. Soviet actions during the course of the war were perceived as representing a cautious and rational calculation of its primary interests.

China's behavior, on the other hand, was not depicted in this way. Peking's actions displayed its revolutionary zeal, inexperience in world affairs, troublemaking capacity in the immediate vicinity of its borders, and exaggerated sense of its own power. The United States had no common ground with a state of this kind, and the corollary was that Moscow would eventually find its coincidence of interest with Peking limited and uncertain, capable of being undermined if the actions of one cut across the other's concerns.

But though the assessment of the qualified nature of Soviet support for its major Asian ally pertained for much of the war, there were times when the alliance between Moscow and Peking did prove vital for China's security. The first occasion was in the period from China's full-scale intervention in the war to the spring of 1951, when the shock of defeat generated widespread fears of an imminent world war for which the United States and the West were ill prepared. The surprise of China's intervention and the setbacks suffered as a result of its entrance into the war, combined with the belief that Moscow was behind the Chinese decision to intervene, caused fear and uncertainty sufficient to deter the U.S. administration from spreading the hostilities. The logic ran somewhat as follows: North Korea was a Soviet satellite, and China had no tangible interests in defending Kim Il-sung's regime; therefore, it had entered the fighting on Moscow's orders, preliminary to the onset of wide-scale hostilities in the Far East or Western Europe while America and its allies in these areas were in disarray. Although some within the Truman administration doubted Moscow's willingness to initiate a general war, the level of uncertainty as to Soviet-Chinese intentions was generally so high, and Communist capabilities in the region reckoned to be so great, that a cautious policy prevailed. The mere existence of the Sino-Soviet treaty with its military clauses was capable of restraining the United States from taking retaliatory action against China, when American and allied military resources were overstretched and world war seemed close at hand.

The Soviet Union's augmentation of China's air strength, its own participation in the air defense of Manchuria, and its probable involvement in the air war over North Korea also contributed to China's security. Though it was not until late 1951 and 1952 that Soviet military assistance to China reached significant levels, this timing turned out to be crucial, since it corresponded with a period when Truman's administrators were becoming disillusioned with the armistice negotiations. Frustrations within the Defense Department had reached a new level of intensity during this period, but Soviet assistance to China had increased Peking's abilities in the air, to complement its already considerable strength on the ground. This fact raised the prospect of a substantial loss of American lives and aircraft if the Chinese border were violated at a time when the U.S. Air Force did not enjoy sufficient strength to guarantee a successful operation. The augmentation of China's air power and air defense system was particularly important because the United States conceived one major component of an expanded war to be the destruction of air bases and communication lines in Manchuria and North China. Not once did America consider using its forces in a land invasion of China; thus it had to be confident of its naval and air power before undertaking such expansion. Not until the late summer and early autumn of 1952, however, did its airplane production reach acceptable levels and F-86 Sabres become available for use in Korea in reasonable numbers. Until that time, America recognized the Communists' MIG 15 as the best jet fighter operating.

The potential efficacy of a naval blockade, especially if unilaterally mounted by the United States, was also in question for some time. Soviet economic support of China, it was reasoned, might well diminish the effectiveness of a blockade. CIA estimates confirmed that Moscow could increase its shipments to China by rail and by sea; moreover, China's level of economic development would facilitate its adaptation to the conditions imposed by a naval interdiction of supplies. By itself, therefore, a naval blockade would not be enough to force concessions out of the Chinese; even if combined with air bombardment, it was not certain to lead to a change of position at the truce talks, although it might possibly diminish the economic and military strength of China and increase the country's problem of domestic control. Both Truman and Eisenhower realized that an expanded war had to be coupled with a ground offensive into North Korea. The prospect of a further loss of North Korean territory, combined with punitive bombing operations against China, was thought to be the only pressure likely to wring concessions out of the Communist negotiators. But this would require additional forces and bring about an increase in U.S. casualties. The Truman administration, reluctant to expand the war after staunchly arguing for the need to limit it, had to weigh these factors, along with allied and domestic criticism. The Eisenhower administration—in a stronger position politically, willing to utilize atomic weapons, and more detached in its attitude toward the allies—was freer to consider the expansion of military options.

Soviet assistance to China's air defense operations and the augmentation of China's military and economic capabilities were important in the prevention of an expanded war in the Far East, and for this indirect method of support, China had good reason to be grateful to the U.S.S.R. In December 1950 it was more the shock associated with the massive nature of China's intervention in Korea than Soviet actions that enhanced the menacing image of a Sino-Soviet alliance, an alliance that had available to it both manpower and technical expertise. This fact, rather than explicit Soviet moves in the winter of 1950, convinced the United States that its objectives in Korea should be limited and that it should diminish its involvement in the conflict as fast as was feasible. But despite the beneficial effects to China of its alliance with the U.S.S.R., the weakness was that its deterrent value could be undermined either by an augmentation of U.S. capabilities and expertise (which occurred by late 1952) or by the passage of time, which showed Moscow's unwillingness to invoke the Sino-Soviet treaty, to initiate tensions and hostilities elsewhere, or to involve itself more directly in the fighting taking place on the peninsula. As a consequence of America's augmented military strength, its willingness to contemplate the use of nuclear weapons, and continuing evidence of the cautious nature of Soviet behavior in the Far East and Korea, China once more became vulnerable. Extensive consideration of an expansion of the war provided the background to Eisenhower's decision to break the stalemate, if necessary, by attacking Chinese territory directly.

Assessments of the probable level and type of Soviet support for China in an expanded war were common to both the Truman and Eisenhower administrations, showing the degree of continuity in foreign policy between the two. So firmly was the resulting view of Soviet reactions held that it still prevailed in 1954 and later. In examining the possibility of direct Chinese intervention in Indochina in 1954, for example, the Eisenhower administration considered an extensive range of actions against China, going beyond those it had examined between March and May of 1953. In June 1954 it assessed the probable effects of undertaking nuclear attacks against widespread military targets in China, a naval blockade of the coast, Chinese Nationalist operations against the mainland, and seizure or neutralization of Hainan. Not surprisingly, the administration thought Peking would make "vigorous efforts to secure the full participation of the USSR," but U.S. officials thought that doing so would, as usual, be a difficult task, and that Moscow would prefer merely to increase its military aid to China while strongly urging Peking to negotiate an end to the hostilities on the basis of China's withdrawal from Indochina.[2] It has been said that the United States became "relatively bolder" in its policy toward the PRC during "the crises over the Taiwan straits, where Peking would lack credible Russian support on the nuclear level."[3] But before then, during the Korean conflict, American estimates of Soviet reactions to attacks on China had shown that this lack of credible support had already been discerned. It was the assessment of Sino-Soviet relations undertaken at that time that most likely contributed to a harsher American stance in subsequent U.S.-China crises and, in turn, probably also hastened the Sino-Soviet split.

Hastening the Sino-Soviet split was the primary aim of the Truman administration's policy toward China prior to the Korean War, and the strategy did not die but changed in form with China's entrance into the fighting in October 1950. The U.S. decision to place the Seventh Fleet in the Taiwan Strait, thereby creating an irredentist issue it had earlier worked hard to avoid, seriously undermined the effort to create rifts between Moscow and Peking. But the "wedge" strategy still existed as a long-term aim, to be accomplished either by the overthrow of the Communist government in China through support for Nationalist and guerilla elements in the southern half of the country, or—more promisingly— by an increase in military, diplomatic, and economic pressure on the PRC in order to force its detachment from the Soviet orbit. Both the Truman and Eisenhower administrations hoped this latter tactic would lead Peking into greater dependence on Moscow and thus alienate sections of the populace and leadership, and/or cause Peking's leaders to discover more speedily that Soviet aid was not disinterested: that China's dependence on the U.S.S.R. would have a price in terms of Soviet encroachments on Chinese territorial integrity and sovereignty.

It was recognized, however, that it would take a long time for this discovery to culminate in an open split between Moscow and Peking, and that despite evident strains in Sino-Soviet wartime relations, the coincidence of interest that a hostile American policy would generate was capable of overcoming any real tension for the time being.

This somewhat contradictory policy—whereby Washington's hostility kept Moscow and Peking together, yet its intensified activity directed at China was also thought likely to drive the Communist allies apart—stemmed from America's fruitful experience of dealing harshly with Tito, from the domestic political setting, and, of course, from the fact that Peking and Washington were at war. These considerations precluded examination of a more conciliatory policy toward Peking. Nevertheless, the contradictions inherent in the policy did lead some within the State Department to consider a wider Far Eastern settlement with Communist China after the truce agreement had been signed in Korea. Dominant figures within the Eisenhower administration received these suggestions unsympathetically, however.[4] The strongly negative reaction exemplified the preference for maintaining pressure on Communist governments in the Cold War years rather than examining creative and innovative approaches involving compromise or real negotiation. Despite President Eisenhower's proclaimed interest in negotiations with Moscow, for example, he lacked the determination or inclination to follow through with his ideas, leaving Dulles to continue his strident public rhetoric, which appeared to rule out any compromise of American hostility toward the Soviet Union.

During the Korean War, the Defense Department's increased prominence in the process of policy formulation further advanced the negative attitude toward negotiation. The military view inevitably acquires additional weight in time of war, and the conflict in Korea was no exception. The selection of the esteemed General

Marshall as Secretary of Defense promoted his department's opinions, as did the appointment of Robert Lovett as his successor. Their increased access to the president ensured that decisions reflected the Pentagon's perspective. Military influence reached its apogee with the election of a general to the presidency (although this is not to imply that Eisenhower had a narrow military conception either of the presidency or of U.S. foreign policy).

Additionally, over the course of the war the U.S. military budget was nearly quadrupled. Although Eisenhower effected some economies after that, the high levels of spending instituted then have never been reversed. The increased budget allowed a more activist foreign policy during the Korean conflict and—subsequently—a condition that required the military to be called upon more frequently for recommendations.

Other factors sustained the influence of the joint chiefs during the Korean crisis. From late 1951, their attitudes mirrored those of the general public and the more vociferous congressional critics of Korean War policy. Public opinion was generally volatile between 1950 and 1953, but frequently displayed a preference for an active policy of bombing within China, provided such action did not imply an intolerable prolongation of the conflict. Near the end of the war, for example, in a close reflection of Defense Department views, the majority of the public were willing to support the use of atomic weapons against the Chinese in the expectation that this method would ensure the speedy and decisive defeat of Peking. The military's position also coincided with the views of certain congressmen, tired of the Korean stalemate and keen to exploit its inconclusiveness for partisan political reasons. With more abandon than the military, they favored a MacArthur-style expansion of the war. Where public opinion was malleable, these congressional critics had their impact on policy: toughening the stance toward Communist China, entangling U.S. administrations with Chiang Kai-shek, and indirectly increasing the pressure for the spread of hostilities and the difficulties of compromise at the truce talks.

Much of the analysis of military opinion in this study has confirmed the conclusion of other students of American foreign policy that once a decision is made to use force, the generals want to use it more quickly and decisively than do their civilian counterparts. This study also confirms the finding that the Navy and Air Force are likely to advocate more aggressive courses of action than the

Army. In addition, it shows that commanders in the field (during other conflicts as well as in Korea) have been more "hawkish" than military officials in Washington, the latter being responsive to the overall strength of and demands on the military establishment.[5] Generals Clark and MacArthur both favored an expanded war in Korea and thought they should be provided with the equipment and troop reinforcements needed to finish the job. General Ridgway was more circumspect in his requests, but he too demanded "more steel and less silk" from his superiors in Washington. Despite the sympathy of the joint chiefs for these positions, however, they remained sensitive to the overall defense priorities of the United States and less willing to draw on resources for use in Korea until the country's total military capabilities had considerably increased.

These divisions within the military and differing military and civilian perspectives did little to enhance the perceived value of diplomacy, however. Civilians in the Truman and Eisenhower administrations frequently rejected the prospect of genuine negotiation with the Communist enemy. The discussions at Panmunjom were regarded by many as a test of America's will, of its ability to prevail; they were often conducted, and their outcome envisaged, in terms of winners and losers. The language used by prominent members of both administrations tended to equate negotiation with appeasement. In policy formulation, U.S. officials displayed a predilection for action over discussion, for boldness over caution, for glorifying strength and denigrating weakness. "Hesitation and timidity" would incur greater risks, Acheson said when the United States considered crossing the 38th Parallel in the face of Chinese threats. Establishing a buffer zone in North Korea was a "sign of weakness" or "appeasement" of the Chinese Communists. Cautious policies were more likely to involve the United States in war with the U.S.S.R. than those dictated by boldness; thus, the United States should cross the 38th Parallel, roll back Communism, and demonstrate its power and the Communist bloc's impotence.

This attitude also helps to explain the attractiveness of the notion of expanding the war into China. Such action could, it was argued at various times, teach China a lesson, destroy its military prestige, force it to concede on the voluntary repatriation of prisoners of war, or—from a longer-term, strategic perspective—provide perhaps the last and best opportunity to undermine and weaken Peking. The language of machismo denied the value of the "softer" art of compromise or exchange, and rejected concern with establishing a fair outcome.[6]

Though Acheson was a more subtle analyst of U.S. foreign policy than Dulles, they both demonstrated this distrust of negotiation with Communist governments unless America was in a position of strength. Acheson displayed his real subtlety when he was negotiating with the Western allies. He recognized the need to appear flexible in order to retain support for U.S. policy positions; to respond to events in ways that would enhance the legitimacy of America's role as leader of the Western world.

Maintaining U.S. national security was seen to depend on the related concepts of credibility and legitimacy. Credibility involved the willingness to take military action in support of allies that came under threat, as shown by the U.S. decision to enter the Korean War; the ability to mount and sustain a successful military operation, such as the victorious run up the Korean peninsula; but also caution in contemplating such a task as tackling a strengthened Chinese air force in Manchuria. Legitimacy could be demonstrated by the ability to gain a high level of international support for U.S. policies so that U.S. goals could be represented in terms of universal interests; this dictated the U.N. involvement in the Korean operations, America's attempts to secure U.N. endorsement of all its actions, and Washington's willingness to compromise—if forced to—in order to maintain a semblance of U.S.-U.N. unity.

Acheson's recognition of the value of these concepts ensured his sensitivity to allied and neutral opinion, and explained in part his reluctance to consider an expanded war against China that these other states rejected. It demonstrated, too, the differing bureaucratic perspectives of the State and Defense Departments, the latter of which chafed at the restrictions imposed by allied and U.N. interventions in policy making. But the differences between State and Defense cannot be understood by referring solely to the diplomatic and military functions of the two departments, since Acheson's sensitivity to allied, and especially British, opinion was also a mark of his concern with the global military position of the United States. He believed that an expanded war with China—the "second team"—would waste U.S. resources, rendering the United States less able to respond to a military threat to Western Europe and less able to build the military strength in Europe deemed essential to America's national security. While it appeared that the Korean conflict was the first phase in a larger war, or (as in the middle of 1951) that it could be fairly speedily concluded and thus permit a return to more urgent security concerns, Acheson's focus on America's global position and the recommendations that stemmed from this focus constituted a powerful guiding force within the Truman administration.

As a consequence, the allies were a major deterrent to an expanded war during this period. A prime example of the operation of allied influence was the retraction of the "hot pursuit" order. It is worth restating that Truman, Acheson, Marshall, and the joint chiefs thought it necessary to grant MacArthur's request on November 6 to cross the Yalu in pursuit of Chinese MIGs. If the border had been breached at that time, the psychological and legal barriers to an expanded war would also have been torn away. It was the crescendo of allied voices warning the United States not to take this unilateral course of action that led to its denial. The Truman administration realized that if it did not pay heed, America would stand virtually alone in the Far East at a time when the probability of world war was seen to have increased. Having once refrained from implementing this course of action, it required serious provocation from the Chinese air force to justify a reversal of the decision.

In retrospect, it can be seen that China's most provocative military action of the whole war was to enter the hostilities in force, and to inflict on the United States the longest retreat in its military history. The avoidance of an expanded war at the moment of its entrance into Korea, therefore, was more valuable to China than was realized at the time. However, once a military balance between U.S./U.N. and Chinese "volunteer" forces had been restored, Peking (and probably Moscow) kept tight control on the conduct of the fighting. China continued to maintain the fiction (as did Washington) that its troops were volunteers; it used its air force only in defensive operations within Manchuria and North Korea, and concentrated on building defensive, not offensive, positions. As Thomas K. Finletter pointed out, U.S./U.N. forces were free to move at will and were never harassed from the air.

As the war dragged on, China's and North Korea's most provocative political acts were to refuse to concede to the U.S. position on the voluntary repatriation of prisoners of war. The effects of this refusal, and the consequent long-drawn-out nature of the negotiations, wore down those attitudes within the United States that had contributed to a fear of spreading the hostilities. As it became apparent that world war would not be initiated by Moscow in response to U.S. actions against North Korea or China, and that this conflict with the Communist world was absorbing America's attention and resources, the mood in the United States changed. Allied opinion lost influence to the point that the U.S. government contemplated a limited reduction of its European commitments in order to effect a military end to the conflict in Korea. There was a resurfacing of the realization (particularly in the Eisenhower administration) that the allies relied more upon the United States than America ultimately did upon its allies. These factors, combined with a belief that an ever expanding U.S. bombing policy would force Communist concessions at the truce talks, culminated in Eisenhower's reluctant decision to break the stalemate and prepare to extend operations both geographically and in terms of the weapons used. The broader notions of legitimacy and credibility were temporarily replaced by a related but baser concern with showing Asia that the United States could inflict a military defeat on China. Fortunately, America did not have to initiate the proposed courses of action; the Communists prevented a further intensification of hostilities by conceding the final issue at the truce talks.

The bombing policy of Presidents Truman and Eisenhower—which in the latter administration included attacks on rice crops and irrigation channels, the life support of a poor nation—recalls the strategy employed during the Vietnam War. There were other significant connections between Korea and Indochina, including the maintenance of the assumption expressed in the 1950s that using increased force can generate concessions at the negotiating table. As General Maxwell Taylor stated during the Vietnam War, he believed that a program of gradually rising military pressures against Hanoi would induce it to end its support for the insurgency in South Vietnam because the North Vietnamese were like the Chinese and North Koreans in that "they would seek an accommodation with us when the cost of pursuing a losing course became excessive."[7]

Furthermore, many of the same military and diplomatic personnel were involved in the two wars. For example, General Mark Clark has recorded that he arranged the visit of France's Marshal Alphonse Juin to Korea in 1953, and that he himself visited Indochina in March 1953. In addition, several officers from the Korean Military Advisory Group went straight from Korea to Vietnam, along with military personnel from the ROK forces.[8]

Within the Washington bureaucracy, the alarmist view of Peking's intentions that its intervention in Korea had generated was transferred to the new area of battle in Southeast Asia. Despite the cautious manner in which China subsequently applied force as an instrument of foreign policy,[9] until the late 1960s the United States still regarded China as an expansionist, violent, and revolutionary power. Since the Communists in Vietnam were simply proxies for the Chinese, the latter could be contained, it was thought, through containment of the former. Some within the military were dissatisfied with this indirect method of dealing with the PRC. Admiral Arthur W. Radford (Eisenhower's chairman of the joint chiefs of staff) summarized the view of many when, during the battle at Dien Bien Phu in 1954, he spoke of bombing China to teach it a lesson "once and for all."[10] In the early 1960s, a group within the Air Force and Navy still felt much the same, regarding China as the major enemy and harboring a desire to wage an air war against the mainland.

In the realization that the United States did contemplate air and naval action against it in 1953, probably to involve the use of atomic weapons, China sought in future Sino-American crises to be more circumspect in its behavior and to signal its intentions to the United States with greater clarity and precision. China could not suffer the negative effects of another such war as that in Korea. Not only did tens of thousands of its young men lose their lives on the battlefield, but the conflict had deleterious effects on all aspects of Chinese policy.[11] Billions of dollars were poured into the military budget at the expense of domestic needs. Consumer and export industries were damaged, the former through a lack of funds, and the latter from the imposition of the trade embargo. Because troops were moved from Kwangtung Province in the south to Manchuria, Chinese Communist Party officials feared that landlords and other political opponents would use the war to resist governmental directives, and U.S. covert operations and support for guerilla and Nationalist forces exacerbated these fears. Hence, harsher policies were introduced into the countryside; peasant hatred of landlords was stirred to new levels of intensity; and land reform policies were radicalized. Mao's stated goal of "entering the new era of socialism unhurriedly" was abandoned in the wake of mobilization campaigns generated to ensure all-out support for the war effort.

China's foreign policy goals also suffered as a result of the war. Its diplomatic and economic isolation led it to become even more dependent upon the Soviet Union, which had already proved suspect as a primary ally. In addition, it incurred a serious financial debt to Moscow as a consequence of the latter's policy of selling weapons to the Chinese. Peking's major objective of recovering Taiwan became impossible to attain and still remains unresolved. The U.N. denunciation of the Chinese as "aggressors" in Korea, and America's subsequent diplomatic action, kept the PRC out of that organization until 1971 and incidentally damaged the principle of universality within the United Nations, as well as its future role in collective security.[12]

Koreans, both North and South, also suffered enormous hardships as the conflict engulfed their country. The "concertina" war, which saw the capital cities change and rechange hands, produced a constant stream of refugees, tracking across a devastated countryside. The saturation bombing technique employed by the U.S. Air Force brought morale in North Korea close to breaking point. To the major powers it may have been a limited war, but to the inhabitants of the country, it must have seemed total. Reflecting the hardships that all major wars generate, income in North Korea diminished by more than a third, and inflation destroyed people's livelihoods and purchasing power; consequent food hoarding and tax evasion brought about confiscatory policies on the part of Kim Il-sung's government.[13] Korea still remains divided and, according to the present U.N. commander there, the demilitarized zone dividing the North from the South continues to be "a primary source of confrontation, tension and hostilities."[14]

Moscow was successful in maintaining its indirect relationship to the conflict in Korea but did so at considerable cost to its relations with both China and North Korea. In the autumn of 1950, Kim Il-sung tried in vain to persuade Moscow to increase its support. The Chinese chafed at delays in the receipt of modern Soviet weaponry, and were critical of the requirement that they should pay for the military equipment. As a result, Mao's and Kim's belief in the value of self-reliance increased, to the eventual detriment of Russia's security.

The U.S.S.R. also witnessed the revitalization and rearmament of Western Europe (including West Germany), the stationing of U.S. troops in Europe, and the establishment of a supreme command for NATO. Moreover, it saw a vast augmentation of the U.S. armed forces and military budget, and an agreement between Tokyo and Washington to build defense forces in Japan and establish American military bases there. As a result of the war, the United States also stepped up its aid to the Philippines, to the French in Indochina, and to the Chinese Nationalists in Taiwan. By 1953, America had become a global power with a matching military capability.

But the United States, too, suffered from its involvement in the hostilities. Approximately 140,000 American casualties were sustained, 45 percent of them after the peace talks had begun. The war brought out a wave of anti-Communist hysteria and added impetus to McCarthyism, itself a phenomenon that destroyed lives and careers. The outbreak of hostilities and China's participation sharpened U.S. perceptions of the threat Communist nations posed, causing the French conflict with Ho Chi Minh to be depicted not as a struggle between colonialists and anticolonialists but as an integral part of an anti-Communist crusade, the burden of which America must bear. Despite the passing of 30 years since the end of the Korean War, the period of détente in East-West relations, and massive military budgets in the United States, U.S. administrations remain skeptical of the worth of negotiating with the Communist "enemy" and have maintained their belief in the necessity of talking only from a position of strength. "Lessons" absorbed during the first major war with Communist nations have endured.

Notes

CHAPTER 1

1. U.S. Senate Committees on Armed Services and Foreign Relations, *Military Situation in the Far East* (Washington, D.C.: GPO, 1951), 82d Cong., 1st sess., 1951, 731–32. The transcript of the hearings has now been declassified in full and is available at the Legislative Branch of the National Archives in Washington, D.C. (hereafter, *Declassified Hearings*).

2. U.S. Senate, *Military Situation in the Far East.*

3. In 1972 the Chinese described Moscow as having been a "merchant of death" during the war years, because it required China to pay for the weapons it received (quoted in Mineo Nakajima, "The Sino-Soviet Confrontation: Its Roots in the International Background of the Korean War," *Australian Journal of Chinese Affairs*, 1979, no. 1:33). In 1973, a "senior Chinese official" was also reported as saying: "In the Korean War, we interfered in the fighting. When we interfered we found ourselves obliged to wait for help from the Soviet Union. The help was delayed at times. We felt torn apart and we suffered. Sometimes we were angry and we begged, but we had to tolerate it because we were on the battlefield and because the modern weapons came from the Soviet Union" (*Foreign Broadcast Information Service*, no. 45, supplement, Washington D.C., March 7, 1973, quoted in Francis H. Heller, ed., *The Korean War: A Twenty-five-year Perspective* [Lawrence: Regents Press of Kansas, 1977], 84).

4. For a discussion of the impact of key events on perceptions see Robert Jervis, *Perception and Misperception in International Politics* (Princeton, N.J.: Princeton University Press, 1976), 217.

5. Alexander L. George, *Presidential Decision Making in Foreign Policy* (Boulder, Colo.: Westview Press, 1980), 126, 151.

6. Fred I. Greenstein, *The Hidden-Hand Presidency: Eisenhower as Leader* (New York: Basic Books, 1982), 108.

7. As described by Robert J. Donovan, *Tumultuous Years: The Presidency of Harry S. Truman, 1949–1953* (New York: Norton, 1982), 62.

8. Richard E. Neustadt, *Presidential Power: The Politics of Leadership from FDR to Carter* (New York: Wiley, 1980), 107.

9. Robert Ferrell, *George C. Marshall* (New York: Cooper Square Publishers, 1966), 260–61; Neustadt, *Presidential Power*, 36.

10. Donovan, *Tumultuous Years*, 36.

[247]

11. Greenstein, *Hidden-Hand Presidency*, 83.

12. Ibid., 87.

13. Ibid., ch. 3.

14. Ole Holsti, "Foreign Policy Formation Viewed Cognitively," in Robert Axelrod, ed., *Structure of Decision: The Cognitive Maps of Political Elites* (Princeton, N.J.: Princeton University Press, 1976), 20.

15. Warren I. Cohen, *Dean Rusk* (Totowa, N.J.: Cooper Square Publishers, 1980), 323.

16. Jervis, *Perception and Misperception*, 219.

17. Ernest May, *"Lessons" of the Past: The Use and Misuse of History in American Foreign Policy* (New York: Oxford University Press, 1973), 81; also in Harry S. Truman, *Memoirs* (Garden City, N.Y.: Doubleday, 1956), 2:332–33. For a discussion of the use of analogical reasoning in U.S. foreign policy making, see Stanley Hoffmann, *Gulliver's Troubles, or, the Setting of American Foreign Policy* (New York: McGraw-Hill, 1968), 135–37.

18. Robert M. Blum, *Drawing the Line: The Origin of the American Containment Policy in East Asia* (New York: Norton, 1982), 13.

19. George, *Presidential Decision Making*, 60, 70.

20. Truman Papers, President's Secretary Files (hereafter cited as PSF), NSC Minutes, October 11, 1951, HSTL.

21. Gaddis Smith, *Dean Acheson* (New York: Cooper Square Publishers, 1972), 423–24.

22. Gaddis Smith, "Reconsiderations: The Shadow of John Foster Dulles," *Foreign Affairs*, 52, Jan. 1974; Ole Holsti, "The 'Operational Code' Approach to the Study of Political Leaders: John Foster Dulles' Philosophical and Instrumental Beliefs," *Canadian Journal of Political Science* 3, no. 1 (March 1970).

23. Warren I. Cohen, "Acheson, His Advisers and China, 1949–1950," in Dorothy Borg and Waldo Heinrichs, eds., *Uncertain Years: Chinese-American Relations, 1947–1950* (New York: Columbia University Press, 1980), 20–21.

24. Holsti, " 'Operational Code' Approach."

25. Smith, *Dean Acheson*, 144.

26. Ibid., 144–45. During the course of an interview on March 15, 1983, in Oxford, England, Lord Franks also pointed to the closeness of Acheson's relations with the Canadian ambassador to the United States, Hume Wrong; he said that the quality of Canadian diplomatic personnel was regarded so highly as to exert considerable diplomatic force in Washington.

27. Greenstein, *Hidden-Hand Presidency*, 47.

28. For a useful survey of the literature on crisis decision making, see Richard G. Head, Frisco W. Short, and Robert C. McFarlane, *Crisis Resolution: Presidential Decision Making in the Mayaguez and Korean Confrontations* (Boulder, Colo.: Westview Press, 1978), esp. ch. 1.

29. For a detailed statement of this view, see Bruce Cumings, *The Origins of the Korean War: Liberation and the Emergence of Separate Regimes, 1945–1947* (Seattle: University of Washington Press, 1981).

CHAPTER 2

1. On this, see Nancy Bernkopf Tucker, *Patterns in the Dust: Chinese-American Relations and the Recognition Controversy, 1949–1950* (New York: Columbia University Press, 1983), esp. 176–77. Tucker notes the scarcity of China specialists, and the

European background and orientation of the China staff in Washington and in the field.

2. U.S. Department of State, *Foreign Relations of the United States* (Washington, D.C.: GPO, 1977), 1950, 1:145 (Feb. 8); hereafter cited as *Foreign Relations*.

3. For the whole text of NSC 68 see ibid., 1:237–92 (April 14).

4. For further details, see Blum, *Drawing the Line*, 112 and ch. 7.

5. See NSC 48/1, Dec. 23, 1949 (quoted in Thomas H. Etzold and John L. Gaddis, *Containment: Documents on American Policy and Strategy, 1945–1950* [New York: Columbia University Press, 1978], 252–69), for a full statement of this problem.

6. Robert Jervis, "The Impact of the Korean War on the Cold War," *Journal of Conflict Resolution* 24, no. 4 (Dec. 1980): 568.

7. Clarence Y. H. Lo, "Military Spending as Crisis Management: The U. S. Response to the Berlin Blockade and the Korean War," *Berkeley Journal of Sociology* 20 (1975–76): 156.

8. Walter S. Poole, *The History of the Joint Chiefs of Staff* 4:77, table 2.

9. For further details of the effects of McCarthy's denouncements on State Department officials and academic advisers, see David Caute, *The Great Fear: The Anti-Communist Purge under Truman and Eisenhower* (New York: Simon and Schuster, 1978), ch. 15; and for details of the Senator's first speech on the matter and its aftermath, see Thomas C. Reeves, *The Life and Times of Joe McCarthy: A Biography* (New York: Stein & Day, 1982), chs. 11–13.

10. Quoted in Stephen Pelz, "When the Kitchen Gets Hot, Pass the Buck: Truman and Korea in 1950," *Reviews in American History*, Dec. 1978, 552.

11. Even Vandenberg denied that there had been any consultation with respect to Asian policy, however: "There was no such liaison. . . . I wish to reiterate it," he said, "because I disassociate myself, as I have publicly done upon previous occasions, from the China policy which we pursued" (*Congressional Record*, June 24, 1949, p. 8294). He restated this position in a letter to a constituent: "I hope you understand that none of the Administration's Far East policies were ever part of our bipartisan program" (Arthur H. Vandenberg, Jr., ed., *The Private Papers of Senator Vandenberg* [Boston: Houghton Mifflin, 1952], 543).

12. Tucker, *Patterns in the Dust*, 89. Many others also helped McCarthy, including J. Edgar Hoover, Richard Nixon, and a number of journalists working for the Hearst, Scripps-Howard, and McCormick newspaper chains (Reeves, *Joe McCarthy*, esp. 245–49).

13. Quoted in Donovan, *Tumultuous Years*, 75.

14. For further details on the formulation and effects of the Truman Doctrine, see Richard H. Freeland, *The Truman Doctrine and the Origins of McCarthyism: Foreign Policy, Domestic Politics, and Internal Security, 1946–1948* (New York: Knopf, 1972); on Nationalist emissary activity, see Tucker, *Patterns in the Dust*, 89.

15. Quoted in Ronald J. Caridi, *The Korean War and American Politics: The Republican Party as a Case Study* (Philadelphia: University of Pennsylvania Press, 1968), 10.

16. Tucker, *Patterns in the Dust*, 156, and esp. ch. 9.

17. *Foreign Relations*, 1948, 8:146–55 (Oct. 13).

18. Tucker, *Patterns in the Dust*, 31.

19. Quoted in Blum, *Drawing the Line*, 86.

20. Chou's message is in *Foreign Relations*, 1949, 8:357–60 (June 1); for details of General Chen's approach, see Tucker, *Patterns in the Dust*, 54.

21. Tucker, *Patterns in the Dust*, 31.

22. U.S. Senate Committee on Foreign Relations, 81st Cong., 1st & 2d sess., *Reviews of the World Situation, 1949–1950*, (Washington, D.C.: GPO, 1974), 273.

23. Bevin Papers, Sept. 13, 1949, Private Collections, Ministers and Officials, FO 800/462, PRO.
24. *Foreign Relations*, 1949, 8:1008 (Nov. 14).
25. Blum, *Drawing the Line*, 86.
26. *Foreign Relations*, 1949, 8:364 (June 2).
27. Ibid., 388 (June 16).
28. Ibid., 363 (June 2).
29. Ibid., 1949, 9:466 (Dec. 29).
30. Ibid., 1950, 6:712 (Feb. 1).
31. Ibid., 1947, 7:840 (June 9).
32. Ibid., 1949, 9:262 (Nov. 24, 1948); ibid., 284–86 (Feb. 10).
33. Ibid., 286.
34. Quoted in Cohen, "Acheson," 26.
35. *Foreign Relations*, 1949, 9:466–67 (Dec. 29).
36. Quoted in William W. Stueck, Jr., *The Road to Confrontation: American Policy toward China and Korea, 1947–1950* (Chapel Hill: University of North Carolina Press, 1981), 142.
37. Koo Papers, Notes of a Conversation, June 3, June 30, 1950, BL.
38. Tucker, *Patterns in the Dust*, 56.
39. *Foreign Relations*, 1950, 6:334–35. (April 26).
40. Ibid., 6:346–47 (May 29).
41. Ibid., 6:350 (May 30).
42. Ibid., 6:349.
43. Ibid., 6:348–49 (May 31).
44. For a detailed discussion of Acheson's position, see Cohen, "Acheson," 48–49.

CHAPTER 3

1. 693.95A China, Feb. 8, 1950, Box 3005, Record Group 59, General Records of the Department of State Decimal File, National Archives (hereafter RG 59, NA).
2. Mao Tse-tung, *Selected Works* (Peking: Foreign Languages Press, 1977), 5: 38–39.
3. Quoted in Allen S. Whiting, *China Crosses the Yalu: The Decision to Enter the Korean War* (Stanford, Calif.: Stanford University Press, 1960), 18.
4. Robert Simmons, *The Strained Alliance: Peking, Pyongyang, Moscow and the Politics of the Korean Civil War* (New York: Free Press, 1975), 31.
5. 795.A North Korea, March 25, 1950, Box 4298, RG 59, NA; *Foreign Relations*, 1950, 7:109–21, esp. 111–12, 119 (June 19).
6. Cumings, *Origins of the Korean War*, xxvi. Indeed, elsewhere Cumings has argued that the Soviet commitment to North Korea was not comparable to the U.S. commitment to South Korea and was of a distinctly different order from Soviet commitments to key Eastern European states (see Bruce Cumings, ed., *Child of Conflict: The Korean-American Relationship, 1943–1953* [Seattle: University of Washington Press, 1983], 55).
7. John Lewis Gaddis, "Korea in American Politics, Strategy and Diplomacy, 1945–50," in Yonosuke Nagai and Akira Iriye, eds., *The Origins of the Cold War in Asia* (New York: Columbia University Press, 1977), 281.

8. Ibid., 284.

9. *Foreign Relations, 1947*, 6:820 (Oct. 1).

10. Ibid., (1949), 7:975 (March 22).

11. Ibid., (1949), 7:1091 (Oct. 21).

12. Nikita Khrushchev, *Krushchev Remembers* (Boston: Little, Brown, 1970), 367–69.

13. *Foreign Relations, 1950*, 7:150 (June 25); 795.00 Korea, June 25, 1950, Box 4262, RG 59, NA.

14. Truman Papers, PSF, June 28, 1950, HSTL.

15. Alexander L. George, "American Policy Making and the North Korean Aggression," *World Politics* 7 (1955):220.

16. Hoffmann, *Gulliver's Troubles*, 142.

17. *Foreign Relations, 1950*, 7: 174–75 (June 26).

18. June 27, 1950, no. 84057, FO 371, PRO. For a discussion of the concept of South Korea as a symbol, see Charles M. Dobbs, *The Unwanted Symbol: American Foreign Policy, the Cold War and Korea, 1945–1950* (Kent, Ohio: Kent State University Press, 1981).

19. *Foreign Relations*, (1950), 7: 152–53 (June 25).

20. Truman Papers, PSF, Aug. 6–8, 1950, HSTL.

21. Ibid., NSC Minutes, June 29, 1950.

22. John A. Munro and Alex I. Inglis, eds., *Mike: The Memoirs of the Right Honourable Lester B. Pearson* (Toronto: University of Toronto Press, 1973), 2:148.

23. C.O.S, (50) Minutes, 101st meeting, July 3, 1950, DEFE 4, PRO.

24. 795.00 Korea, June 26, 1950, Box 4262, RG 59, NA.

25. Ibid., June 29, 1950, Box 4263.

26. *Foreign Relations, 1950*, 1:329 (June 29).

27. Connelly Papers, Cabinet Minutes, July 8, 1950, HSTL.

28. *Foreign Relations, 1950*, 7:315 (July 6).

29. Simmons, e.g. (*Strained Alliance*, 150), has described Peking as "most emphatic about its desire for non-involvement"; Whiting (*China Crosses the Yalu*, 56–57) has written that China analyzed the first months of the war "in sober tones."

30. *Foreign Relations, 1950*, 1:327 (June 29); 1:332 (July 1).

31. 795.00 Korea, July 9, 1950, Box 4264, RG 59, NA; 795A.5 North Korea, July 9, 1950, Box 4298, RG 59, NA.

32. 793.00 China, July 28, 1950, Box 4196, RG 59, NA.

33. *Foreign Relations, 1950*, 7: 157–61, 178–83, 248–50, 255 (June 25–30).

34. John E. Mueller, *War, Presidents, and Public Opinion* (New York: Wiley, 1973), 51; Pelz, "When the Kitchen Gets Hot," 553.

35. Caridi, *Korean War and American Politics*, 33, 37; *New York Times*, June 28, 1950.

36. James T. Patterson, *Mr. Republican: A Biography of Robert A. Taft* (Boston: Houghton Mifflin, 1972), 452; Caridi, *Korean War and American Politics*, 65–71.

37. Alonzo L. Hamby, *Beyond the New Deal: Harry S. Truman and American Liberalism* (New York: Columbia University Press, 1973), 403.

38. *Washington Post*, June 28, July 1, 1950.

39. James Aronson, *The Press and the Cold War* (Indianapolis, Ind.: Bobbs-Merrill, 1970), 107.

40. *Foreign Relations, 1950*, 7:181 (June 26).

41. For a discussion of these contingency plans, see John Lewis Gaddis, "The Strategic Perspective: The Rise and Fall of the 'Defensive Perimeter' Concept, 1947–1951," in Borg and Heinrichs, *Uncertain Years*, esp. 85–86.

42. *Foreign Relations, 1950,* 7:349–51 (July 10).
43. See, e.g., ibid., 7:379–80 (July 14), for one of many Indian attempts to encourage the United States to resolve the Taiwan issue.
44. Ibid., 7:325 (July 7).
45. See, e.g., ibid., 7:331–32 (July 8–10), esp. 347–51.
46. Whiting, *China Crosses the Yalu,* 54.
47. Ibid., 58.
48. MacArthur Papers, July 30, 1950, Box 8, RG 6, MML.
49. See for example editorials in *New York Times,* June 28, 1950; *Washington Post,* June 29, 1950.
50. Suggested by Stueck, *Road to Confrontation,* 197.
51. *Foreign Relations, 1950,* 7:180 (June 26); see also 7:158 (June 25).
52. Truman, *Memoirs,* 2:342.
53. 793.00 China, July 29, 31, 1950, Box 4196, RG 59, NA.
54. *Foreign Relations, 1950,* 6:534–36 (Oct. 23).
55. Ibid., 7:373 (July 13).
56. Ibid., 7:410 (July 17).
57. C.O.S. (50) Minutes, 162d Meeting, Oct. 5, 1950, DEFE 4, PRO.
58. *Department of State Bulletin* (Aug. 28, 1950): 330–31.
59. Caridi, *Korean War and American Politics,* 55. See also *Congressional Record* (e.g., July 19, p. 10608; July 13, p. A5111) for typical use of the Yalta theme; Senator Wiley also hinted (July 10, p. 9738) that there might be a Pearl Harbor–type investigation of the administration's policy toward South Korea.
60. Reeves, *Joe McCarthy,* 328; *Washington Post,* Aug. 18, 1950.
61. Patterson, *Mr. Republican,* 455.
62. *Congressional Record,* Sept. 21, 1950, p. 15412.
63. Ayers Papers, Aug. 14, 1950, HSTL; Reeves, *Joe McCarthy,* 331–32.
64. Connelly Papers, Sept. 29, 1950, HSTL.
65. Records of the Office of Public Opinion Studies, July 26, 1950, Box 39, RG 59, NA; see, e.g., *New York Times,* Oct. 2, 6, 8, 1950; *Washington Post,* Oct. 4, 6, 1950.
66. *New York Times,* Oct. 5, 1950; Public Opinion Studies, Oct. 5–11, 1950, Box 26, RG 59, NA.
67. J. Lawton Collins, *War in Peacetime: The History and Lessons of Korea* (Boston: Houghton Miffin, 1969), 82–83.
68. Harry S. Truman, *Public Papers of the Presidents of the United States: Harry S Truman, 1950:* 531, 536, 539.
69. *Foreign Relations, 1950,* 7: 502–3, 506 (July 31).
70. Division of Chinese Affairs, Sept. 19, 1950, Box 17, RG 59, NA.
71. *Foreign Relations, 1950,* 7:386 (July 14).
72. Ibid., 7:272 (July 1).
73. 795.00 Korea, July 22, 1950, Box 4266, RG 59, NA.
74. *Foreign Relations, 1950,* 7:460–61 (July 24).
75. Records of the Policy Planning Staff (hereafter PPS Records), Aug. 8, 1950, Box 8, RG 59, NA.
76. *Foreign Relations, 1950,* 7:473 (July 25).
77. 795.00 Korea, July 27, 1950, Box 4266, RG 59, NA.
78. Stueck, *Road to Confrontation,* 205.
79. *Foreign Relations, 1950,* 7:624 (Aug. 21).
80. Dean Acheson, *Present at the Creation: My Years in the State Department* (New York: Norton, 1969), 451.

81. *Foreign Relations*, 1950, 7:712–21 (Sept. 9).

82. Ibid., 7:716.

83. Ibid., 7:826 (Sept. 29).

84. Ibid., 7:714 (Sept. 9).

85. V. K. Wellington Koo, Chinese Oral History Project, 7:A108–9, BL.

86. *Foreign Relations*, 1950, 7:575 (Aug. 14).

87. Records of the Army Staff, G3 091 Korea TS, Aug. 21, 1950, Box 36A, RG 319, NA.

88. *Foreign Relations*, 1950, 7:600 (Aug. 18).

89. 795.00 Korea, Sept. 7, 1950, Box 4268, RG 59, NA; *Foreign Relations*, 1950, 7:721–22 (Sept. 11).

90. Simmons, *Strained Alliance*, 156; Stueck, *Road to Confrontation*, 227.

91. *Foreign Relations*, 1950, 7:921 (Oct. 10).

92. See Foreign Service Posts of the Department of State, Moscow, Secret, Box 1335, RG 84, (Washington National Records Center) (WNRC), Suitland, Md.

93. *Foreign Relations*, 1950, 7:878 (October 5).

94. Foreign Service Posts, Moscow, Secret, Oct. 19, 1950, Box 1335, RG 84, WNRC.

95. Division of Chinese Affairs, Sept. 19, 1950, Box 17, RG 59, NA.

96. See, e.g., *Foreign Relations*, 1950, 7:600–603 (Aug. 18).

97. Ibid., 7:935–38 (Oct. 12).

98. Ibid., 7:953 (Oct. 15).

99. Whiting, *China Crosses the Yalu*, 93.

100. Kavalam M. Panikkar, *In Two Chinas: Memoirs of a Diplomat* (London: George Allen & Unwin, 1955), 110; *Foreign Relations*, 1950 7:864 (Oct. 4). For indications of the State Department's unfavorable view of Panikkar, see Division of Chinese Affairs, Oct. 12, 1950, Box 18, RG 59, NA.

101. *Foreign Relations*, 1950, 7:868 (Oct. 4).

102. Truman Papers, PSF, NSC Minutes, July 7, 1950, HSTL.

103. Division of Chinese Affairs, July 12, 1950, Box 17, RG 59, NA.

104. 795A.5 North Korea, Sept. 29, 1950, Box 4298, RG 59, NA; 795.00 Korea, Box 4268, RG 59, NA.

105. *Foreign Relations*, 1950, 7:864 (Oct. 4).

106. 795.00 Korea, July 12, 1950, Box 4265, RG 59, NA.

107. *Foreign Relations*, 1950, 7:848–49 (Oct. 3).

108. 793.00 China, Sept. 12, 1950, Box 4196, RG 59, NA.

109. *Foreign Relations*, 1950, 7:933 (Oct. 12).

110. Records of the Army Staff, G3 091 Korea TS, July 11, 1950, Box 34A, RG 319, NA.

111. *Foreign Relations*, 1950, 7:934 (Oct. 12).

112. Records of the Army Staff, G3 091 Korea TS, July 11, 1950, Box 34A, RG 319, NA.

113. Smith, *Dean Acheson*, 201.

114. *Foreign Relations*, 1950, 7:934 (Oct. 12).

115. Ibid., 7:765 (Sept. 22).

116. Ibid., 7:934 (Oct. 12).

117. Kennan Papers, Box 24, June 30, 1950, SGML.

118. *Foreign Relations*, 1950, 1:334 (July 1).

119. Division of Chinese Affairs, July 12, 1950, Box 17, RG 59, NA.

120. Acheson Papers, July 12, 1950, HSTL.

121. *Foreign Relations*, 1950, 1:375–89, (Aug. 25), esp. 388.

122. Ibid., 7:671–79 (Aug. 31).

123. Ibid., 7:781 (Sept. 26); 7:793n (Sept. 27).

124. Ibid., 7:915 (Oct. 9).

125. Acheson Papers, Aug. 23, 1950, HSTL.

126. Oct. 3, 1950, no. 84099, FO 371, PRO.

127. Matthew B. Ridgway, *The Korean War* (Garden City, N.Y.: Doubleday, 1967), 38.

128. *Foreign Relations*, 1950, 7:931–32 (Oct. 11).

129. Ibid., 7:949, 955 (Oct. 15).

CHAPTER 4

1. 795.00 Korea, Oct. 3, 1950, Box 4269, RG 59, NA.

2. Kennan Papers, SGML; also George F. Kennan, *Memoirs, 1950–1963* (Boston: Little, Brown, 1972), 34.

3. Stueck, *Road to Confrontation*, 242.

4. James F. Schnabel, *Policy and Direction: The First Year* (Washington, D.C.: GPO, 1972), 241.

5. MacArthur Papers, Nov. 4, 1950, Box 1, RG 6, MML.

6. *Foreign Relations*, 1950, 7:1058n (Nov. 6).

7. Schnabel, *Policy and Direction*, 243.

8. Acheson Papers, Memorandum of Conversation, Nov. 6, 1950, HSTL.

9. Bombing just one end of the bridges was so difficult that after the first attempts, the airmen decided to ignore the stricture. See Roy K. Flint, "The Tragic Flaw: MacArthur, the Joint Chiefs and the Korean War" (Ph.D. diss., Duke University, 1975), 383n.

10. Edward Friedman, "Problems in Dealing with an Irrational Power: America Declares War on China," in Mark Selden and Edward Friedman, *America's Asia: Dissenting Essays on Asian-American Relations* (New York: Random House, 1971).

11. "Selected Records of the Department of State and the Department of Defense Relating to the Korean War, 1947–1952," Nov. 17, 1950, Box 8, HSTL.

12. *Foreign Relations*, 1950, 7:1077, 1077n (Nov. 7).

13. Division of Chinese Affairs, Nov. 16, 1950, Box 18, RG 59, NA.

14. Nov. 24, 1950, no. 84104, FO 371, PRO.

15. *Foreign Relations*, 1950, 7:1108–9 (Nov. 9).

16. Records of the Army Staff, G3 091 Korea TS, Nov. 20, 1950, Box 36A, RG 319, NA.

17. Truman Papers, PSF, NSC Minutes, Nov. 10, 1950, HSTL.

18. *Foreign Relations*, 1950, 7:1229 (Nov. 24); 7:1212 (Nov. 21).

19. Deuel Writings, Nov. 13, 1950, Box 11, LC.

20. *Foreign Relations*, 1950, 7:1216–17 (Nov. 23).

21. Office of the Executive Secretariat, Nov. 8, 1950, Box 11, RG 59, NA.

22. Records of the Army Staff, G3 091 Korea TS, Nov. 8, 1950, Box 33A, RG 319, NA.

23. *Foreign Relations*, 1950, 7:1126 (Nov. 10).

24. Ibid., 7:1127.

25. Ibid., 7:1119 (Nov. 9); Truman Papers, PSF, NSC Minutes, Nov. 10, 1950, HSTL.

26. *Foreign Relations*, 1950, 7:1121 (Nov. 9).

27. Caridi, *Korean War and American Politics*, 95; Hamby, *Beyond the New Deal*, 418–22; Reeves, *Joe McCarthy*, 332–34; Patterson, *Mr. Republican*, 465.

28. *Foreign Relations*, 1950, 7:1030 (Nov. 3).

29. Ibid., 7:1091–92 (Nov. 7).

30. Ibid., 7:1125 (Nov. 10); 7:1168–70 (Nov. 17).

31. 793.00 China, Oct. 30, 1950, Box 4196, RG 59, NA.

32. *Foreign Relations*, 1950, 7:1082–83 (Nov. 7).

33. PPS Records, Nov. 14, 1950, RG 59, FOIA.

34. *Foreign Relations*, 1950, 7:1182 (Nov. 17).

35. Ibid., 7:1101–6 (Nov. 8).

36. Ibid., 7:1122 (Nov. 9); Truman Papers, PSF, NSC Minutes, Nov. 10, 1950, HSTL.

37. *Foreign Relations*, 1950, 7:1085 (Nov. 7); PPS Records, Nov. 14, 1950, RG 59, FOIA.

38. *Foreign Relations*, 1950, 7:1221 (Nov. 24).

39. Ibid., 7:1205–6 (Nov. 21).

40. Ibid., 7:1207–8.

41. Ibid., 7:1223–24 (Nov. 24).

42. Ibid., 7:1232–33 (Nov. 25).

43. See Whiting, *China Crosses the Yalu*, ch. 7, for details.

44. James F. Schnabel and Robert J. Watson, *History of the Joint Chiefs of Staff*, 3:356.

45. Foreign Service Posts, Moscow, Secret, Dec. 5, 1950, Box 1336, RG 84, WNRC.

46. 795.00 Korea, Dec. 14, 9, 1950, Box 4270, RG 59, NA. The public appeared to agree with this assessment: according to a Gallup poll on Dec. 30, 81 percent thought the Chinese had entered the fighting in Korea on Moscow's orders; only 5 percent disagreed (Public Opinion Studies, Dec. 30, 1950, Box 33, RG 59, NA).

47. *Foreign Relations*, 1950, 7:1292 (Dec. 1); 1951, 1:4–7 (Dec. 11, 1950).

48. Ibid., 1950, 7:1309 (Dec. 2).

49. MacArthur Papers, Dec. 7, 1950, Box 9, RG 6, MML.

50. *Foreign Relations*, 1950, 7:1246 (Nov. 28).

51. Office of the Executive Secretariat, Nov. 29, 1950, Box 11, RG 59, NA.

52. *Foreign Relations*, 1950, 7:1401–2 (Dec. 5).

53. Acheson Papers, Memorandum of Conversation, Dec. 1, 1950, HSTL.

54. Marshall D. Shulman, *Stalin's Foreign Policy Reappraised* (Cambridge, Mass.: Harvard University Press, 1963), 169; Acheson Papers, Memorandum of Conversation, Dec. 1, 1950, HSTL.

55. Robert F. Futrell, *The United States Air Force in Korea, 1950–1953* (New York: Duell, Sloan & Pearce, 1961), 231.

56. Records of the U.S. Joint Chiefs of Staff (hereafter JCS Records), CCS USSR 3-27-45, Sec. 54. Dec. 8, 1950, RG 218, NA. For a Soviet assessment of its air support of Chinese troops during the Korean War, see comments in Stephen S. Kaplan, et al., *Diplomacy of Power: Soviet Forces as a Political Instrument* (Washington, D.C.: Brookings Institution, 1981), 331–32.

57. Elsey Papers, Dec. 11, 1950, Box 73, HSTL.

58. Schnabel, *Policy and Direction*, 295.

59. Acheson Papers, Memorandum of Conversation, Nov. 28, 1950, HSTL.

60. *Foreign Relations*, 1950, 7:1253–54 (Nov. 29).

61. Schnabel, *Policy and Direction*, 318.

62. Office of the Executive Secretariat, Dec. 8, 1950, Box 11, RG 59, NA: Reeves,

Joe McCarthy, 348; Mueller, *War, Presidents*, 52. Poll data are in *The Gallup Poll*, vol. 2. (New York: Random House, 1972).

63. Caridi, *Korean War and American Politics*, 108, 111–12, 116; Patterson, *Mr. Republican*, 454, 485.

64. Reeves, *Joe McCarthy*, 347–48.

65. See, e.g., *Washington Post*, Nov. 27, 29, 1950. On the 27th the Alsops described Acheson as "the baby, the innocent sacrifice that must in the end be made."

66. PPS Records, Dec. 11, 1950, Box 23, RG 59, NA.

67. Ibid.

68. Dulles Papers, Nov. 30, 1950, SGML.

69. MacArthur Papers, Dec. 26, 1950, Box 3, RG 5, MML.

70. *Foreign Relations*, 1950, 7:1630–33 (Dec. 30).

71. Ibid., 7:1345–46 (Dec. 4).

72. Deuel Writings, January 10, 1951, Box 12, LC.

73. *Foreign Relations*, 1950, 7:1383 (Dec. 5).

74. Ibid.

75. Ibid., 7:1382.

76. Ibid., 7:1519 (Dec. 11).

77. Acheson, *Present at the Creation*, 513. See also his statement to the press, Jan. 17, 1951.

78. Quoted in Jan Kalicki, *The Pattern of Sino-American Crises* (London: Cambridge University Press, 1975), 70; *Foreign Relations*, 1951, 7:91 (Jan. 17).

79. *Foreign Relations*, 1950, 7:677 (Aug. 31); Acheson Papers, Memorandum of Conversation, Nov. 28, 1950, HSTL.

80. *Foreign Relations*, 1950, 7:1563 (Dec. 17).

81. Records of the Army Staff, G3 091 Korea TS, Sec. 12, Dec. 30, 1950, Box 126, RG 319, NA.

82. PPS Records, Jan. 19, 1951, RG 59, FOIA; *Foreign Relations*, 1951, 7:98 (Jan. 18).

83. Jan. 16, 1951, no. 92067, FO 371, PRO.

84. *Foreign Relations*, 1951, 7:27–28 (Jan. 5).

85. Ibid., 7:1885–87 (Jan. 20).

86. Ibid., 7:1617 (Dec. 28).

87. Connelly Papers, Jan. 26, 1951, HSTL.

88. January 12, 1951, no. 1439, PREM 8, PRO.

89. *Foreign Relations*, 1950, 7:1332 (Dec. 3).

90. 795.00 Korea, December 14, 1950, Box 4270, RG 59, NA.

91. January 2, 3, 1951, no. 92067, FO 371, PRO.

92. *Foreign Relations*, 1950, 7:1631 (Dec. 30). See also JCS message, ibid., 7:1626 (Dec. 29).

93. Reported in Records of the Army Staff, G3 091 Korea TS, July 5, 1951, Box 38A, RG 319, NA.

94. Hamby, *Beyond the New Deal*, 423.

95. Quoted in Richard F. Haynes, *The Awesome Power: Harry S Truman as Commander in Chief* (Baton Rouge: Louisiana State University Press, 1973), 219.

96. Cited in Buhite, *Soviet-American Relations in Asia, 1945–1954* (Norman: University of Oklahoma Press, 1981), 181n.

97. *New York Herald Tribune*, Nov. 29, 1950.

98. NSC 100, NA. See also *Foreign Relations*, 1951, 1:7–18 (Jan. 11).

99. As Rusk said on a later occasion, when the fig leaf is pulled off, you have to be prepared to deal with what's behind it (quoted in Deuel Writings, Jan. 10, 1951, Box 12, LC).

100. Truman Papers, PSF, NSC Minutes, Jan. 25, 1951, HSTL.

101. Records of the Army Staff, G3 091 Korea TS, Nov. 16, 1950, Box 34A, RG 319, NA.

102. JCS Records, Recently Declassified Army Documents, Korea, G3 files, Nov. 28, 1950, RG 218, NA.

103. Records of the Army Staff, G3 091 Korea TS, Dec. 1, 1950, Box 34, RG 319, NA. G3 also recommended the immediate acceptance of the 30,000 troops offered by Chiang Kai-shek.

104. Acheson Papers, Memorandum of Conversation, Nov. 28, 1950, HSTL.

105. *Foreign Relations*, 1950, 7:1328 (Dec. 3).

106. Ibid., 7:1330.

107. Ibid., 7:1457 (Dec. 7).

108. Ibid., 7:1330 (Dec. 3).

109. Ibid., 7:1335; see also Vandenberg's views on Dec. 19, 1950, 795.00 Korea, Box 4271, RG 59, NA.

110. Records of the Office of the Secretary of Defense (hereafter Defense Records), CD 092.3 (NATO) General #2, Dec. 5, 1950, RG 330, NA.

111. JCS Records, CCS 381 Far East (11-28-50), Sec. 1, Dec. 27, 1950, RG 218, NA.

112. Ibid., Jan. 3, 1951.

113. Truman Papers, PSF, NSC Minutes, Jan. 18, 1951, HSTL. There is also an inadequate summary of this discussion, produced by the State Department representative on the NSC staff, in *Foreign Relations*, 1951, 7:93–94 (Jan. 19).

114. Dec. 11, 1950, no. 1200, PREM 8, PRO; Bevin Papers, Dec. 10, 1950, FO 800/571, PRO.

115. Dec. 8, 1950, no. 83018, FO 371, PRO.

116. Ibid.

117. 795.00 Korea, Dec. 25, 1950, Box 4271, RG 59, NA.

118. *Foreign Relations*, 1950, 7:1603–4 (Dec. 27).

119. Ibid., 7:1327 (Dec. 3).

120. Ibid., 7:1385 (Dec. 5).

121. 611.93 China, Nov. 27, 1950, Box 2860, RG 59, NA; 795.00 Korea, Dec. 9, 14, 1950, Box 4270, RG 59, NA.

122. *Foreign Relations*, 1950, 6:162–64 (Nov. 30); Dulles Papers, SGML.

123. 793.00 China, Dec. 27, 1950, Box 4197, RG 59, NA.

124. *Foreign Relations*, 1950, 7:1309 (Dec. 2).

125. Ibid., 7:1023–25, 1038–41, 1087–93, 1125, 1170 (Nov. 1–16).

126. Ibid., 7:1163 (Nov. 16).

127. Ibid., 7:1246 (Nov. 28); 7:1276–81 (Dec. 1).

128. Ibid., 7:1321 (Dec. 3).

129. Ibid., 7:1324.

130. Ibid., 7:1326. See also Acheson Papers, Memorandum of Conversation, Dec. 1, 1950, HSTL.

131. *Foreign Relations*, 1950, 7:1335–36 (Dec. 3).

132. Ibid., 7:1384 (Dec. 5).

133. Ibid., 7:1603–4 (Dec. 27).

134. Foreign Service Posts, Moscow, Secret, Jan. 15, 1951, Box 169, RG 84, WNRC.

135. *Foreign Relations*, 1950, 7:1631 (Dec. 30).

136. Defense Records, CD 092 Korea, Dec. 4, 1950, Box 180, RG 330, NA.

137. *Foreign Relations*, 1950, 7:1470 (Dec. 8).

138. Truman Papers, PSF, NSC Minutes, Jan. 18, 1951, HSTL; PPS Records,

Memorandum from Merchant to Fisher reporting questions raised at NSC Staff meeting to consider NSC 101 on January 15 (dated April 30, 1951), RG 59, FOIA.

139. 793.00 China, Jan. 11, 1951, Box 4197, RG 59, NA.

140. 795.00 Korea, Jan. 19, 1951, Box 4271, RG 59, NA.

141. *Foreign Relations*, 1951, 7:1567–68 (Feb. 6).

142. 793.00 China, Feb. 8, 1951, Box 4197, RG 59, NA; *Foreign Relations*, 1951, 7:156 (Feb. 6); 7:177 (Feb. 13).

143. The CIA and the State and Defense Departments were asked to get together to resolve this question and to determine "what action we can take [against China] without serious risk of Soviet intervention" *Foreign Relations*, 1951, 7:177 (Feb. 13).

CHAPTER 5

1. *Foreign Relations*, 1951, 7:192–93 (Feb. 23).

2. PPS Records, Marshall to Nitze, Feb. 12, 1951, RG 59, FOIA.

3. Ibid., Jan. 30, 1951; for detailed description of first party, second party, and third party discussions, see *Foreign Relations*, 1951, 7:1476ff.

4. PPS Records, Marshall to Nitze, Feb. 12, 1951, RG 59, FOIA.

5. Truman Papers, PSF, NSC Minutes, March 21, 1951, HSTL.

6. *Foreign Relations*, 1951, 7:241–43 (March 17).

7. Foreign Service Posts, Moscow, March 20, 1951, Box 1339, and March 15, 1951, Box 1341, RG 84, WNRC; PPS Records, Negotiated Settlement of the Korean Conflict, March 24 1951, RG 59, FOIA.

8. *Foreign Relations*, 1951, 7:304–5 (April 5); 7:376 (April 23).

9. Text in ibid., 7:265–66 (March 24); *New York Times*, March 25, 1951; Truman, *Memoirs*, 2:440–41.

10. Truman, *Memoirs*, 2:439–40, 442; Connelly Papers, March 20 [*sic*], 1951, HSTL.

11. Truman, *Public Papers, 1951:* 223; *Department of State Bulletin* (April 30, 1951): 683.

12. *Foreign Relations*, 1951, 7:483–86 (May 31); 7:507–11 (June 5). See also Acheson, *Present at the Creation*, 532–33.

13. NSC 48/5, May 17, 1951, NA; *Foreign Relations*, 1951, 7:439–42 (May 17).

14. *Foreign Relations*, 1951, 7:419–20 (May 6).

15. Ibid., 1951, 7:357, 366 (April 18).

16. Ibid., 7:426 (May 10).

17. David Rees, *Korea: The Limited War* (New York: St. Martin's Press, 1964), 273, ch. 15.

18. *Declassified Hearings*, 2579–83, 4193. See also the useful article by John E. Wiltz, "The MacArthur Hearings of 1951: The Secret Testimony," *Military Affairs* 39 (Dec. 1975).

19. *Declassified Hearings*, 3952.

20. U.S. Senate, *Military Situation in the Far East*, 731.

21. Quoted in John W. Spanier, *The Truman-MacArthur Controversy and the Korean War* (Cambridge, Mass.: Harvard University Press, 1959), 247; see also U.S. Senate, *Military Situation in the Far East*, 1719.

22. *Declassified Hearings*, 1626.

23. Spanier, *Truman-MacArthur Controversy*, 248–49; U.S. Senate, *Military Situation in the Far East*, 1719.

24. *Declassified Hearings*, 4011.

25. Ibid., 3945–46.

26. Ibid., 2311.

27. Ibid., 877.

28. U.S. Senate, *Military Situation in the Far East*, 887.

29. Schnabel and Watson, *History of the JCS*, 3: 454.

30. *Declassified Hearings*, 1733, 3217.

31. Public Opinion Studies, June 14–20, 1951, Box 27, and Monthly Survey, June 1951, Box 12, RG 59, NA.

32. Ibid., May 25, June 21, Dec. 30, 1951, Box 39; *Foreign Relations*, 1951, 1:90 (June 5).

33. Truman Papers, PSF, NSC Minutes, May 3, 1951, HSTL.

34. *Foreign Relations*, 1951, 7:448 (May 23); 795.00 Korea, May 23, 1951, Box 4273, RG 59, NA.

35. Rusk and Dulles speeches in *Department of State Bulletin* (May 28, 1951): 843–48.

36. Cohen, *Dean Rusk*, 63.

37. *Foreign Relations*, 1951, 7:1672 (May 21).

38. Office of the Executive Secretariat, May 21, 1951, Box 2, RG 59, NA.

39. Weekly Political Summary, May 19–25, 1951, no. 90904, FO 371, PRO.

40. *Declassified Hearings*, 807.

41. Ibid., 2324–25, 2445, 2671–72.

42. *Foreign Relations*, 1951, 7:385–86 (April 27 and 28).

43. PPS Records, Memorandum for the NSC submitted by JCS, March 21, 1951, RG 59, FOIA; *Foreign Relations*, 1951, 7:1598–1605 (March 21).

44. *Foreign Relations*, 1951, 7:1608–9 (March 25); see also 7:1616–19 (April 4).

45. 793.00 China, April 13, 1951, Box 4198, RG 59, NA.

46. Ibid., April 25, 1951; see also May 7, 1951.

47. *Foreign Relations*, 1951, 7:1673–82 (May 22).

48. PPS Records, Memorandum for Nitze, Feb. 28, 1951, RG 59, FOIA.

49. JCS Records, CCS 381 Far East (11-28-50), Sec. 4, Feb. 16, 1951, RG 218, NA.

50. April 6, 1951, no. 92063, FO 371, PRO.

51. C.O.S. (51), 42, 73d meeting, April 30, 1951, DEFE 4, PRO; see also *Foreign Relations*, 1951, 7:338–42 (April 12).

52. April 6, 1951, no. 92757, FO 371, PRO.

53. May 1, 1951, no. 92063, FO 371, PRO.

54. Ibid., May 4, 1951.

55. *Foreign Relations*, 1951, 7:353–62 (April 18).

56. Ridgway Papers, April 27, 28, 1951, Box 20, AMHI; *Foreign Relations*, 1951, 7:385–87 (April 27, 28).

57. *Foreign Relations*, 1951, 7:399–400 (May 2).

58. Records of the Army Staff, G3 091 Korea TS, Sec. IX, Box 38, Case 167, April 5, 1951, RG 319, NA; *Foreign Relations*, 1951, 7:295–96 (April 5).

59. *Foreign Relations*, 1951, 7:296,n.1 (April 5).

60. PPS Records, Memorandum for the NSC, April 10, 1951, RG 59, FOIA.

61. NSC 48/5, May 17, 1951, pp. 6–7, NA.

62. John L. Gaddis, *Strategies of Containment: A Critical Appraisal of Post-War American National Security Policy* (New York: Oxford University Press, 1982), 122.

63. *Foreign Relations*, 1950, 7:1326 (Dec. 3).

64. Ibid., 1951, 7:1990 (May 29). Two days later the commander of the Pacific Fleet was asked to develop a plan for a blockade of the China coast (793.00 China, June 1, 1951, Box 4199, RG 59, NA).

65. *Foreign Relations*, 1951, 7:470–72 (May 29).

66. JCS Records, CCS 383.21 Korea (3-19-45), Sec. 53, July 13, 1951, RG 218, NA; *Foreign Relations, 1951*, 7:667–68 (July 13).

67. *Foreign Relations, 1951*, 7:718–19, 730–31 (July 21, 25).

68. Defense Records, CD 092 Korea, Aug. 4, 10, 1951, Box 233, RG 330, NA.

69. *Foreign Relations, 1951*, 7:771–74, 835–41 (Aug. 3, 18); 795.00 Korea, Aug. 3, 1951, Box 4274, RG 59, NA.

70. PPS Records, Memorandum for the Secretary of Defense, Aug. 29, 1951, RG 59, FOIA.

71. Ibid., State–Joint Chiefs meeting, Aug. 29, 1951, p. 17, FOIA; *Foreign Relations, 1951*, 7:859–64 (Aug. 29).

72. *Foreign Relations, 1951*, 7:862, 861 (Aug. 29).

73. Ibid., 7:862, 863.

74. Defense Records, CD 092 Korea, enclosed with letter from Matthews (deputy undersecretary of state) to secretary of defense, Sept. 10, 1951, Box 233, RG 330, NA; *Foreign Relations, 1951*, 7:889–91 (Sept. 8); but see also 7:911–14 (Sept. 12).

75. PPS Records, Meeting of the U.S.-U.K. Foreign Ministers, Washington, D.C., Sept. 10, 1951, RG 59, FOIA; *Foreign Relations, 1951*, 7:893–99 (Sept. 11).

76. *Foreign Relations, 1951*, 7:976–80 (Oct. 1).

77. PPS Records, Memorandum, Ferguson to Webb, Sept. 4; Memorandum, Watts to Sohm, Oct. 19; Letter, Gray to Acheson, Sept. 19, 1951, RG 59, FOIA.

78. Isidor F. Stone, *The Hidden History of the Korean War* (New York: Monthly Review Press, 1952), 297.

79. See, e.g., Records of the Army Staff, G3 091 Korea TS, Oct. 26, 1951, Box 34, RG 319, NA.

80. Ibid., Nov. 3, 1951, Box 38A; Defense Records, CD 092.3 NATO (Gen), Nov. 12, 1951, RG 330, NA.

81. PPS Records, JCS comments on position paper "Courses of Action in Korea in the Event No Armistice Is Achieved," Nov. 7, 1951, RG 59, FOIA; see also *Foreign Relations, 1951*, 7:1107–9 (Nov. 3).

82. *Foreign Relations, 1951*, 7:1177–80 (Nov. 26).

83. JCS Records, Omar Bradley Files, Dec. 1, 1951, Box 4, RG 218, NA.

84. Dec. 20, 1951, no. 92760, FO 371, PRO.

85. Acheson Papers, Memorandum of Conversation, Jan. 7, 1952, HSTL. As late as Nov. 20, and as a result of Operation Hudson Harbor, the Department of the Army had confirmed that the means available for tactical employment of atomic weapons were inadequate and that timely identification of large masses of troops had been extremely rare; it recommended that this deficiency be remedied through more effective intelligence-gathering procedures and the development of a ground-to-ground vehicle capable of delivering atomic missiles in support of ground troops. Records of the Army Staff, G3 091 Korea TS, Nov. 20, 1951, Box 38A, RG 319, NA. See also Schnabel and Watson, *History of the JCS*, 3: 613–14.

86. Truman Papers, PSF, NSC Minutes, Jan. 7, 1952, HSTL.

87. Acheson Papers, Memorandum of Conversation, Jan. 7, 1952, HSTL; *Foreign Relations, 1951*, 7:1254–57 (Dec. 6).

88. 795.00 Korea, Oct. 5, 1951, Box 4275, RG 59, NA.

89. PPS Records, State–Joint Chiefs meeting, Nov. 26, 1951, RG 59, FOIA. Vandenberg was most likely referring to the production of the F-86 Sabre jet, the only U.S. aircraft that would truly rival the MIG; Sabres had been in short supply since the start of the war.

90. Public Opinion Studies, Public Attitudes on U.S. Policy towards China, April–

Aug. 1951, Box 33, Box 12, RG 59, NA; Mueller, *War, Presidents,* 230; Reeves, *Joe McCarthy,* 370–72.

91. *Congressional Record,* Oct. 11, 1951, p. 12938; Public Opinion Studies, June 21–27, 1951, Box 27, RG 59, NA.

92. *Congressional Record,* Jan. 29, 1952, p. 570; Jan. 15, pp. A128–29.

93. Quoted in Caridi, *Korean War and American Politics,* 198.

94. *Foreign Relations,* 1951, 7:1864 (Dec. 8).

95. 611.93 China, Sept. 26, 1951, Box 2861, RG 59, NA.

96. NSC 118, Nov. 3, 1951, NA.

97. NSC 118/2, Dec. 20, 1951, NA.

98. Truman Papers, PSF, Special Intelligence Estimate 9004, April 6, 1951, HSTL.

99. NSC 48/5, May 17, 1951, NA.

100. 611.93 China, May 7, 1951, Box 2861, RG 59, NA.

101. PPS Records, Embassy Dispatch, April 25, 1951, RG 59, FOIA.

102. Truman Papers, PSF, Special Estimate 8, July 6, 1951, HSTL.

103. JCS Records, CCS 383.21 Korea (3-19-45), Sec. 51, July 2 1951, RG 218, NA.

104. 795.00 Korea, July 14, 19, 1951, Box 4274, RG 59, NA.

105. Foreign Service Posts, Moscow, July 16, 1951, Box 1340, RG 84, WNRC.

106. *Foreign Relations,* 1951, 1:108–9 (July 28).

107. Foreign Service Posts, Moscow, Aug. 11, 1951, Box 1340, RG 84, WNRC.

108. In September the Far East command estimated that 25,900 Caucasian troops had arrived in Korea, of which 15,400 were probably Soviet, but at the end of the month, there was no new information on the status of this estimate (*Foreign Relations,* 1951, 7:922, 967 [Sept. 18,28]).

109. JCS Records, CCS 383.21 Korea (3-19-45), Sec. 59, Aug. 20, 1951, Box 34, RG 218, NA.

110. Ibid., Sec. 58, Aug. 16, 1951.

111. Truman Papers, PSF, Intelligence, Aug. 6, 1951, HSTL.

112. Ibid.

113. Ibid., Korean War Files, Special Estimate 20, Dec. 15, 1951.

114. Ibid.

115. PPS Records, "NSC agenda for meeting on Wednesday, Dec. 19," Dec. 17, 1951, RG 59, FOIA.

116. *Foreign Relations,* 1951, 1:203 (Sept. 24); 7:1737–43 (July 10).

117. Ibid., 7:449 (May 23).

118. 793.00 China, Sept. 17, 1951, Box 4199, RG 59, NA.

119. *Foreign Relations,* 1951, 1:197–98 (Sept. 24); Shulman, *Stalin's Foreign Policy,* 172–73, 177.

120. Truman Papers, PSF, Intelligence, Aug. 6, 1951, HSTL.

121. Futrell, *U.S. Air Force in Korea,* 266.

122. October 26, 1951, no. 92807, FO 371, PRO.

123. Morton H. Halperin, "The Limiting Process in the Korean War," in Allen H. Guttman, ed., *Korea and the Theory of Limited War* (Boston: Heath, 1967), 94.

124. James A. Field, *History of United States Naval Operations: Korea* (Washington,D.C.: GPO, 1962), 372–73.

125. NSC 118/2, Dec. 20, 1951, NA.

126. *Foreign Relations,* 1951, 7:1292 (Dec. 10).

127. Ibid., 7:1264 (Dec.7).

128. Ibid., 7:962 (Sept. 26).

129. Ibid., 7:2050 (Nov. 21).

130. PPS Records, NSC Agenda, Dec. 17, 1951, RG 59, FOIA.
131. Nov. 30, 1951, no. 92759, FO 371, PRO.
132. *Foreign Relations*, 1951, 7:943 (Sept. 25).
133. NSC 118/2, Dec. 20, 1951, NA.

CHAPTER 6

1. Foreign Service Posts, Moscow, Intelligence Report, no. 5751.2, March 14, 1952, Box 169, RG 84, WNRC.
2. Barton J. Bernstein, "Truman's Secret Thoughts on Ending the Korean War," *Foreign Service Journal*, Nov. 1980, and his valuable article, "The Struggle over the Korean Armistice: Prisoners of Repatriation?" in Cumings, *Child of Conflict*.
3. Bernstein, "Struggle over the Korean Armistice," esp. 284–85. According to a report by Phil W. Manhard, who was in Korea on interrogation duty for the State Department between July and December 1951 and the first week of February 1952, the trustees in the Chinese POW camps, appointed by U.S. Army camp authorities, were selected for their anti-Communist stance. They were former Chinese Nationalist MPs, most of whom had been captured by the Communists on Hainan Island and in South China, and company-grade officer graduates of the Chinese Nationalist Military Academy. They exercised discretionary control over food, clothing, fuel, and medical treatment in the camps; moreover, for several months they had conducted a drive to collect petitions for transfer to Taiwan. Often using brute force, beatings, and torture, Manhard said, they announced: "It has been officially decided that all who wish to do so will be guaranteed an opportunity to go to Formosa—those who do not wish to fight Communism will remain in the POW camp indefinitely" (Foreign Service Posts, Korea, Seoul, March 14, 1952, Box 9, RG 84, NA). In addition, see Stelle's memorandum confirming that the leaders in the camps were "practically all former Nationalist troops" and that they conducted "a reign of terror over the other inmates." Stelle also points to the anomaly of the U.S. position on the voluntary repatriation of the prisoners of war: it was "the thugs" who ran the camps that were the objects of U.S. concern in the POW issue, "aside from our own U.S. prisoners" (PPS Records, Stelle to Nitze, Jan. 24, 1952, RG 59, FOIA).
4. PPS Records, June 11, 1952, RG 59, FOIA; 795.00 Korea, July 9, 1952, Box 4282, RG 59, NA.
5. 795.00 Korea, Box 4279, May 8, 1952, RG 59, NA; PPS Records, June 11, Sept. 3, 2, 1952, RG 59, FOIA.
6. Truman Papers, PSF, Longhand Notes File, Jan. 27, May 18, 1952, Box 333, HSTL.
7. JCS Records, Recently Declassified JCS Documents, Korea, April 3, 1952, RG 218, NA.
8. PPS Records, Memorandum of Conversation, Feb. 20, 1952, RG 59, FOIA.
9. Truman Papers, PSF, NSC Minutes, April 3, 1952, HSTL.
10. 795.00 Korea, May 14, 1952, Box 4279, RG 59, NA.
11. Futrell, *U.S. Air Force in Korea*, 448.
12. Ibid.
13. Ibid., 481.
14. Ibid., 490, 492; 795.00 Korea, Aug. 26, Sept. 2, 1952, Box 4283, RG 59, NA; Aug. 26, Sept. 30, 1952, no. 99602, FO 371, PRO.
15. Bradley said to Lord Alexander that the president thought the bombings

would induce a more cooperative attitude at the truce negotiations, and to Selwyn Lloyd that the bombing would "ginger up" the peace talks (June 24, 1952, no. 99598, FO 371, PRO; 795.00 Korea, June 24, 1952, Box 4281, RG 59, NA). For an interesting discussion of the theorizing within the Johnson administration about coercive warfare and the problems with the assumptions behind this policy, see Wallace Thies, *When Governments Collide: Coercion and Diplomacy in the Vietnam Conflict, 1964–68* (Berkeley: University of California Press, 1980).

16. Schnabel and Watson, *History of the JCS*, 3:845.

17. Ibid.

18. Simmons, *Strained Alliance*, 216.

19. June 24–July 17, 1952, nos. 99599, 99600, FO 371, PRO.

20. Schnabel and Watson, *History of the JCS*, 3:847.

21. July 1, 1952, no. 111, PREM 11, PRO.

22. 795.00 Korea, June 24, 25, 1952, Box 4281, RG 59, NA.

23. Royal Institute of International Affairs, *Survey of International Affairs 1952*, (London: Oxford University Press, 1953), 322.

24. *New York Times*, Oct. 15, 16, 1952.

25. Oct. 25, 1952, no. 99232, FO 371, PRO; *New York Times*, Oct. 16, 1952. A *New York Times* report (Dec. 7, 1952) on Nationalist raids details 53 raids between June 1 and October 14, 1952.

26. M. Gravel, *The Pentagon Papers: The Defense Department History of the United States Decision Making on Vietnam* (Boston: Beacon Press, 1971), 1:381–82.

27. Ibid., 386, 389–90.

28. PPS Records, Aug. 14, 1952, RG 59, FOIA; 795.00 Korea, Aug. 14, 1952, Box 4283, RG 59, NA.

29. 795.00 Korea, Oct. 2, Box 4284, RG 59, NA; PPS Records, Sept. 10, 1952, FOIA.

30. Acheson Papers, Memorandum of Conversation, Sept. 17, 1952, Box 67, HSTL.

31. This and the two following paragraphs are based on the account in Schnabel and Watson, *History of the JCS*, 3:892–903; Haynes, *Awesome Power*, 237–38; Bernstein, "Struggle over the Korean Armistice," 299–300; Truman Papers, PSF, NSC Minutes, Sept. 24, 1952, HSTL.

32. Selected Records of the Department of State and Department of Defense, Sept. 23, 1952, 7:1229, HSTL.

33. JCS Records, Omar Bradley Files, Oct. 9, 1952, Box 4, RG 218, NA.

34. *New York Times*, July 9, 1952.

35. JCS Records, 383.21 Korea (3-19-45), Oct. 16, 1952, Box 41, RG 218, NA; Schnabal and Watson, *History of the JCS*, 3:932–33.

36. Records of the Army Staff, 1951–52, 091.Korea, Nov. 7, 1952, RG 319, NA.

37. 793.00 China, Oct. 20, 1952, Box 4202, RG 59, NA.

38. Nov. 11, 1952, no. 111, PREM 11, PRO; CAB 129/57, Dec. 15, 1952, no. 441, PRO; Bernstein, "Struggle over the Korean Armistice," 303.

39. David Carlton, *Anthony Eden: A Biography* (London: Allen Lane, 1981), 321; *Foreign Relations, 1952–1954*, 15:644 (Nov. 16, 1952).

40. Munro and Inglis, *Lester Pearson*, 327.

41. PPS Records, Dec. 4, 1952, RG 59, FOIA; Joseph C. Goulden, *Korea: The Untold Story of the War* (New York: Times Books, 1982). 620; *New York Times*, Nov. 11, 1952.

42. Schnabel and Watson, *History of the JCS*, 3:933–34.

43. *Foreign Relations*, 1951, 1:132–38 (Aug. 8).

44. JCS Records, CCS 381 Far East (11-28-50), Sec. 15, May 16, 1952, RG 218, NA.

45. Futrell, *U.S. Air Force in Korea*, 230.

46. Connelly Papers, Sept. 12, 1952, HSTL.

47. Acheson Papers, Memorandum of Conversation, Sept. 17, 1952, Box 67, HSTL.

48. Ibid.

49. Records of the Army Staff, 1951–52, 091.Korea, Nov. 19, 1952, RG 319, NA.

50. Quoted in Hamby, *Beyond the New Deal*, 485.

51. *The Gallup Poll*, 1952; 1050, 1052.

52. Public Opinion Studies 1948–1956, Box 12, RG 59, NA. The State Department's opinion surveys showed, however, that there was a significant difference in male and female responses to the war. In April 1952, 45 percent of the women polled thought it had been right to send troops to Korea, compared with 54 percent of the men; 42 percent of women thought it had been wrong, compared with 38 percent of men. When asked about extending the war to Manchuria, 45 percent of women and 63 percent of men were in favor; 33 percent of women and 28 percent of men were against (Public Opinion Studies, April 17, 1952, Box 39, RG 59, NA).

53. Ibid., Box 39, RG 59; Haynes, *Awesome Power*, 237. Mueller (*War, Presidents*, 103) points out, however, that the public supported an expanded war only when the question was phrased in a way that did not link the idea of expansion to a longer war.

54. 795.00 Korea, Sept. 15, 1952, Box 4283, RG 59, NA; *Christian Science Monitor*, quoted in *Congressional Record*, March 19, 1952 p. A1739; *New York Times*, June 22, 1952; Public Opinion Studies, May 15–21, 1952, Box 27, RG 59, NA; *Time* magazine quoted in 795.00 Korea, June 19, 1952, Box 4281, RG 59, NA.

55. *Congressional Record*, May 15, 1952, p. A3007; Robert A. Divine, *Foreign Policy and U.S. Presidential Elections, 1952–1960* (New York: New Viewpoints, 1974), 34.

56. *New York Times*, Oct. 3, 1952.

57. Caridi, *Korean War and American Politics*, 205.

58. Ibid., 206.

59. John Foster Dulles, "A Policy of Boldness," *Life*, May 19, 1952, quoted in Caridi, *Korean War and American Politics*, 185.

60. 695A.0024 North Korea, Feb. 8, 1952, RG 59, NA; see also Bernstein, "Struggle over the Korean Armistice," esp. 279ff.

61. Divine, *Foreign Policy*, 64; Reeves, *Joe McCarthy*, 451, 445.

62. Reeves, *Joe McCarthy*, 452–53.

63. Divine, *Foreign Policy*, 51; Patterson, *Mr. Republican*, 556–57.

64. Reeves, *Joe McCarthy*, 439–40. For further details regarding the "Marshall" speech and the campaign between September and November 1952, see Stephen E. Ambrose, *Eisenhower: Soldier, General of the Army, President-Elect, 1890–1952* (New York: Simon & Schuster, 1983), ch. 27.

65. Divine, *Foreign Policy*, 70.

66. *New York Times*, Nov. 1, 1952.

67. 795.00 Korea, Dec. 17, 1952, Box 4284, RG 59, NA; Futrell, *U.S. Air Force in Korea*, 487.

68. Declassified Documents Reference System (1981), 543C, Aug. 27, 1952 (hereafter DDRS).

69. PPS Records, quoting conclusions of NIE 58, Aug. 21, 1952, RG 59, FOIA.

70. 795.00 Korea, Oct. 30, 1952, Box 4284, RG 59, NA.

71. Truman Papers, PSF, Intelligence, NIE 55/1, July 30, 1952, HSTL; 795.00 Korea, May 18, 1952, Box 4279; June 30, 1952, Box 4281; June 9, 1952, Box 4280, RG 59, NA.

72. DDRS (1980), 346A, Dec. 11, 1952.
73. Shulman, *Stalin's Foreign Policy*, 197–98 and esp. ch. 10.
74. Speech to the Junior Chamber of Commerce, March 20, 1952.
75. Truman Papers, PSF, Korean War File, General, Aug. 28, 1952, HSTL.
76. Koo, Chinese Oral History, 7:E155, BL.
77. JCS Records, 383.21 Korea (3-19-45), Sept. 29, 1952, Box 48, RG 218, NA.
78. *New York Times*, Oct. 30, 1952.
79. Feb. 29, 1952, no. 99218, FO 371, PRO.
80. Gravel, *Pentagon Papers*, Doc. 14, July 14, 1952, 1:391.
81. Connelly Papers, Dec. 5, 1952, HSTL.
82. Barton J. Bernstein, "New Light on the Korean War," *International History Review*, April 1981, 273.
83. An official State Department spokesman said as much to U.S. diplomatic correspondents on July 8, 1952. See Deuel Writings, July 8, 1952, Box 12, LC.
84. PPS Records, Dec. 16, 22, 1952, RG 59, FOIA; 695A.0024 North Korea, Dec. 24, 1952, Box 3026, RG 59, NA.
85. Mark Clark, Eisenhower Administration Oral History Project, 25–26, BL.
86. Finletter speech of June 19, 1952, quoted in *Congressional Record*, June 24, 1952, p. A4014; Malcolm W. Cagle and Frank A. Manson, *The Sea War in Korea* (Annapolis, Md.: U.S. Naval Institute, 1957), 449.
87. Mueller, *War, Presidents*, 252.
88. This is not to say that other issues were not important in the election result of 1952. Caridi has noted that the high level of government spending, taxation, and inflation also contributed to the downfall of the Democrats (Caridi, *Korean War and American Politics*, 240). See also Hamby, *Beyond the New Deal*, ch. 22, for a description of the campaign.

CHAPTER 7

1. Acheson, *Present at the Creation*, 633.
2. Clark, Oral History Project, BL, 9.
3. Dwight D. Eisenhower, *The White House Years: Mandate for Change, 1953–1956* (Garden City, N.Y.: Doubleday, 1963), 1:96; *Foreign Relations, 1952–1954*, 5:1651 (July 12, 1953).
4. Eisenhower, *White House Years*, 1:179–80.
5. Caridi, *Korean War and American Politics*, 253.
6. Eisenhower, *White House Years*, 1:180; "Memorandum on Ending the Korean War" (considering both political and military matters), Dec. 14, 1952, RG 10, MML.
7. JCS Records, CCS 383.21 Korea (3-19-45), Sec. 125, March 23, 1953, RG 218, NA.
8. NSC 147, NSC Planning Board, "Analysis of Possible Courses of Action in Korea," April 2, 1953, NA. The NSC Planning Board emerged to replace the senior staff in the reorganization of NSC machinery ordered by President Eisenhower in March 1953.
9. SE-37, CIA, March 9, 1953, FOIA.
10. JCS Records, CCS 383.21 Korea (3-19-45), Sec. 128, May 20, 1953, RG 218, NA; Schnabel and Watson *History of the JCS*, 3:948–62; *Foreign Relations, 1952–1954*, 15:1059–64 (May 19, 1953); 15:1065 (May 20).

11. NSC Action no. 794, May 20, 1953, NA; Schnabal and Watson, *History of the JCS*, 3:961–62; *Foreign Relations, 1952–1954*, 15:1067–68 (May 20, 1953); 15:1068 (May 21).

12. Barry M. Blechman and Robert Powell, "What in the Name of God Is Strategic Superiority?" *Political Science Quarterly* 97 (Winter 1982–83):591; Schnabel and Watson, *History of the JCS*, 3: 979–80; John Gittings, "Talks, Bombs and Germs—Another Look at the Korean War," *Journal of Contemporary Asia* 5, no. 2 (1975): 215–16; Mark Clark, Oral History, 1972, 13, AMHI.

13. Schnabel and Watson, *History of the JCS*, 3:982, 980; letter from Clark in Blechman and Powell, "Strategic Superiority," 595, n. #17; 695.0029 North Korea, May 22, 1953, Box 3024, RG 59, NA.

14. Eisenhower papers, NSC, 139th meeting, April 8, 1953, Whitman Files, Box 4, DDEL.

15. Deuel Writings, April 6, 1953, Box 13, LC.

16. DDRS 1951–53 (1981), 625B, March 21, 1953; Eisenhower papers, Discussion at Special Meeting of National Security Council, March 31, 1953 (dated April 7), FOIA, DDEL.

17. 795.00 Korea, April 21, 1953, Box 4285, RG 59, NA.

18. Eisenhower papers, NSC, 139th meeting, April 8, 1953, "Action on item 4," Whitman Files, Box 4, DDEL.

19. 795.00 Korea, Jan. 23, Feb. 16, April 15, 1953, Box 4285, RG 59, NA; 611.95 Korea, March 27, 1953, Box 2882A, RG 59, NA; 793.00 China, May 26, June 12, 1953, Box 4204, RG 59, NA.

20. 793.00 China, June 18, 1953, Box 4205, RG 59, NA.

21. Emmet J. Hughes, *The Ordeal of Power: A Political Memoir of the Eisenhower Years* (New York: Atheneum, 1963), 104–5; see also Dulles's statement at the Bermuda meeting with French and British government ministers, DDEL, John Foster Dulles Files, Subject Series, Alphabetical Subseries, Dec. 7, 1953, Box 1, SGML.

22. Goulden, *Korea*, 628. The exact date at which tactical atomic weapons were available to the United States is unclear, since in July 1952 General Collins had reported them available for use. (*New York Times*, July 9, 1952).

23. Eisenhower papers, NSC, 131st meeting, Feb. 11, 1953, Whitman Files, Box 4, DDEL.

24. *Foreign Relations, 1952–1954*, 15:827 (March 31, 1953).

25. Carlton, *Anthony Eden*, 335.

26. Charles C. Alexander, *Holding the Line: The Eisenhower Era, 1952–1961* (Bloomington: Indiana University Press, 1975), 68.

27. David A. Rosenberg, "The Origins of Overkill: Nuclear Weapons and American Strategy, 1945–1960," *International Security* 7, pt. 4 (Spring 1983): 66.

28. I am grateful to Professor Robert Jervis for reminding me of this fact.

29. Eisenhower papers, Discussion at special NSC meeting, March 31, 1953, FOIA, DDEL.

30. *Foreign Relations, 1952–1954*, 15:1014 (May 13, 1953).

31. Eisenhower, *White House Years*, 1:180.

32. Sherman Adams, *Firsthand Report: The Inside Story of the Eisenhower Administration* (London: Hutchinson, 1962), 55.

33. DDEL, John Foster Dulles Files, Subject Series, Alphabetical Subseries, Dec. 7, 1953, SGML; also in *Foreign Relations, 1952–1954*, 5:1811–13 (Dec. 7, 1953).

34. See NSC 170/1, Nov. 20, 1953, NA; Gaddis, *Strategies of Containment*, 169; comments to Churchill at Bermuda in Dec. 1953, *Foreign Relations, 1952–1954*, 5:1739 (Dec. 4, 1953).

35. Eisenhower papers, NSC, 139th meeting, April 8, 1953, Whitman Files, Box 4, DDEL.

36. Ibid.

37. *News Chronicle,* May 20, 1953, Royal Institute of International Affairs, Press Library.

38. 695A.0024, May 2, 6, 8, 1953, Box 3024, RG 59, NA.

39. 795.00 Korea, May 18, 1953, Box 4286, RG 59, NA.

40. Ibid., May 4, 9, 1953, Box 4285, NA.

41. Foster Rhea Dulles, *American Policy toward Communist China: The Historical Record, 1949–1969* (New York: Thomas Y. Crowell, 1972), 132; Denis Stairs, *The Diplomacy of Constraint: Canada, the Korean War and the United States* (Toronto: University of Toronto Press, 1974), 273–74.

42. Caridi, *Korean War and American Politics,* 262–63.

43. NSC 147, April 2, 1953, NA.

44. Eisenhower, *White House Years,* 1:180; *Foreign Relations, 1952–1954,* 15:1015 (May 13, 1953).

45. Eisenhower papers, NSC, 131st meeting, Feb. 11, 1953, Whitman Files, Box 4, DDEL.

46. Richard H. Immerman, "Eisenhower and Dulles: Who Made the Decisions?" *Political Psychology,* Autumn 1979.

47. Gaddis, *Strategies of Containment,* 153.

48. *Foreign Relations, 1952–54,* 13:437 (March 28, 1953).

49. 695.0029 North Korea, May 22, 1953, Box 3024, RG 59, NA.

50. *Foreign Relations, 1952–1954,* 15:1302, (July 2, 1953); NSC 154/1, July 7, 1953, NA.

51. Greenstein, *Hidden-Hand Presidency,* 99.

52. Clark, Oral History, 9, BL.

53. Eisenhower papers, NSC, 139th meeting, April 8, 1953, Whitman Files, Box 4, DDEL.

54. 795.00 Korea, May 20, 1953, Box 4286, RG 59, NA; Public Opinion Studies, Jan. 29, March 23, 1953, Box 39, R59, NA.

55. NSC 147, April 2, 1953, NA.

56. Mueller, *War, Presidents,* 105.

57. *Congressional Record,* April 10, 1953, pp. 2952–53; 611.95A241 North Korea, May 11, 1953, Box 2885, RG 59, NA; C. D. Jackson Records 1954–56, March 19, 1953, Box 2, Cutler, Robert, DDEL; DDRS 1951–53 (81) 625B, March 21, 1953.

58. Koo, Chinese Oral History, 7:F36, BL.

59. *New York Herald Tribune,* Jan. 9, 1953.

60. Caridi, *Korean War and American Politics,* 258–59.

61. Donovan, *Eisenhower,* 117.

62. Ibid.

63. Eisenhower, *White House Years,* 1:109–10.

64. Hughes, *Ordeal of Power,* 72.

65. Schnabel and Watson, *History of the JCS,* 3:948, 957; see also Eisenhower, *White House Years,* 1:180.

66. NSC 147, April 2, 1953, NA.

67. SE-37, CIA, March 9, 1953, FOIA; see also DDRS (1981), 165A, March 28, 1953.

68. NSC 147, April 2, 1953, NA.

69. DDRS (1979), 124B, NIE 80, April 3, 1953.

70. Eisenhower papers, NSC, 139th meeting, April 8, 1953, Whitman Files, Box 4, DDEL.

71. *Foreign Relations, 1952–1954*, 15:1140–41. (June 4, 1953).

72. Blanche Wiesen Cook, *The Declassified Eisenhower: A Divided Legacy* (Garden City, N.Y.: Doubleday, 1981), 178–79.

73. DDEL, Dulles Files, Telephone Conversations Memoranda, March 31, 1953, Box 1, SGML; 695A.0024 North Korea, March 30, 1953, Box 3027, RG 59, NA.

74. PPS Records, April 25, 1953, Box 9, RG 59, NA.

75. Foreign Service Posts, Moscow, May 28, 1953, Box 1391, RG 84, WNRC.

76. 795.00 Korea, June 3, 1953, Box 4268, RG 59, NA.

77. Foreign Service Posts, Moscow, April 20, 1953, Box 1392, RG 84, WNRC.

78. Cook, *Declassified Eisenhower*.

79. 795.00 Korea, May 18, 26, 28, June 3, 1953, Box 4268, RG 59, NA.

80. In the view of a highly placed social scientist from the People's Republic, it was the fear of an expanded war and U.S. use of nuclear weapons that led Peking to modify its position on the question of voluntary repatriation.

81. Schnabel and Watson, *History of the JCS*, 3:1006–7; 795.00 Korea, June 21, 1953, Box 4287, RG 59, NA. Rhee's action contributed to the U.S. decision to investigate his possible overthrow. See Box 4287 *passim* for discussion of this and Operation Everready: see also Minnich cabinet notes, June 19, 1953, DDEL.

82. Dulles Files, 1952–59, Telephone Calls Series, July 15, 1953, Box 1, DDEL.

83. The Eisenhower administration reaffirmed at the end of the year that a violation of the armistice would result in an expanded war and the implementation of the measures decided upon at the NSC meeting of May 20. NSC 170/1 of November 20 said that if a violation occurred, the United States should "*a.* Invoke the joint declaration. . . . *b.* Make clear to the world the necessity of expanding the war to China by air and naval action as the only feasible way of honoring our collective security commitments to the United Nations and our security commitments to the Republic of Korea. *c.* Implement the military and diplomatic measures referred to in NSC Action no 794 of May 20 1953. . . . *d.* Call on other UN members for effective manpower and other military assistance appropriate to the expanded war against China."

84. NSC 154/1, Agreed Greater Sanctions Statement, July 7, 1953, NA.

CHAPTER 8

1. Quoted in Kaplan et al., *Diplomacy of Power*, 332.

2. *Foreign Relations*, Special National Intelligence Estimate, (1952–1954), 13:1702–9 (June 15, 1954).

3. Kalicki, *Sino-American Crises*, 68.

4. 793.00 China, e.g., May 26, June 12, 1953, Box 4204, and reactions, June 18, 1953, Box 4205, RG 59, NA.

5. Richard K. Betts, *Soldiers, Statesmen and Cold War Crises*, (Cambridge, Mass.: Harvard University Press, 1977).

6. For a discussion of this type of language, see Dale Spender, *Man Made Language* (London: Routledge & Kegan Paul, 1980).

7. Thies, *When Governments Collide*, 219.

8. Jon Halliday, "What Happened in Korea? Rethinking Korean History, 1945–1953," *Bulletin of Concerned Asian Scholars*, 5, no. 3 (1973): 41.

9. For further discussion, see Peter Van Ness, *Revolution and Chinese Foreign Policy: Peking's Support for Wars of National Liberation* (Berkeley: University of California

Press, 1970); Allen S. Whiting, "The Use of Force in Foreign Policy by the People's Republic of China," *Annals of the American Academy of Political and Social Science* 402 (July 1972).

10. Carlton, *Anthony Eden*, 345–56.

11. Byong-moo Hwang and Melvin Gurtov, *China under Threat: The Politics of Strategy and Diplomacy* (Baltimore, Md.: Johns Hopkins University Press, 1980); Lawrence C. Weiss, "Storm around the Cradle: The Korean War and the Early Years of the People's Republic of China, 1949–1953" (Ph.D diss., Columbia University, 1981).

12. Roderick Ogley, *The United Nations and East-West Relations* (Brighton, England: University of Sussex, 1972).

13. Robert A. Scalapino and Chong-sik Lee, *Communism in Korea*, pt. 1 (Berkeley: University of California Press, 1972), esp. 413–22.

14. *New York Times*, May 22, 1983.

Bibliography

PRIMARY SOURCES

Manuscript Collections

Acheson, Dean. Papers. Harry S Truman Library (HSTL), Independence, Missouri.

Almond, Edward M. Papers. U.S. Army Military History Institute (AMHI), Carlisle Barracks, Pennsylvania.

Alsop, Joseph, and Alsop, Stewart. Papers. Library of Congress (LC), Washington, D.C.

Ayers, Eben A. Papers. Harry S Truman Library (HSTL), Independence, Missouri

Bevin, Ernest. Papers. Private Collections, Ministers and Officials, FO 800, Public Record Office (PRO), London.

Bradley, Omar. Files. Modern Military Branch, National Archives (NA), Washington, D.C.

Byers, Clovis E. Papers. Hoover Institution on War, Revolution and Peace (HI), Stanford, California.

Clark, Mark. Papers. Dwight D. Eisenhower Library (DDEL), Abilene, Kansas.

Connelly, Matthew J. Papers. Harry S Truman Library (HSTL), Independence, Missouri.

Deuel, Wallace. Writings and Journals. Library of Congress (LC), Washington, D.C.

Drumwright, Everett F. Papers. Hoover Institution on War Revolution and Peace (HI), Stanford, California.

Dulles, John Foster. Files. Dwight D. Eisenhower Library (DDEL), Abilene, Kansas.

Dulles, John Foster. Papers. Files. Seeley G. Mudd Library (SGML), Princeton University, Princeton, New Jersey.

Eisenhower, Dwight D. Papers as President of the United States, 1953–61. Dwight D. Eisenhower Library, Abilene, Kansas. Freedom of Information Act (FOIA) requests.

Eisenhower, Dwight D. Papers as President of the United States, 1953–61. Dwight D. Eisenhower Library (DDEL), Abilene, Kansas.

Elsey, George M. Papers. Harry S Truman Library (HSTL), Independence, Missouri.

Feis, Herbert. Papers. Library of Congress (LC), Washington, D.C.

Jackson, C. D. Records. Dwight D. Eisenhower Library (DDEL), Abilene, Kansas.

Jessup, Philip C. Papers. Library of Congress (LC), Washington, D.C.

Joy, Charles Turner. Diary. Hoover Institution on War, Revolution and Peace (HI), Stanford, California.

Kennan, George. Papers. Seeley G. Mudd Library (SGML), Princeton University, Princeton, New Jersey.

Koo, Wellington, V. K. Papers. Butler Library (BL), Columbia University, New York, New York.

Krock, Arthur. Papers. Seeley G. Mudd Library (SGML), Princeton University, Princeton, New Jersey.

Lloyd, David D. Files. Harry S Truman Library (HSTL), Independence, Missouri.

MacArthur, Douglas A. Papers. MacArthur Memorial Library (MML), Norfolk, Virginia.

Minnich, Arthur. Cabinet Notes. Dwight D. Eisenhower Library (DDEL), Abilene, Kansas.

Pulitzer, J., Jr. Papers. Library of Congress (LC), Washington, D.C.

Reid, Helen Rogers. Papers. Library of Congress (LC), Washington, D.C.

Ridgway, Matthew B. Papers. U.S. Army Military History Institute (AMHI), Carlisle Barracks, Pennsylvania.

Selected Records Department of State and Department of Defense. Harry S Truman Library (HSTL), Independence, Missouri.

Smith, H. Alexander. Papers. Seeley G. Mudd Library (SGML), Princeton University, Princeton, New Jersey.

Taft, Robert A. Papers. Library of Congress (LC), Washington, D.C.

Truman, Harry S. Papers. President's Secretary Files. Harry S Truman Library (HSTL), Independence, Missouri.

Willoughby, Charles A. Papers. U.S. Army Military History Institute (AMHI), Carlisle Barracks, Pennsylvania.

Public Records: Unpublished

National Archives, Legislative Branch
RG 46, MacArthur Hearings.

National Archives, Diplomatic Branch
RG 59, General Records of the Department of State, 1950–1954. Decimal File:
611.93 China.
611.95 Korea.
611.95A North Korea.
611.95B South Korea.
693.00 China.
694.A Formosa.
695.00 North Korea.
695.B South Korea.
793.00 China.
793.A Manchuria.
795.00 Korea.
795.A North Korea.
795.B South Korea.
RG59, Office of the Executive Secretariat, Summaries of the Secretary's Daily Meetings, 1949–1952; RG59, Undersecretary's Meetings, Summaries; RG59, Under-

secretary's Meetings, Minutes, Memoranda; RG59, Division of Chinese Affairs; RG59, Records of the Policy Planning Staff, Country and Area Files, (U.S.S.R.); RG59, Office of Intelligence Research Reports; RG59, Records of the Office of Public Opinion Studies; RG59, Records of the Policy Planning Staff 1947–1953, Freedom of Information Act (FOIA) Requests:
Country and Area Files, China 1950–1953.
Country and Area Files, Korea 1947–1952.
Country and Area Files, Korea 1953.
Minutes of Meetings 1950–1952.
State-JCS Meetings 1951–1952.
(Please note that certain of these FOIA documents have now become available in *Foreign Relations of the United States.* Washington, D.C.: GPO. FR1952–1954, Vol. 15: Korea [two parts]. 1984.)
RG84, Foreign Service Posts of the Department of State:
Korea–Seoul. Washington, D.C., National Archives.
Moscow. Washington National Records Center, Suitland, Md.
Tokyo. Washington National Records Center, Suitland, Md.

National Archives, Modern Military Branch
RG 218, Records of the U.S. Joint Chiefs of Staff; RG 319, Records of the Army Staff; RG 330, Records of the Office of the Secretary of Defense; RG 338, Far East Command.
NSC Documents and NSC Action Memoranda.

The History of the Joint Chiefs of Staff
The Joint Chiefs of Staff and National Policy, vol. 3. The Korean War, Parts I and II, by James F. Schnabel and Robert J. Watson, Historical Division, Joint Secretariat, JCS, April 1978, March 1979. (Washington, D.C., National Archives).
The Joint Chiefs of Staff and National Policy, vol. 4, 1950–52, by Walter S. Poole, Historical Division, Joint Secretariat, JCS, December 1979. (Washington, D.C., National Archives).

Central Intelligence Agency, Washington, D.C., Freedom of Information Act (FOIA).

Public Record Office, London, 1950–1953
FO 371. Foreign Office Files: Far Eastern–China, Korea; American–United States.
PREM 11, 8. Prime Minister's Office.
DEFE 4. Chiefs of Staff Committee, Minutes of Meetings.
DEFE 5. Chiefs of Staff Committee, Memoranda.
DEFE 6. Chiefs of Staff Committee, Joint Planning Staff Reports.
CAB 128. Cabinet, Minutes.
CAB 129. Cabinet, Memoranda.
CAB 131. Cabinet Defence Committee.
CAB 134. Far Eastern Official Committee.

Declassified Documents Reference System.
Retrospective Collection. Collections 1975–81. Carrollton Press, Virginia.

Congressional Record 1950–53.

Eisenhower, Dwight D. *Public Papers of the Presidents of the United States: Dwight D. Eisenhower, 1953–1961.* 8 vols. Washington, D.C.: GPO, 1960–61.

Truman, Harry S. *Public Papers of the Presidents of the United States: Harry S Truman, 1950–1953.* 3 vols. Washington, D.C.: GPO, 1965–66.

United Kingdom. *Parliamentary Debates.* House of Commons. 1950–53. Fifth series. Vols. 476–518.

U.S. Congress. Senate. Committee on Foreign Relations. *Economic Assistance to China and Korea: 1949–1950,* Washington, D.C.: GPO, 1974.

——. Committee on Foreign Relations. *Executive Sessions.* 81st Cong., 1st & 2d sess., 1949–50 (Historical Series). Washington, D. C.: GPO, 1976.

——. Committee on Foreign Relations. *Reviews of the World Situation: 1949–1950.* Hearings in executive session. 81st Cong., 1st & 2d sess. (Historical Series). Washington, D.C.: GPO, 1974.

——. Committee on Foreign Relations, Subcommittee. *Hearings on the Nomination of Philip C. Jessup to be United States Representative to the Sixth General Assembly of the United Nations.* 82nd Cong., 1st sess., 1951.

——. Committees on Armed Services and Foreign Relations. *Military Situation in the Far East.* 82nd Cong., 1st sess., 1951. Washington, D.C.: GPO, 1951.

——. Committee on Foreign Relations. *The United States and the Korean Problem: Documents 1943–1953.* 83rd Cong., 1st sess., 1953. Washington, D.C: GPO, 1953.

U.S. Department of State. *American Foreign Policy, 1950–1955: Basic Documents.* Washington, D.C.: GPO, 1957.

——. *Department of State Bulletin.* Washington, D.C.: GPO.

——. *Foreign Relations of the United States.* Washington, D.C.: GPO.

FR 1947, Vol. 6: *The Far East.* 1972.

FR 1947, Vol. 7: *The Far East: China.* 1972.

FR 1948, Vol. 6: *The Far East and Australasia.* 1974.

FR 1948, Vol. 8: *The Far East: China.* 1973.

FR 1949, Vol. 7: *The Far East and Australasia* (two parts). 1976.

FR 1949, Vol. 8: *The Far East: China.* 1978.

FR 1949, Vol. 9: *The Far East: China.* 1975.

FR 1950, Vol. 1: *National Security Affairs.* 1977.

FR 1950, Vol. 3: *Western Europe.* 1976.

FR 1950, Vol. 6: *East Asia and the Pacific.* 1976.

FR 1950, Vol. 7: *Korea.* 1976.

FR 1951, Vol. 1: *National Security.* 1979.

FR 1951, Vol. 2: *The United Nations; the Western Hemisphere.* 1979.

FR 1951, Vol. 6: *Asia and the Pacific* (two parts). 1977.

FR 1951, Vol. 7: *China and Korea* (two parts). 1983.

FR 1952–1954, Vol. 3: *United Nations Affairs.* 1979.

FR 1952–1954, Vol. 5: *Western European Security* (two parts). 1979.

FR 1952–1954, Vol. 13: *Indochina* (two parts). 1982.

FR 1952–1954, Vol. 15: *Korea* (two parts). 1984.

——. *United States Policy in the Korean Crisis.* Washington, D.C.: GPO, 1950.

——. *United States Policy in the Korean Conflict.* Washington, D.C.: GPO, 1951.

Oral Histories and Interviews

Almond, Edward M. U.S. Army Military History Institute, Carlisle Barracks, Pennsylvania.

Ayers, Eben A. Harry S Truman Library (HSTL), Independence, Missouri.

Bell, David E. Harry S Truman Library (HSTL), Independence, Missouri.

Bolté, Charles. U.S. Army Military History Institute (AMHI), Carlisle Barracks, Pennsylvania.

Clark, Mark. Eisenhower Administration Oral History Project, Butler Library (BL), Columbia University, New York, New York.

Clark, Mark. Oral History. U.S. Army Military History Institute (AMHI), Carlisle Barracks, Pennsylvania.

Clubb, O. Edmund. Harry S Truman Library (HSTL), Independence, Missouri.

Elsey, George M. Harry S Truman Library (HSTL), Independence, Missouri.

Finletter, Thomas K. Harry S Truman Library (HSTL), Independence, Missouri.

Franks, Lord Oliver. Harry S Truman Library (HSTL), Independence, Missouri.

_____. Interview with author, March 15, 1983, Oxford, England.

Gross, Ernest. Oral History Project, Butler Library (BL), Columbia University, New York, New York.

Henderson, Loy. Harry S Truman Library (HSTL), Independence, Missouri.

Hickerson, John D. Harry S Truman Library (HSTL), Independence, Missouri.

Johnson, U. Alexis. Harry S Truman Library (HSTL), Independence, Missouri.

Judd, Walter. Oral History Project, Butler Library (BL), Columbia University, New York, New York.

Knowland, William. Oral History Project, Butler Library (BL), Columbia University, New York, New York.

Koo, V. K. Wellington. Chinese Oral History Project, Butler Library (BL), Columbia University, New York, New York.

Muccio, John J. Harry S Truman Library (HSTL), Independence, Missouri.

Murphy, Charles S. Harry S Truman Library (HSTL), Independence, Missouri.

Pace, Frank. Harry S Truman Library (HSTL), Independence, Missouri.

Pace, Frank. U.S. Army Military History Institute (AMHI), Carlisle Barracks, Pennsylvania.

Princeton Seminars, 1953–54, Dean Acheson Papers. Harry S Truman Library (HSTL), Independence, Missouri.

Ridgway, Matthew B. U.S. Army Military History Institute (AMHI), Carlisle Barracks, Pennsylvania.

Robertson, Walter S. Eisenhower Administration Oral History Project, Butler Library (BL), Columbia University, New York, New York.

Sprouse, Philip. Harry S Truman Library (HSTL), Independence, Missouri.

Taylor, Maxwell. U.S. Army Military History Institute (AMHI), Carlisle Barracks, Pennsylvania.

Newspaper Collections

Butler Library, Columbia University, New York, New York.

Royal Institute of International Affairs, Chatham House Press Library, London, England.

SECONDARY SOURCES

Books

Acheson, Dean. *Present at the Creation: My Years in the State Department.* New York: Norton, 1969.

Adams, Sherman. *Firsthand Report: The Inside Story of the Eisenhower Administration.* London: Hutchinson, 1962.

Alexander, Charles C. *Holding the Line: The Eisenhower Era 1952–1961.* Bloomington: Indiana University Press, 1975.

Allison, Graham T. *Essence of Decision: Explaining the Cuban Missile Crisis.* Boston: Little, Brown, 1971.

Allison, Graham, and Peter Szanton. *Remaking Foreign Policy: The Organizational Connection.* New York: Basic Books, 1976.

Allison, John M. *Ambassador from the Prairie, or, Allison Wonderland.* Boston: Houghton Mifflin, 1973.

Alsop, Joseph, and Stewart Alsop. *The Reporter's Trade.* London: Bodley Head, 1960.

Ambrose, Stephen E. *Eisenhower: Soldier, General of the Army, President-Elect, 1890–1952.* New York: Simon & Schuster, 1983.

Appleman, Roy E. *South to the Naktong, North to the Yalu.* Washington D.C.: GPO, 1961.

Aron, Raymond. *The Imperial Republic: The United States and the World, 1945–1973.* Englewood Cliffs, N.J.: Prentice-Hall, 1974.

Aronson, James. *The Press and the Cold War.* Indianapolis, Ind.: Bobbs-Merrill, 1970.

Attlee, Clement. *Twilight of Empire: Memoirs of Prime Minister Clement Attlee.* New York: Barnes, 1962.

Axelrod, Robert, ed. *Structure of Decision: The Cognitive Maps of Political Elites.* Princeton, N.J.: Princeton University Press, 1976.

Bell, Coral. *Negotiation from Strength: A Study in the Politics of Power.* Westport, Conn.: Greenwood Press, 1977.

Bernstein, Barton J., ed. *Politics and Policies of the Truman Administration.* Chicago: Quadrangle Books, 1970.

Betts, Richard K. *Soldiers, Statesmen and Cold War Crises.* Cambridge, Mass.: Harvard University Press, 1977.

Blum, Robert M. *Drawing the Line: The Origin of the American Containment Policy in East Asia.* New York: Norton, 1982.

Boardman, Robert. *Britain and the People's Republic of China, 1949–1974.* London: Macmillan, 1976.

Bohlen, Charles E. *Witness to History, 1929–1969.* New York: Norton, 1973.

Borg, Dorothy, and Waldo Heinrichs, eds. *Uncertain Years: Chinese-American Relations, 1947–1950.* New York: Columbia University Press, 1980.

Bowles, Chester. *Ambassador's Report.* London: Victor Gollancz, 1954.

Bradley, Omar N., and Clay Blair. *A General's Life: An Autobiography.* New York: Simon & Schuster, 1983.

Brodie, Bernard. *War and Politics.* London: Macmillan, 1973.

Buhite, Russell D. *Soviet-American Relations in Asia, 1945–1954.* Norman: University of Oklahoma Press, 1981.

Cagle, Malcolm W., and Frank A. Manson. *The Sea War in Korea.* Annapolis, Md.: U.S. Naval Institute, 1957.

Caridi, Ronald J. *The Korean War and American Politics: The Republican Party as a Case Study*. Philadelphia: University of Pennsylvania Press, 1968.

Carlton, David. *Anthony Eden: A Biography*. London: Allen Lane, 1981.

Caute, David. *The Great Fear: The Anti-Communist Purge under Truman and Eisenhower*. New York: Simon & Schuster, 1978.

Challener, Richard D., ed. *The Legislative Origins of American Foreign Policy*. U.S. Senate Foreign Relations Committee Historical Series. Reviews of the World Situation, 1949–50. New York: Garland, 1979.

Cho Soon Sung. *Korea in World Politics, 1940–1950*. Los Angeles: University of California Press, 1967.

Choy Bong-youn. *Korea—A History*. Rutland, Vt.: Charles E. Tuttle, 1971.

Clark, Mark W. *From the Danube to the Yalu*. New York: Harper, 1954.

Clubb, O. Edmund. *Twentieth Century China*. New York: Columbia University Press, 1964.

Cohen, Warren I. *Dean Rusk*. American Secretaries of State and Their Diplomacy, ed. Robert Ferrell, vol. 19. Totowa, N.J.: Cooper Square Publishers, 1980.

_____, ed. *New Frontiers in American–East Asian Relations: Essays Presented to Dorothy Borg*. New York: Columbia University Press, 1983.

Collins, J. Lawton. *War in Peacetime: The History and Lessons of Korea*. Boston: Houghton Mifflin, 1969.

Cook, Blanche Wiesen. *The Declassified Eisenhower: A Divided Legacy*. Garden City, N.Y.: Doubleday, 1981.

Cumings, Bruce. *The Origins of the Korean War: Liberation and the Emergence of Separate Regimes, 1945–1947*. Princeton, N.J.: Princeton University Press, 1981.

_____, ed. *Child of Conflict: The Korean-American Relationship, 1943–1953*. Seattle: University of Washington Press, 1983.

Dallek, Robert. *The American Style of Foreign Policy*. New York: Knopf, 1983.

Davies, John Paton, Jr. *Dragon by the Tail*. New York: Norton, 1972.

Dean, William F. (as told to William L. Worden). *General Dean's Story*. New York: Viking, 1954.

Divine, Robert A. *Foreign Policy and U.S. Presidential Elections, 1952–1960*. New York: New Viewpoints, 1974.

_____. *Eisenhower and the Cold War*. New York: Oxford University Press, 1981.

Dobbs, Charles M. *The Unwanted Symbol: American Foreign Policy, the Cold War and Korea, 1945–1950*. Kent, Ohio: Kent State University Press, 1981.

Donovan, Robert J. *Eisenhower: The Inside Story*. New York: Harper, 1956.

_____. *Tumultuous Years: The Presidency of Harry S Truman, 1949–1953*. New York: Norton, 1982.

Dulles, Foster Rhea. *American Policy toward Communist China: The Historical Record, 1949–1969*. New York: Thomas Y. Crowell, 1972.

Dulles, John Foster. *War or Peace*. New York: Macmillan, 1950.

East, Maurice A.; Stephen A. Salmore; and Charles F. Hermann, eds. *Why Nations Act*. Beverly Hills, Calif.: Sage Publications, 1978.

Eden, Anthony. *Full Circle*, London: Cassell, 1960.

Eisenhower, Dwight D. *The White House Years: Mandate for Change, 1953–1956*, vol. 1. Garden City, N.Y.: Doubleday, 1963.

Etzold, Thomas H., and John L. Gaddis. *Containment: Documents on American Policy and Strategy, 1945–1950*. New York: Columbia University Press, 1978.

Ferrell, Robert H. *George C. Marshall*. American Secretaries of State and Their Diplomacy, ed. Robert Ferrell, vol. 15. New York: Cooper Square Publishers, 1966.

_____. *Harry S Truman and the Modern American Presidency*. Boston: Little, Brown, 1983.

_____, ed. *The Eisenhower Diaries*. New York: Norton, 1981.

_____, ed. *Off the Record: The Private Papers of Harry S Truman*. New York: Harper, 1980.

Field, James A. *History of United States Naval Operations: Korea*. Washington, D.C.: GPO, 1962.

Finletter, Thomas K. *Power and Policy: U.S. Foreign Policy and Military Power in the Hydrogen Age*. New York: Harcourt Brace, 1954.

Fleming, David F. *The Cold War and Its Origins 1917–1960*. 2 vols. Garden City, N.Y.: Doubleday, 1961.

Fogdick, Dorothy. *Common Sense and World Affairs*. New York: Harcourt Brace, 1955.

Freeland, Richard H. *The Truman Doctrine and the Origins of McCarthyism: Foreign Policy, Domestic Politics, and Internal Security, 1946–1948*. New York: Knopf, 1972.

Futrell, Robert F. *The United States Air Force in Korea 1950–1953*. New York: Duell, Sloan & Pearce, 1961.

Gaddis, John L. *Strategies of Containment: A Critical Appraisal of Post-War American National Security Policy*. New York: Oxford University Press, 1982.

The Gallup Poll, vol. 2: *Public Opinion, 1949–1953*. New York: Random House, 1972.

Gardner, Lloyd C., ed. *The Korean War*. Chicago: Quadrangle Books, 1972.

George, Alexander L. *The Chinese Communist Army in Action: The Korean War and its Aftermath*. New York: Columbia University Press, 1967.

_____. *Presidential Decision Making in Foreign Policy*. Boulder, Colo.: Westview Press, 1980.

George, Alexander L., and Richard Smoke. *Deterrence in American Foreign Policy: Theory and Practice*. New York: Columbia University Press, 1974.

Gittings, John. *The Role of the Chinese Army*. London: Oxford University Press, 1967.

_____. *The World and China, 1922–1972*. London: Eyre Methuen, 1974.

Goodrich, Leland M. *Korea: A Study of United States Policy in the United Nations*. New York: Council on Foreign Relations, 1956.

Gordenker, Leon. *The United Nations and the Peaceful Unification of Korea: The Politics of Field Operations, 1947–1950*. The Hague: Martinus Nijhoff, 1959.

Gosnell, Harry F. *Truman's Crises: A Political Biography of Harry S Truman*. Westport, Conn.: Greenwood Press, 1980.

Goulden, Joseph C. *Korea: The Untold Story of the War*. New York: Times Books, 1982.

Graebner, Norman A. *The New Isolationism*. New York: Ronald Press, 1956.

Gravel, Morton. *The Pentagon Papers: The Defense Department History of the United States Decision Making on Vietnam*. Vol. 1. Boston: Beacon Press, 1971.

Greenstein, Fred I. *The Hidden-Hand Presidency: Eisenhower as Leader*. New York: Basic Books, 1982.

Guttmann, Allen, ed. *Korea and the Theory of Limited War*. Boston: Heath, 1967.

Halperin, Morton H. *Bureaucratic Politics and Foreign Policy*. Washington, D.C.: Brookings Institution, 1974.

Hamby, Alonzo L. *Beyond the New Deal: Harry S Truman and American Liberalism*. New York: Columbia University Press, 1973.

Harriman, W. Averell. *America and Russia in a Changing World*. Garden City, N.Y.: Doubleday, 1971.

Haynes, Richard F. *The Awesome Power: Harry S Truman as Commander in Chief*. Baton Rouge: Louisiana State University Press, 1973.

Head, Richard G.; Frisco W. Short; and Robert C. McFarlane. *Crisis Resolution:*

Presidential Decision Making in the Mayaguez and Korean Confrontations. Boulder, Colo.: Westview Press, 1978.

Heller, Francis H., ed. *The Korean War: A 25 Year Perspective*. Lawrence: Regents Press of Kansas, 1977.

Henderson, Gregory. *Korea: The Politics of the Vortex*. Cambridge, Mass.: Harvard University Press, 1968.

Hermes, Walter G. *Truce Tent and Fighting Front*. Washington, D.C.: GPO, 1966.

Higgins, Trumbull. *Korea and the Fall of MacArthur: A Precis in Limited War*. New York: Oxford University Press, 1960.

Hinton, Harold C. *Communist China in World Politics*. London: Macmillan, 1966.

Hoffmann, Stanley. *Gulliver's Troubles, or, The Setting of American Foreign Policy*. New York: McGraw-Hill, 1968.

Hoopes, Townsend. *The Devil and John Foster Dulles*. Boston: Atlantic/Little, Brown, 1973.

Hughes, Emmet J. *The Ordeal of Power: A Political Memoir of the Eisenhower Years*. New York: Atheneum, 1963.

Hwang Byong-moo, and Melvin Gurtov. *China under Threat: The Politics of Strategy and Diplomacy*. Baltimore, Md.: Johns Hopkins University Press, 1980.

Ireland, Timothy P. *Creating the Entangling Alliance: The Origins of the North Atlantic Treaty Organisation*. London: Aldwych Press, 1981.

Janis, Irving L., and Leon Mann. *Decision Making: A Psychological Analysis of Conflict, Choice and Commitment*. New York: Free Press, 1977.

Jebb, Gladwyn. *The Memoirs of Lord Gladwyn*. New York: Weybright and Talley, 1972.

Jervis, Robert. *Perception and Misperception in International Politics*. Princeton, N.J.: Princeton University Press, 1976.

Jessup, Philip C. *The Birth of Nations*. New York: Columbia University Press, 1974.

Joy, C. Turner. *How Communists Negotiate*. New York: Macmillan, 1955.

Jurike, Stephen, Jr., ed. *From Pearl Harbor to Vietnam: The Memoirs of Admiral Arthur W. Radford*. Stanford, Calif.: Hoover Institution Press, 1980.

Kalicki, Jan. *The Pattern of Sino-American Crises*. London: Cambridge University Press, 1975.

Kaplan, Lawrence S. *A Community of Interests: NATO and the Military Assistance Program, 1948–1951*. Washington, D.C.: GPO, 1980.

Kaplan, Stephen S., Michel Tatu, et al. *Diplomacy of Power: Soviet Forces as a Political Instrument*. Washington, D.C.: Brookings Institution, 1981.

Karig, Walter; Malcolm W. Cagle; and Frank A. Manson. *Battle Report: The War in Korea*. New York: Rinehart, 1952.

Kennan, George F. *Memoirs, 1925–1950*. Boston: Little, Brown, 1967.

———. *Memoirs, 1950–1963*. Boston: Little, Brown, 1972.

Khrushchev, Nikita. *Khrushchev Remembers*. Boston: Little, Brown, 1970.

Kirkendall, Richard S., ed. *The Truman Period as a Research Field*. Columbia: University of Missouri Press, 1967.

Kissinger, Henry. *Nuclear Weapons and Foreign Policy*. Abridged ed. New York: Norton, 1969.

Kolko, Joyce, and Gabriel Kolko. *The Limits of Power: The World and United States Foreign Policy, 1945–1954*. New York: Harper & Row, 1972.

LaFeber, Walter. *America, Russia and the Cold War, 1945–1980*. 4th ed. New York: Wiley, 1980.

Lebow, Richard N. *Between Peace and War: The Nature of International Crisis.* Baltimore, Md.: Johns Hopkins University Press, 1981.

Leckie, Robert. *Conflict: The History of the Korean War, 1950–1953.* New York: Putnam, 1962.

MacArthur, Douglas A. *Reminiscences.* New York: McGraw-Hill, 1964.

McLellan, David S. *Dean Acheson: The State Department Years.* New York: Dodd, Mead, 1976.

Mahurin, Walker M. *Honest John: The Autobiography of Walker M. Mahurin.* New York: Putnam, 1962.

Manchester, William. *American Caesar, Douglas MacArthur, 1880–1964.* New York: Dell, 1978.

Mao Tse-tung, *Selected Works.* Vol. 5. Peking: Foreign Languages Press, 1977.

Marshall, Samuel L. A. *The River and the Gauntlet: Defeat of the Eighth Army by the Chinese Communist Forces, November 1950, in the Battle of the Chongchon River, Korea.* New York: Morrow, 1953.

May, Ernest R. *"Lessons" of the Past: The Use and Misuse of History in American Foreign Policy.* New York: Oxford University Press, 1973.

———. *The Truman Administration and China 1945–1949.* Philadelphia: Lippincott, 1975.

May, Ernest R., and James C. Thomson, Jr. *American-East Asian Relations: A Survey.* Cambridge, Mass.: Harvard University Press, 1972.

Mueller, John E. *War, Presidents, and Public Opinion.* New York: Wiley, 1973.

Munro, John A., and Alex I. Inglis, eds. *Mike: The Memoirs of the Right Honourable Lester B. Pearson.* Vol. 2: *1948–1957.* Toronto: University of Toronto Press, 1973.

Murphy, Robert. *Diplomat among Warriors.* Garden City, N.Y.: Doubleday, 1964.

Nagai, Yonosuke, and Akira Iriye, eds. *The Origins of the Cold War in Asia.* New York: Columbia University Press, 1977.

Neustadt, Richard E. *Presidential Power: The Politics of Leadership from FDR to Carter.* New York: Wiley, 1980.

Noble, Harold Joyce, ed. *Embassy at War.* Seattle: University of Washington Press, 1975.

Ogley, Roderick. *The United Nations and East-West Relations.* Institute for the Study of International Organisation Monographs, 1st ser., no. 6. Brighton, England: University of Sussex, 1972.

Osgood, Robert. *Limited War.* Chicago: University of Chicago Press, 1956.

Paige, Glenn D. *The Korean Decision.* New York: Free Press, 1968.

Panikkar, Kavalam M. *In Two Chinas: Memoirs of a Diplomat.* London: George Allen & Unwin, 1955.

Patterson, James T. *Mr. Republican: A Biography of Robert A. Taft.* Boston: Houghton Mifflin, 1972.

Phillips, Cabell. *The Truman Presidency.* New York: Macmillan, 1966.

Pogue, Forrest. *George C. Marshall.* 3 vols. New York: Viking Press, 1963–73.

Poots, Rutherford M. *Decision in Korea.* New York: McBridge, 1954.

Porter, Brian. *Britain and the Rise of Communist China: A Study of British Attitudes, 1945–1954.* London: Oxford University Press, 1967.

Pruessen, Ronald W. *John Foster Dulles: The Road to Power.* New York: Free Press, 1982.

Rankin, Karl Lott. *China Assignment.* Seattle: University of Washington Press, 1964.

Rees, David. *Korea: The Limited War.* New York: St. Martin's Press, 1964.

Reeves, Thomas C. *The Life and Times of Joe McCarthy: A Biography.* New York: Stein & Day, 1982.

Ridgway, Matthew B. *The Korean War.* Garden City, New York: Doubleday, 1967.

Rovere, Richard H., and Arthur M. Schlesinger, Jr. *The MacArthur Controversy and American Foreign Policy.* New York: Noonday Press, 1965.

Royal Institute of International Affairs. *Survey of International Affairs: 1952.* London: Oxford University Press, 1953.

Scalapino, Robert A., and Chong-sik Lee. *Communism in Korea.* Pt. 1. Berkeley: University of California Press, 1972.

Schilling, Warner R.; Paul Y. Hammond; and Glenn H. Snyder. *Strategy, Politics and Defense Budgets.* New York: Columbia University Press, 1962.

Schnabel, James F. *Policy and Direction: The First Year.* Washington, D.C.: GPO, 1972.

Sebald, William. *With MacArthur in Japan: A Personal History of the Occupation.* New York: Norton, 1965.

Shulman, Marshall D. *Stalin's Foreign Policy Reappraised.* Cambridge, Mass.: Harvard University Press, 1963.

Simmons, Robert. *The Strained Alliance: Peking, Pyongyang, Moscow and the Politics of the Korean Civil War.* New York: Free Press, 1975.

Smith, Gaddis. *Dean Acheson.* American Secretaries of State and their Diplomacy, ed. Robert Ferrell, vol. 16. New York: Cooper Square Publishers, 1972.

Spanier, John W. *The Truman-MacArthur Controversy and the Korean War.* Cambridge, Mass.: Harvard University Press, 1959.

Spender, Dale. *Man Made Language.* London: Routledge & Kegan Paul, 1980.

Stairs, Denis. *The Diplomacy of Constraint: Canada, the Korean War and the United States.* Toronto: University of Toronto Press, 1974.

Stebbins, Richard P. *The United States in World Affairs.* New York: Council on Foreign Relations, 1950–54.

Steel, Ronald. *Walter Lippmann and the American Century.* Boston: Little, Brown, 1980.

Stoessinger, John G. *Nations into Darkness: China, Russia, and America.* New York: Random House, 1978.

Stone, Isidor F. *The Hidden History of the Korean War.* New York: Monthly Review Press, 1952.

Stueck, William W., Jr. *The Road to Confrontation: American Policy toward China and Korea, 1947–1950.* Chapel Hill: University of North Carolina Press, 1981.

Sulzberger, Cyrus L. *A Long Row of Candles: Memoirs and Diaries.* New York: Macmillan, 1969.

Taubman, William. *Stalin's American Policy.* New York: Norton, 1982.

Taylor, Maxwell D. *Swords and Plowshares.* New York: Norton, 1972.

Thies, Wallace. *When Governments Collide: Coercion and Diplomacy in the Vietnam Conflict, 1964–68.* Berkeley: University of California Press, 1980.

Truman, Harry S. *Memoirs.* Vol. 2: *Years of Trial and Hope.* Garden City, N.Y.: Doubleday, 1956.

Tucker, Nancy Bernkopf. *Patterns in the Dust: Chinese-American Relations and the Recognition Controversy, 1949–1950.* New York: Columbia University Press, 1983.

Ulam, Adam B. *The Rivals: America and Russia since World War II.* New York: Viking Press, 1971.

———. *Expansion and Coexistence: Soviet Foreign Policy 1917–1973.* New York: Praeger, 1974.

Bibliography

Vandenburg, Arthur H., Jr., ed. *The Private Papers of Senator Vandenburg*. Boston: Houghton Mifflin, 1952.

Van Ness, Peter. *Revolution and Chinese Foreign Policy: Peking's Support for Wars of National Liberation*. Berkeley: University of California Press, 1970.

Whiting, Allen S. *China Crosses the Yalu: The Decision to Enter the Korean War*. Stanford, Calif.: Stanford University Press, 1960.

Whitney, Courtney. *MacArthur: His Rendezvous with History*. New York: Knopf, 1956.

Willoughby, Charles A., and John Chamberlain. *MacArthur, 1941–1951*. New York: McGraw-Hill, 1954.

Young, Kenneth. *Negotiating with the Chinese Communists: The United States Experience, 1953–1967*. New York: McGraw-Hill, 1968.

Articles

Bernstein, Barton J. "The Week We Went to War: American Intervention and the Korean Civil War." *Foreign Service Journal*, Jan. 1977.

———. "The Policy of Risk: Crossing the 38th Parallel and Marching to the Yalu." *Foreign Service Journal*, March 1977.

———. "Syngman Rhee: The Pawn as Rook—The Struggle to End the Korean War." *Bulletin of Concerned Asian Scholars* 10, no. 1 (1978).

———. "Truman's Secret Thoughts on Ending the Korean War." *Foreign Service Journal*, Nov. 1980.

———. "New Light on the Korean War." *International History Review*, April 1981.

———. "The Struggle over the Korean Armistice: Prisoners of Repatriation?" In Bruce Cumings, ed., *Child of Conflict: The Korean-American Relationship, 1943–1953*. Seattle: University of Washington Press, 1983.

Blechman, Barry M., and Robert Powell. "What in the Name of God Is Strategic Superiority?" *Political Science Quarterly* 97 (Winter 1982–83).

Bridgham, Philip; Arthur Cohen; and Leonard Jaffe. "Mao's Road and Sino-Soviet Relations: A View from Washington 1953." *China Quarterly* 51 (Oct.–Dec. 1972).

Buhite, Russell D. "Major Interests: American Policy toward China, Taiwan and Korea, 1945–1950." *Pacific Historical Review* 47, no. 3 (1978).

Caldwell, Dean. "Bureaucratic Foreign Policy Making." *American Behavioral Scientist*, Sept.–Oct. 1977.

Carpenter, William M. "The Korean War: A Strategic Perspective." *Comparative Strategy* 2, no. 4 (1980).

Clubb, O. Edmund. "Formosa and the Offshore Islands in American Policy, 1950–1955." *Political Science Quarterly* 74, no. 4 (1959).

Cohen, Warren I. "Acheson, His Advisers, and China, 1949–1950." In Dorothy Borg and Waldo Heinrichs, eds., *Uncertain Years: Chinese-American Relations, 1947–1950*. New York: Columbia University Press, 1980.

Cottrell, Alvin J., and James E. Dougherty. "The Lessons of Korea: War and the Power of Man." *Orbis*, Spring 1958.

Dingman, Roger. "Truman, Attlee and the Korean War Crisis." In *The East Asian Crisis, 1945–1951, International Studies* (1982/1), International Centre for Economics and Related Disciplines, London School of Economics.

Endicott, Stephen L. "Germ Warfare and the 'Plausible Denial': The Korean War 1952–1953." *Modern China* 5, no. 1 (Jan. 1979).

Freedman, Lawrence. "Logic, Politics and Foreign Policy Processes: A Critique of the Bureaucratic Politics Model." *International Affairs* 52, no. 3 (July 1976).

Friedman, Edward. "Problems in Dealing with an Irrational Power: America Declares War on China." In Mark Selden and Edward Friedman, eds., *America's Asia: Dissenting Essays on Asian-American Relations.* New York: Random House, 1971.

———. "Nuclear Blackmail and the end of the Korean War." *Modern China* 1, no. 1 (Jan. 1975).

Gaddis, John Lewis. "Reconsiderations—Was the Truman Doctrine a Real Turning Point?" *Foreign Affairs* 52 (Jan. 1974).

———. "Korea in American Politics, Strategy and Diplomacy, 1945–50." In Yonosuke Nagai and Akira Iriye, eds., *The Origins of the Cold War in Asia.* New York: Columbia University Press, 1977.

———. "The Strategic Perspective: The Rise and Fall of the 'Defensive Perimeter' Concept, 1947–1951." In Dorothy Borg and Waldo Heinrichs, eds., *Uncertain Years: Chinese-American Relations, 1947–1950.* New York: Columbia University Press, 1980.

George, Alexander L. "American Policy Making and the North Korean Aggression." *World Politics* 7 (1955).

Gittings, John. "Talks, Bombs and Germs—Another Look at the Korean War." *Journal of Contemporary Asia* 5, no. 2 (1975).

Halliday, Jon. "What Happened in Korea? Rethinking Korean History, 1945–1953." *Bulletin of Concerned Asian Scholars* 5, no. 3 (1973).

———. "The Korean War: Some Notes on Evidence and Solidarity." *Bulletin of Concerned Asian Scholars* 11, no. 3 (1979).

Halperin, Morton H. "The Limiting Process in the Korean War." In Allen H. Guttmann, ed., *Korea and the Theory of Limited War.* Boston: Heath, 1967.

Holsti, Ole. "The 'Operational Code' Approach to the Study of Political Leaders: John Foster Dulles' Philosophical and Instrumental Beliefs." *Canadian Journal of Political Science* 3, no. 1 (March 1970).

Immerman, Richard H. "Eisenhower and Dulles: Who Made the Decisions?" *Political Psychology,* 1979, no. 1 (Autumn).

Jervis, Robert. "The Impact of the Korean War on the Cold War." *Journal of Conflict Resolution* 24, no. 4 (Dec. 1980).

Koh Biyung Chul. "The Korean War as a Learning Experience for North Korea." *Korea and World Affairs* 3, no. 3 (Fall 1979).

LaFeber, Walter. "Crossing the 38th: The Cold War in Microcosm." In Lynn Miller and Ronald W. Pruessen, eds., *Reflections on the Cold War.* Philadelphia: Temple University Press, 1974.

Lichterman, Martin. "To the Yalu and Back." In Harold Stein, ed., *American Civil-Military Decisions: A Book of Case Studies.* Birmingham: University of Alabama Press, 1963.

Lo, Clarence Y. H. "Military Spending as Crisis Management: The U.S. Response to the Berlin Blockade and the Korean War." *Berkeley Journal of Sociology* 20 (1975–76).

Lofgren, Charles A. "Mr. Truman's War: A Debate and Its Aftermath." *Review of Politics* 31 (April 1969).

McLellan, David S. "Dean Acheson and the Korean War," *Political Science Quarterly* 83, no. 1 (March 1968).

Matray, James. "Truman's Plan for Victory: National Self Determination and the 38th Parallel Decision in Korea." *Journal of American History* 66 (Sept. 1979).
———. "America's Reluctant Crusade: Truman's Commitment of Combat Troops in the Korean War." *Historian* 42, no. 3 (May 1980).
Nakajima, Mineo. "The Sino-Soviet Confrontation: Its Roots in the International Background of the Korean War." *Australian Journal of Chinese Affairs*, 1979, no. 1.
Nikitin, I. "From the Notes of a Soviet Diplomat." *Far Eastern Affairs*, 1979, no. 1.
Park Hong-kyu. "Korean War Revisited—Survey of Historical Writing." *World Affairs* 137, no. 4 (Spring 1975).
Pelz, Stephen E. "When the Kitchen Gets Hot, Pass the Buck: Truman and Korea in 1950." *Reviews in American History*, Dec. 1978.
Rosenberg, David A. "U.S. Nuclear Stockpile 1945 to 1950." *Bulletin of the Atomic Scientists* 38, no. 5 (May 1982).
———. "The Origins of Overkill: Nuclear Weapons and American Strategy, 1945–1960." *International Security* 7, no. 4 (Spring 1983).
Smith, Beverly. "The White House Story: Why We Went to War in Korea." *Saturday Evening Post*, Nov. 10, 1951.
Smith, Gaddis. "Reconsiderations: The Shadow of John Foster Dulles." *Foreign Affairs* 52 (Jan. 1974).
Stueck, William Whitney, Jr. "The Soviet Union and the Origins of the Korean War." *World Politics* 28 (1975–76).
Swartout, Robert, Jr. "American Historians and the Outbreak of the Korean War: An Historiographical Essay." *Asia Quarterly*, 1979, no. 1.
Warner, Geoffrey. "The Korean War." *International Affairs* 56, no. 1 (Jan. 1980).
Wells, Samuel F., Jr. "Sounding the Tocsin: NSC 68 and the Soviet Threat." *International Security* 4, no. 2 (Fall 1979).
Whiting, Allen S. "The Use of Force in Foreign Policy by the People's Republic of China." *Annals of the American Academy of Political and Social Science* 402 (July 1972).
Wiltz, John E. "The MacArthur Hearings of 1951: The Secret Testimony." *Military Affairs* 39 (Dec. 1975).

Unpublished Papers

Baron, Michael L. "Tug of War: The Battle over American Policy Toward China, 1946–1949." Ph.D. diss., Columbia University, 1980.
Elowitz, Larry. "Korea and Vietnam: Limited War and the American Political System." Ph.D. diss., University of Florida, 1972.
Flint, Roy K. "The Tragic Flaw: MacArthur, the Joint Chiefs and the Korean War." Ph.D. diss., Duke University, 1975.
Kotch, John. "The Origins of the American Security Commitment to Korea." Ph.D. diss., Columbia University, 1975.
Lo, Clarence Y. H. "Truman's Military Budgets during the Korean War." Ph.D. diss., University of California, Berkeley, 1978.
Mantell, Matthew. "Opposition to the Korean War: A Study of American Dissent." Ph.D. diss., New York University, 1973.
Matray, James. "The Reluctant Crusade: American Foreign Policy in Korea, 1941–1950." Ph.D. diss., University of Virginia, 1977.
Mauck, Kenneth R. "The Formation of American Foreign Policy in Korea, 1945–1953." Ph.D. diss., University of Oklahoma, 1978.

Pelz, Stephen E. "America Goes to War, Korea, June 24–30, 1950." Henry Luce Fellow, East Asian Institute, Columbia University, n.d.

——. "America Goes to War, Korea, July 1–October 9, 1950: Truman's Decision to Cross the 38th Parallel." Henry Luce Fellow, East Asian Institute, Columbia University, n.d.

Weiss, Lawrence S. "Storm around the Cradle: The Korean War and the Early Years of the People's Republic of China, 1949–1953." Ph.D. diss., Columbia University, 1981.

Index

Acheson, Dean: and aggressor resolution, 111–114; and allies, 146, 151, 154, 161–162, 200, 241; and armistice negotiations, 174, 176, 182, 200; atomic bomb, use of, 116; and ceasefire resolution, 111; and China (Nationalist), 45–47, 50, 52–53, 67, 87, 139 (see also U.S. administration, policy toward); and China (PRC), 157–158 (see also U.S. administration, policy toward; Sino-Soviet relations, perceptions of); and China's entry into war, 79, 102–103; and China White Paper, 44; and Chinese in Indochina, 180–181, 198; and Congress, 69; and crossing the 38th Parallel, 70, 73–74, 240; decision-making style, 33–35; and demilitarized zone, 92–93, 98–99, 240; and election campaign, 192; and Europe, 34, 40, 103–104, 119, 124–125, 241; and expanding war into China, 84, 95, 114–115, 119–121, 124–130, 145, 154–155, 166, 240–242; and "hot pursuit," 90; and Indian POW resolution, 185–186, 201; and Korean War, intervention in, 59, 61–62; and limiting war, 134; at MacArthur hearings, 137; and McCarthy, 107, 156; before National Press Club, 47, 58; and NSC 68, 40; and public opinion, 107–108; and Rashin bombing, 76, 150; relations with colleagues, 28, 30–31, 43, 201; Seventh Fleet decision, 62, 64–67; and Sino-Soviet relations, 46–48, 81, 83, 86–87, 124–126, 137, 160, 197–198; and "Titoism" in China (PRC), 48–50,
53–54, 198, 233; at Truman-Attlee discussions, 110–111; and Yalu power installations, 179

Adams, Sherman, 214

Allison, John M., 72–73, 86, 166, 171, 198

Alsop, Joseph, 70, 108

Armistice negotiations. See United Nations, and POW issue; under U.S. administration

Atomic weapons. See under China (PRC); U.S. administration; U.S. Congress

Attlee, Clement. See Truman-Attlee discussions

Austin, Warren, 69, 111–112, 139, 166

Australia, 111, 152, 167, 216–217

Barbour, Walworth, 77, 125–126

Barrett, Edward W., 97

Baruch, Bernard, 115

Bendetson, Karl, 196

Bevin, Ernest, 64, 68, 92, 112–113, 145

Bohlen, Charles, 39, 59, 65, 73, 133, 162, 228, 230

Bolte, Charles L., 93, 95, 116

Bradley, Omar, 23, 30; aggressor resolution, 112; and atomic bomb, 124, 155; and Britain, 146, 154; and China's entry into war, 88, 93; and Congress, 128; in Eisenhower administration, 204; and expanding war into China, 117, 119, 121, 146, 148, 150–151, 170–171, 196, 262n; at MacArthur hearings, 136–138, 141; Rashin, 76, 150; Taiwan, 50–51; at Wake Island conference, 78

Brewster, Owen, 115

Library of Congress Cataloging in Publication Data

Foot, Rosemary, 1948–
    The wrong war.

    (Cornell studies in security affairs)
    Bibliography: p.
    Includes index.
    1. Korean War, 1950–1953—Diplomatic history. 2. United States—Foreign
relations—1945–1953. I₇ Title. II. Series.
DS918.F62 1985   951.9′042   84–29305
ISBN 978–1–5017–7206–1

Milton Keynes UK
Ingram Content Group UK Ltd.
UKHW011828160823
426985UK00003B/91